# Shame and Honor in the Book of Esther

*SOCIETY*
*OF BIBLICAL*
*LITERATURE*

## DISSERTATION SERIES
Michael V. Fox, Old Testament Editor
E. Elizabeth Johnson, New Testament Editor

**Number 165**

SHAME AND HONOR IN THE
BOOK OF ESTHER
by
Timothy S. Laniak

# Timothy S. Laniak

# SHAME AND HONOR IN THE BOOK OF ESTHER

Society of Biblical Literature
Dissertation Series

Scholars Press
Atlanta, Georgia

# SHAME AND HONOR IN THE BOOK OF ESTHER

## Timothy S. Laniak

Th.D., 1997
Harvard Divinity School

Advisor:
Dr. Jon D. Levenson

**Library of Congress Cataloging in Publication Data**
Laniak, Timothy S.
    Shame and honor in the book of Esther / Timothy S. Laniak.
        p.    cm. — (Dissertation series / Society of Biblical
    Literature ; no. 165)
    Includes bibliographical references.
    ISBN 0-7885-0505-X (cloth : alk. paper)
    1. Bible. O.T. Esther—Criticism. I. Title. II. Series:
Dissertation series (Society of Biblical Literature) ; no. 165.
BS1375.3.L37    1998
222'.906—dc21                                    98-30969
                                                CIP
        ISBN 1-58983-240-X (paper : alk. paper)

Printed in the United States of America
on acid-free paper

# Table of Contents

# Preface

In a society where shame is synonymous with embarrassment and honor is equated with a school "roll," it is difficult to conceive to times and communities in which death is preferred to dishonor. Yet, anthropological and historical data confirm that honor and shame are fundamental sentiments and organizing values in the Far East, Middle East and in traditional cultures around the world. They regularly function as "master symbols."

My investigation of these subjects began in the context of a two-year journey around the world beginning in 1985. Numerous unofficial "informants" helped explain the significance of "family name" in Arab villages, "saving face" in Chinese relationships, "seppuku" (ritual suicide) in Japan, etc. The extent to which the values of shame and honor dominated the daily lives of persons in these societies deeply impressed me.

My interest in the topic of shame in the Bible was easily piqued as a result of these personal experiences. It soon became apparent how pervasive the themes of shame and honor were, especially in biblical texts which referred to the traumatic, marginalizing experience of exile. During the spring of 1994 I began formal research on the topic during a seminar on the book of Esther with Professor Jon Levenson.

It has become increasingly clear both to me and my readers that research on the book of Esther has much to gain from social-scientific reflection on these topics. In fact, the vocabulary and structure of the story *invites* such interdisciplinary discussion. Scholarship on Esther has examined many important historical, religious and literary issues but there has been no sustained exploration of these very values which the author persistently emphasizes. It is our intention to bring an anthropological sensitivity to these social dynamics which are typically alien to the reader in the modern West.

Bertram Wyatt-Brown (1982) created a storm of controversy in the study of the American Civil War by taking seriously the concepts of shame and honor in the Old South. These were terms familiar to other historians but ones which had been relegated to the category of propaganda or imagination. The following study on the book of Esther suggests that the time for biblical scholars to take seriously these concepts is long overdue. Though perhaps marginal in modern consciousness, the values of shame and honor are ubiquitous in scripture and explicitly central in the book of Esther.

# Acknowledgments

This thesis would never have seen completion without the support of several individuals. Professor Jon Levenson offered his expertise on the book of Esther and his widely respected scholarly sense. For his consistent encouragement and open-mindedness I am deeply grateful. Professor Gary Anderson brought the kind of interdisciplinary instincts which are so amply demonstrated in *A Time to Mourn, A Time to Dance*. His breadth of interest, openness and collegial spirit have been warmly appreciated. Professor Lawrence Sullivan was willing to remain with the project even though we were separated by thousands of miles during his sabbatical year in Florence. His internationally recognized background in anthropology and the history of religions only begins to explain the quality of insight he brings to a discussion of this kind. My sincere appreciation to all three of these faculty readers.

There are three other readers who deserve recognition (honor, that is) for helping to render comprehensible my analysis. David Baer sacrificed some of his own precious research hours at Cambridge University for me. Jody Walker provided the kind of careful, comprehensive editing every author covets.

My best critic and most faithful supporter has been my wife, Maureen. She knows not only what, but more importantly, when to criticize. She unhesitatingly encouraged this venture which created a greater burden on her than on anyone else. Without her this seven-year doctoral journey would not have been successfully completed. The following dissertation is affectionately dedicated to her.

אשת־חיל מי ימצא ורחק מפנינים מכרה

# Abbreviations

| | |
|---|---|
| ABD | *Anchor Bible Dictionary* |
| ANET | *Ancient Near Eastern Texts Relating to the Old Testament* |
| ATANT | Abhandlungen sur Theologie des Alten und Neuen Testaments |
| b. | *Babylonian Talmud* |
| BDB | *Brown-Driver-Briggs-Gesenius Hebrew-English Lexicon* |
| BH | Biblical Hebrew |
| CBQ | *Catholic Biblical Quarterly* |
| HTS | Harvard Theological Studies |
| ICC | International Critical Commentary |
| JBL | *Journal of Biblical Literature* |
| JSOT | *Journal for the Study of the Old Testament* |
| KAT | Kommentar sum Alten Testament |
| LXX | *Septuagint* |
| Meg. | Tractate *Megillah* |
| MT | *Masoretic Text* |
| NT | New Testament |
| OT | Old Testament |
| Sanh. | *Sanhedrin* |
| SBL | Society of Biblical Literature |
| TDOT | *Theological Dictionary of the Old Testament* |
| VT | *Vetus Testamentum* |
| WZKM | *Wiener Zeitschrift für die Kunde des Morgenlandes* |
| YNER | Yale Near Eastern Researches |
| ZAW | *Zeitschrift für die alttestamentliche Wissenschaft* |

# Introduction

The following is a critical assessment of the structural and thematic centrality of shame and honor in the biblical story of Esther. The pursuit of honor and the avoidance of shame are widely attested human motivations, but evidence of these values in the modern West has diminished (Berger 1973). As a result, scholarship has contributed little more than word studies to a topic of vast socio-historical and theological significance. By combining a close reading of the text with an ongoing social scientific dialogue on selected topics, this commentary will suggest that a crisis of identity lay at the heart of the Jewish experience of Diaspora. This crisis is central to the social background of the book of Esther.

The introduction will provide a brief survey of the history of biblical scholarship on Esther with a particular interest in current research trends. A discussion of the structural and thematic pattern which Esther shares with a number of other biblical (and non-biblical) texts *across* formal boundaries follows this overview. This pattern traces the life of a chosen character from the periphery of society to the very heights of power, a symbolic movement from the margin to the middle. In that section, our purpose is to identify the common interests of different authors from different periods. These interests—all of which revolve around the themes of shame and honor—are particularly acute in texts which refer to the exile.

After isolating the *themes* of honor and shame, the analysis will focus on the *semantics* of relevant terms within biblical lexicography. Although many of these terms will not be featured in the discussion of the text of Esther, they will provide conceptual categories by which we can think comprehensively about the dynamics of these pivotal values.

The final portion of the introduction engages the insights of psychology and anthropology. While reflection about shame and honor is still new to most biblical scholars, the topic is commonplace in the journals of social anthropology and psychology. A brief survey of the pertinent social scientific literature will bring precision to the methodology of this study which seeks to look not only *at* a text, but also *through* it into the realities of the societies and communities which it reflects.

## Review of Scholarship on Esther

The urge to explain—or fill in—literary and theological gaps has accompanied the reading of Esther since it was first written. The earliest versions and translations of Esther reveal interpretive impulses at the onset of the story's "career." The additions to Esther in the Septuagint (LXX) are clearly intended to explain some of the problems in the earlier MT version (Levenson 1997:27ff.). The first priority was to make the role of God more explicit; the MT version of Esther never mentions him at all. Two Aramaic Targums followed with elaborate expansions of their own. Targum *Sheni*, the second of the two, is *twice* as long as the received text of Esther.

Esther had a mixed reception in the early centuries of the Common Era. Always a featured text in Jewish liturgy, Esther has always been re-read during Purim, the festival which it was ostensibly written to authorize. Yet, in the Talmud there is a question about whether or not the book "defiled the hands."[1] Sentiment in the early Christian community was more consistently negative. Esther is the only OT book which is not quoted in the NT.[2] Since the days of the early church fathers, criticism for ethnocentric nationalism and "secularism" has colored Christian readings of the book. Luther's (1914) assessment that Esther demonstrates excessive "Judaizing" and "pagan impropriety" represents a long-standing perspective. Distaste for the violence and revenge at the end of the book brings the place of Esther in the canon into open question by Christian scholars in the modern era (Pfeiffer 1941:747; B.

---

[1] See the remarks in b. Meg. 7a and b. Sanh. 100a. Unfortunately, the precise meaning of this phrase is uncertain.

[2] Its similar absence at Qumran is also noteworthy.

Anderson 1950; L. E. Browne 1962:381; Eissfeldt 1965:511–12. Compare the comments of the Jewish scholar, Sandmel [1972:44]).

In the wake of modern historical-critical scholarship Esther bore its share of predictable criticism. The book was challenged not only for its religious credibility but also (quite aggressively) for its historical credibility (Berg 1979:1–14). Historicity was a central concern for two centuries of critical commentators.[3] No one doubted that the book possessed an historical *quality* to it; its style, authentic terminology, and many specific details made a Persian provenance quite possible. However, doubts about much of the data festered.[4] Evidence for a queen named Esther, a Persian empire with 127 provinces, and a tradition of unalterable law are just a few of the historical problems which raised suspicion in the standard commentaries. These specific items, together with the many improbable events that the story records, created a common assessment voiced by Paton (1908:75) that, "the book of Esther is not historical, and it is doubtful whether even a historical kernel underlies its narrative." Most of critical scholarship accepted this judgment[5] and turned to other issues.

Several Scandinavian scholars at the turn of the century had another set of interests which they brought to the study of Esther. The associations of Esther with Ishtar, Mordecai with Marduk, and Haman with Humman (the chief Elamite deity) propelled a search for a myth-and-ritual precedent for the book. Zimmern (1891), Jensen (1892) and Gunkel (1916) each suggested distinct reconstructions of the pagan origins of Purim. The evidence, although highly suggestive, was consistently inconclusive. Without the determination of a ritual *Sitz im Leben*, the project floundered.

More recent scholarship on Esther has focused less on the world described by the text and more on the text itself. As one would expect, the technical concerns of source and redaction

---

[3] The first formal attack on the historical credibility of Esther came from Semler in 1773.

[4] See Paton's (1908:64–77) review of the problems.

[5] I do not count myself among those who reject the book of Esther as a source of history.

analysis are well represented. The relationship of the Hebrew and (two) Greek *texts* received a fairly unified assessment. Moore (1967:351–58), Clines (1984:72), Fox (1991b:9) and Levenson (1997:27–34) generally agree that the Greek alpha (A) text circulated at the same time as the MT. This A-text reflects a Greek tradition distinct from the LXX (which followed the MT). The LXX additions were added as separate units after MT Esther took its present shape.[6]

The possibility of originally separate *stories* of Esther and Mordecai also complicates the picture. It is possible that the story of Esther and the regulations of Purim were originally separate traditions, joined at a later time (Paton 1908:57–60). Discussion about separate Mordecai-Haman and Esther-Haman tales and royal edicts which might have been combined (Cazelles 1961; Bardtke 1963; Bickerman 1967; Clines 1984; Wills 1990; Fox 1991b) is much more speculative.

Many of the recent analyses of Esther have focused their attention on specific literary elements such as chiasm (Radday 1973; Berg 1979; Fox 1993a), irony (Goldman 1990; Huey 1990), humor (Jones 1977; Radday 1990), motif (Berg 1979; Craig 1995) and characterization (Fox 1993a; L. M. Day 1995). Dommershausen (1968) provides a sustained analysis of the rhetoric and style of the book. As a result of these various efforts, there is substantial consensus with regard to many literary topics. Any new discussion of Esther must begin with an appreciation for the chiastic structure of the story, its patterned reversals and its set of stock motifs.

The genre classification of Esther includes "historicized wisdom" (Talmon 1963); "oriental tale" Bickerman 1973); "court-conflict tale"; (Humphreys 1973); "novella" (Humphreys 1985); "*Diasporanovelle*" (Meinhold 1975, 1976, 1983); novel (Loader 1978, 1991; Wills 1995); "Persian chronicle" (Gordis 1981);

---

[6] While the following thesis comments on both Hebrew and Greek texts of Esther (as well as the Latin, Greek and Aramaic versions), it will follow the MT as the primary text. This is the canonical text for both Jews and Protestant Christians. Comparative comments will demonstrate that the issues of honor and shame are more explicit in the other texts and versions and that, therefore, the observations relate to all the stories of Esther.

*"novelle"* (Siegel 1985); "court legend" (Wills 1990) (cf. C. V. Dorothy 1989). Humphreys' classification of "court-conflict" story has been fairly well received. Esther and the stories of Daniel 3 and 6 belong to this category in which the protagonists face — and overcome — the rivalrous challenge of accusing equals.[7] "Court-contest" stories (i.e., Daniel 2 and 4), in contrast, feature a supernatural display of God's power *vis à vis* the court magicians. In both cases, the final scene emphasizes the precedence of Jews in the court while it offers a parody of their rivals. These categorizations may not meet all of the requirements of genre classification, but they are heuristic designations which are useful for the comparative task.

G. Gerleman (1973) analyzed the relationship of Esther to the story of Moses in a unique way. The book of Esther is explained as an attempt to supersede Passover with Purim. Although this theory has not met with wide acceptance, many of the suggested links between the two stories are undeniable. It is much more likely that the tradition of a deliverance holiday was not replaced by but rather *continued* by the story of Esther.

For some scholars, the question of genre helped answer the problem of historicity. The suggestion that Esther is a "historical novel" (i.e., Eissfeldt 1965:507, n. 3) created a way to accept the historical quality of the book without being troubled by perceived inaccuracies or unlikelihoods.[8] The concept of Jewish novels was pursued by Wills (1990, 1995), who describes the Second Temple period as one of increased literacy. The stories of Esther, Joseph and Asenath, Daniel, Bel and the Dragon, and a host of others were popular hero stories which reflected the norms of Jewish life in the Diaspora.

Discussion of genre cast new light on the function of the story and its social *Sitz im Leben*. Meinhold (1975,76) identified the Esther and Joseph stories as examples of *Diasporanovelle*.

---

[7] Another classic (non-biblical) example is the story of Ahiqar.

[8] As much as genre is a useful indicator of historicity, the book of Esther should not be regarded as a-historical simply because it is a story. "Story-telling," in the words of Wyatt-Brown (1982:xiv), "is the oldest form of history." The literary quality of Israel's varied historiography is being increasingly appreciated.

Humphreys (1973) and White (1989) see a very intentional purpose to these Jewish short-novels: they not only describe but also *prescribe* a lifestyle for the Diaspora (cf. Jer. 29:4–7). In the words of Humphreys (ibid., 223), Esther presents:

> ... a style of life for the Diaspora Jew which affirms most strongly that at one and the same time the Jew can remain loyal to his heritage and God and yet can live a creative, rewarding and fulfilled life precisely within a foreign setting, and in interaction with it ...

This observation, now assumed by many commentators, is important for the study at hand. While some question the book of Esther as an historical document, it is undoubtedly more than an entertaining "tale." Its account of two Jews in the days of Ahasuerus constitutes a carefully designed characterization of the social realities of the Diaspora and one which provides direction for living in those realities. According to the analysis that follows, the book accomplishes even more. The final chapter expresses a comprehensive *vision* for the way life *should be* in the Diaspora. Accepting the realities of exile is only one side of the story; seeing the tables turned is the other (Greenstein 1987:237). Esther is an example of what the Jews occasionally enjoyed and always hoped for.

The social realities portrayed and perpetrated by the book of Esther are frequent topics in feminist scholarship (Craghan 1982; Camp 1982; White 1989; LaCocque 1990; L. R. Klein 1990;[9] Bellis 1994). Gender analysis has sharpened the focus of inquiry with regard to the relationships, roles and behavior of the female protagonist(s). The question is often asked whether or not Esther *subverts* or *supports* the dominant patriarchal paradigm.[10] While Esther is honored as a truly exceptional woman, most would agree that the story returns, in chapter 10, to the male-dominated, hierarchical orientation of chapter 1. This leaves Esther as a feminist heroine only for some. Vashti usually

---

[9] Klein's is one of several "feminist" contributions about Esther in Brenner (1995).

[10] E. Fuchs (1982) has put this question to the text most specifically.

receives more praise for what she did *not* do. We will return to this discussion in the commentary on Esther 8–10 below.

The area of inquiry which this dissertation seeks to pursue shares some common ground with several of the categories mentioned above. It is both a literary and social-scientific venture. It aims first to understand the world of the text with all of its subtlety and multivalence. It seeks, then, to understand the world *behind* the text, that is the social context suggested by the various themes, motifs and characters of the story.[11] Ours is not simply an historical question ("What *really* happened?"); neither is it only a literary question ("What makes the story *work*?"). It is rather a joint inquiry into the concerns and values about which the narrator insists we reflect.

## A Literary Pattern

Attempts to define the genre of Esther have been both helpful and limiting. Humphreys' category of court-conflict tale, for example, accurately identifies a collection of motifs which the reader can easily find, but only in a select few biblical stories. This may keep the comparativist on track, but it also confines his/her view to a very small sampling. We might accept this handicap if we were sure that the categorization is not anachronistic.[12]

In the case of Esther, it will prove fruitful to cast the comparative net wider than is usually done. The search for comparable motifs and parallel movements exposes a more general socio-literary pattern, one that cuts across various genres. To "sacrifice" the (sometimes false) precision of limiting categorizations is to free up our study to reveal a fundamental

---

[11] For this author, good hermeneutics pays attention to three "horizons" (cf. Thiselton 1992): text, context, and the presuppositions of the reader. This commentary seeks understanding through a creative movement between these poles. Anthropology will aid the study of ancient context but also, more subtly, it will expose some of the modern reader's predispositions.

[12] These are typical liabilities of form-criticism. One often wonders, "Is it the ancient or the modern who defines the 'exception' and the 'rule'?"

dynamic in ancient Jewish life and thought, particularly in the
Second Temple period.

There are two plots or patterns in Israel's Scripture that re-
emerge in different literary settings. The first follows a
sin>alienation>reconciliation pattern. The goal of the movement
is a return to the original state of grace/favor with both God and
community. Found most clearly in the ritual laws regarding
sacrifice, this pattern is common in the stories of Israel's
historiographers as well. It informs the narrative cycles of the
Judges and the kings of Israel. It is as useful a pattern for a
disobedient prophet (Jonah) as for a rebellious nation.

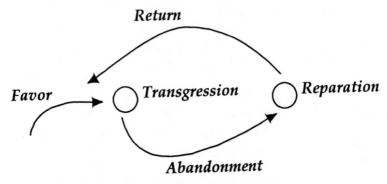

*Pattern #1: Guilt and Reconciliation*

The prophets repeatedly use this pattern to describe the
history of Israel, especially with reference to the exile. The
prophetic metaphor which pictures the nation as an unfaithful
wife (Hosea; Ezekiel 16) describes a breach of covenant which
leads to the abandonment of "divorce."[13] Abandonment or
separation, in the case of Israel, takes place through exile.
National exile is viewed as a temporary, punitive state which is
eventually followed by a renewal of the covenant (Ezk. 16:60–63;
Hos. 14:4–7; cmp. Jer. 31:31–34).A

A second "plot" in the Bible might be called the pattern of
challenge and honor. While the first pattern presumes guilt-

---

[13] It is important to notice the common biblical association of shame and
guilt in Ezekiel 16 (Odell 1992; cf. Klopfenstein 1972; Burton 1988).

based shame, the second one features a crisis of suffering and shame "without cause."[14] The chosen servant is an *innocent* victim of injustice through some insult or attack on his/her life.[15] Only after divine intervention is there vindication and re-emergence as the representative leader of the community (see the following diagram).[16] The laments follow this pattern,[17] typically featuring a person in the stage of "abandonment," a seemingly endless moment of shameful alienation. The psalmist cries out to the divine Patron who alone can bring deliverance from "the enemy." The hope of deliverance is usually expressed in words of trust and praise at the close of the psalm.

This pattern[18] underlies numerous stories in the Bible (see Chart #1). The story of Job provides a classic example of the

---

[14] See the frequent use of the term חנם in the psalms of lament.

[15] According to M. Odell (1992), the subtle message at the end of Ezekiel 16 (vv. 59–63) is that God will not permit Israel to use a lament (which presumes their innocence and God's "guilt") but rather shames Israel for her very real guilt.

[16] The story of Miriam's leprosy in Numbers 12 combines both patterns. From the narrator's point of view, the story is about the vindication of Moses and it is, therefore, an example of pattern # 2. Miriam's own experience reflects the first pattern and may even function as a kind of parable of Israel. She suffers a period of alienation because she has challenged her brother's leadership. Only after he intercedes for her is she allowed to return to her previous position.

[17] The precedent for reading biblical narrative together with the psalms of lament began with their ancient superscriptions (Childs 1971). Readers were led to correlate the "religious" coordinates of the psalms with episodes in the lives of David. For the relationship between narrative and lament, see also Westermann (1974).

[18] It is not the intention of this discussion to reconstruct rigid, formal, literary categories. These patterns are heuristic devices to trace a collection of themes in the biblical literature. While pattern #1 primarily follows a guilt-based grid, "innocent" forms of cultic impurity also fit best in this category. Pattern #2 usually turns on the innocence of the threatened victim. However, lamentations are not only recited in mourning for the dead but also in despair over the consequences of Israel's sin (cf. Lamentations). Daniel, Nehemiah and Judith offer prayers of repentance for national sin, although their own personal stories follow most closely the plot line of pattern #2. Having granted these ambiguities, the following

pattern from the wisdom collection. Westermann (1981:6) insightfully describes the book of Job as a dramatized lament. Job is a righteous and God-fearing person who suffers inexplicably at the hands of "the Accuser" (*hassatan*). His friends offer him no true comfort during his estrangement from God. Finally, God reveals himself. Job's suffering ends and he is vindicated before his friends, for whom he then intercedes. Everything that was taken away is returned several times over. Peace and abundance follow.

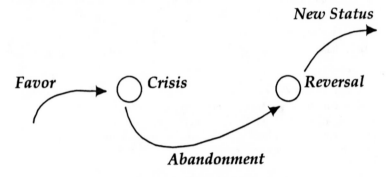

*Pattern #2: Challenge and Honor*

There are accounts in the historical books which follow this second pattern as well. David's rise to power follows a movement from ignominy to divine call, to threat, to final vindication and prominence.[19] The Goliath episode is a cryptic example of the pattern of David's whole life. As a result of what appears to be an uneventful duty, he finds himself at the scene of a conflict. It is a war which threatens his kin and country. While the enemy Goliath defies the armies of Israel, David's own brothers deride him.[20] Unable to use the traditional equipment of war, David trusts in the God who has previously empowered

---

survey will highlight the very predictable ways the motifs of this pattern continually recur.

[19] See Stansell's (1992) discussion of David's rise to power.

[20] Like Joseph, David's early life is marked by conflict with members of his own family.

him. The enemy's challenge meets with courageous faith, and a bloody victory grants freedom and sovereignty to the Israelites.

Nehemiah, a surprisingly well-situated Jewish exile in Persia, is blessed with favor in the court. Crisis comes in the form of a word of the desolate condition of Jerusalem. When he responds to the crisis, false accusations about his efforts to rebuild the city eventually turn into military threats. Finally, with the help of the God to whom Nehemiah prays throughout the book, the Jews experience confounding success and reap the rewards of public vindication and material and religious prosperity.

The court stories provide another set of examples of the challenge and honor pattern which range from pre-monarchic to post-exilic settings. Joseph is the recipient of favor early in his life but his brothers turn on him with jealousy and eventually plan to murder him. After selling him off as a slave they declare his death to their father. Far from home, Joseph rises to prominence in Potiphar's house only to return to the "pit" of prison[21] after false accusation. Even in jail, however, he finds that God gives him favor with his superiors and special abilities which enable him one day to enter the palace. Ultimately, as Prime Minister of Egypt, he becomes a source of blessing for the chosen seed and the larger world. The life of Moses similarly follows the pattern of grace, threat, wilderness, vindication and deliverance. Whereas Joseph (like Job) is called to intercede for/bless those who caused his pain, Moses (like David) executes judgment on the enemies of God's people.

The pattern of Joseph's life echoes throughout the other court stories of Daniel and Esther. In the book of Daniel we find several accounts of the Jewish exiles whose experience of sudden favor is followed by an unexpected threat or challenge from their rivals in the court. Trusting God in each case, the Jews are eventually vindicated and promoted to a higher rank in the end.

As an orphan and exile in a strange land, Esther is also an unlikely candidate for royal favor, yet she becomes queen of Persia. Consistent with the pattern, Esther's rise to prominence

---

[21] Joseph's "pit" experiences resemble those of Jeremiah, the contours of whose life also illustrate the dynamics of shame and lament.

## CHART #1

HONOR GRANTED>CHALLENGED>VINDICATED>ENHANCED

| | Divine Choice | Object of Favor | Threat Descent | Lament | Reversal & Vindication | Prosperity & Order |
|---|---|---|---|---|---|---|
| Job | 1:8; 2:3 | 1:2-3 | 1:13-19 <br> 2:7 | 1:20-21 <br> 2:8,11-13 | 38:1-41:9 | 42:10-17 |
| Moses (Ex.) | 2:1,2 | 2:5-10 | 2:11-15a | 2:15b | 12:29-36 <br> 14:19-31 | (12:24-27) |
| Joseph (Gen.) | 37:5-9 <br> 39:2 | 37:3 <br> 39:2-6;21-2 | 37:18-24 <br> 39:7-18 | 37:4 | | |
| David (I Sam.) | 16:12,13 | 16:18-23 <br> 18:2,3 | 18:8-11ff | 22:1ff | I Sam. 31- <br> 2 Sam. 4 | 2 Sam 7-8 |
| Daniel | 1:9,17 | 1:9ff <br> 6:3 | 3:12-15 <br> 6:6-9 | 3:21-23 <br> 6:16 | 3:24-27 <br> 6:24 | 3:29-30 <br> 6:25-28 |
| Nehemiah | | 2:8,18 | 1:3 <br> (2:19; 4:1-14; <br> 6:1-14) | 1:4 | 6:15,16 | 8:10-12 <br> (chps. 10-13) |
| Susanna | vv.2,3 | v.4 | vv.20,21 | vv.35,42-43 | vv.61-62 | v.64 |
| Esther/ Mordecai | 2:5-7* | 2:9,15-18 | 3:1-15 | 4:1-17 | 6:1-12; 7:10; <br> 9:1-2ff | 10:1-3 |

* Divine Choice may be implied by the identification of the protagonist as a Jew or by a description of serendipitous events.

(and very life) is threatened by Haman's plot. After fasting, Esther courageously coordinates the deliverance of her people from their enemies. The end, again, according to pattern, results in more power and prosperity in the hands of the Jewish protagonists than was ever anticipated. The stories of Judith and Susanna also portray the lives of beautiful but unlikely Jewish heroines who rise in the face of threat, creating a way to save themselves and/or their people. In each case, the tables are turned on the oppressors and threat gives way to vindication.

Our survey encourages a closer look at the structural and thematic similarities which these various stories share. Each of the four dramatic phases or movements in these various passages has characteristic themes.[22] The first phase of the plot illustrates (or assumes) the *chosenness* of the protagonist. The plea of the lament typically begins by reminding God that he is "*My* God."[23] "In the deepest despair, in a situation where all evidence speaks against any claim on a relationship, the psalmist holds to it, presupposes it, and indeed seems to stake everything on it" (P. Miller 1986:101). In narrative, the simple identification of a character *as a Jew* is sufficient to implicate YHWH, *the God of the Jews*, in the outcome of the events at hand.

The relationship that is presumed typically involves an *unlikely* choice. The main character begins as a *marginal* character. David is the youngest of eight sons. Joseph is the eleventh of twelve. Moses is the hidden son of a Jewish slave. Job is an Edomite. Nehemiah, Esther, Mordecai, Daniel and his

---

[22] Nickelsburg (1972:48–58) and Collins (1975:224–25) describe the pattern shared by Joseph, Esther and Ahiqar: (1) Hero prospers (2) Conspiracy endangers hero (3) Hero condemned/imprisoned (4) Hero released, recognized and exalted. The following discussion follows these same categories but examines their respective elements in more detail. Our analysis also reflects more versatility across genres.

[23] The typical designation of the "*righteous* sufferer" may distort the emphasis in the biblical text. Job was a good man who sacrificed to God, one who, in wisdom discourse, "fears God." Yet while this "righteousness" is emphasized, it is usually understood in the socio-theological context of election, covenant or patronage. One might more appropriately speak of the "*related* sufferer" for it is the client's relationship with God which is called into question.

friends are all exiles. This popular characterization of unlikely
Jewish heroes at the beginning of a given story dramatically
highlights their rise to eventual prominence at the end. The
movement to the center begins at the extremes of the periphery.

Divine choice is characteristically accompanied by an
initial spate of unanticipated human favor. Moses is brought up
in the palace. Joseph is the favorite of his father. Esther, like
Daniel and his friends, receives special treatment by a royal
eunuch. David is invited to the palace by Saul. And Job is the
wealthiest man in the Near East. Favor is a key concept in this
introductory stage, marked, for example, by the terms חן in
Daniel and Esther, צלח in Genesis, and ברך in Job. Favor follows,
and is a result of, divine election.

The second phase describes a threat/challenge to the
protagonist. The challenge may be verbal or physical or both. It
destabilizes the reputation of the subject and puts life itself at
risk. The innocent sufferer is disgraced. The threat may come
from real enemies or from "friends" who act like enemies. The
mistreatment is undeserved and is as unexpected as the original
experience of grace. The laments describe a virtual type-scene of
such unjust suffering. The stereotypic role of the "enemy" (אויב,
צר, etc.) in the laments (and throughout the Psalms) is quite
clearly visible in story form as well. In terms of dramatic roles,
one might say that Sanballat is to Nehemiah what Saul is to
David and what Haman is to Esther. Each of these characters
plays the role of the personal enemy of God's chosen one(s).

The hero may be thrown into a literal pit (Gen. 37:24; Dan.
6:16; cmp. Jer. 18:20,22; Lam. 3:53,55; Ps. 30:4[3]) or suffer a
metaphorical version of death. Thus, the common reference to
mourning is found together with fasting and prayer. In this state
there is a haunting fear of God's absence:[24] "Why do you hide
yourself in times of trouble?!" (Ps. 10:1). God's concern for his
own name and his commitment to his chosen ones form the
basis of an appeal for intervention: "Help us, O God of our
salvation, for the honor (כבד) of your name; Deliver us, and

---

[24] God's "absence" is, for the biblical writers, a synonym for his silence. Job,
in his desperation, cries out in complaint against God, but never doubts his
existence, *per se*. The laments of Jeremiah follow the same assumptions.

forgive our sins, for your name's sake" (Ps. 79:9). The afflicted one cries out for life itself *and* he pleads as well that the enemies receive their just deserts.

The third phase recounts the reversal of fortunes and the beginning of divine deliverance. Circumstances which have pushed the protagonist away from security and blessing are now turned into conditions which promise peace and prosperity. The psalmist is assured of both deliverance and vindication. There is a breakthrough in heaven; the waiting is over. God finally speaks to Job. Joseph and Esther gain a hearing with the king. David is proclaimed king in Hebron.

The reversal in this movement necessarily affects both parties; vindication of the hero is accompanied by — *and accomplished through* — the humiliation and silence of the enemies. Nehemiah prays that God would turn the insults of his accusers back on their own heads (4:5). Execution intended for Susanna becomes the sentence for her accusers (Sus. 61–62). Daniel's accusers are thrown to their deaths in the very pit they had prepared for Daniel. David feeds Goliath's body to the birds — the disgrace which Goliath had vowed for David. And Haman expires on the gallows which he had ordered to be constructed for Mordecai.

The fourth and final phase is the denouement. The chosen one is honored by promotion, power, wealth and public respect. Joseph, Daniel, and Mordecai are all named Prime Ministers. David ultimately takes full kingship over a united Israel. Job's fortunes are doubled. Nehemiah presides as governor over a purified, defensible Judah. In some cases there is feasting and holiday celebration (Exodus, Esther, Nehemiah, Job, Judith) and the ranks of the Jews may swell with those who seek to join them (Exodus, Esther, Judith). In each example the final situation is an improvement over the first. While pattern #1 seeks a return to the original state (i.e. of purity, reintegration), pattern #2 moves toward an *increase* in prosperity and prominence.

## A *Socio*-Literary Pattern?

The purpose of the above comparisons is not to flatten out historical or literary particularity but rather to highlight the fundamental values and interests which motivated the veneration of characters and events in canonical history. The prevalence of this literary pattern which transcends traditional, formal boundaries strongly suggests a corresponding social pattern. Certain dimensions of Israel's corporate consciousness and sense of national identity are reflected in the historical accounts of the nation's ancestors and heroes. Their lives become representative mirrors and models for the entire community.

In all of the examples above there is a clear concern for status as each story comes to its conclusion. Stories that begin with shepherds, slaves and exiles end with Prime Ministers, kings and queens. Common to them all is an initial experience of unexpected favor that foreshadows a higher, final state of prominence in the end. Status is a pivotal and consistent concern throughout.

Between the first brief experience of favor and the final state of prosperity there lies a conflict with enemies that pushes the protagonist below the level where he/she started to a state akin to death. The overall movement from *low* to *higher* to *lower-than-before* to *higher-than-before* confirms the hypothesis that a concern for social honor is fundamental. This assessment is more fully confirmed when threat pushes each protagonist into a state associated with shame. Esther and Daniel are under the sentence of death. Joseph is a slave and then a prisoner. Moses moves from prince to shepherd. Job is robbed of his wealth and health. David roams with a band of criminals.

The acquisition of honor following a state of shame seems to be an organizing element of the pattern. This is demonstrated not only by the journey of the protagonist up and down and up again but also by the shaming of the enemy, an element which is dramatically emphasized in the final phases of the plot. Those who oppose God's servants inevitably find themselves, in the end, as servants of Israel ... or dead. David and Judith hold the head of their enemies in their hands. The head of Esther's enemy hangs in a noose. This offensive (from the modern's perspective) dimension to the historical episodes has its counterpart in the psalms of lament.

> The righteous will rejoice when they see retribution (וְקָם);
>> When they bathe their feet in the blood of the wicked.
> And people will say,
>> "Surely there is a reward for the righteous;
>> Surely there is a God who does justice on earth."
>>> (Ps. 58:12)

Deliverance is inextricably tied to vindication; promotion and prosperity require the execution of justice.

## The Semantics of Honor

With these general, structural themes in mind, we now turn to a survey of terms for honor and shame in biblical lexicography. Such an overview will create the conceptual categories necessary for our analysis of the particular text of Esther.

The most comprehensive root for honor in Hebrew is כבד. Derivatives of this root can connote weight, wealth, radiant glory, prestige and righteousness. For the sake of clarity, these various meanings will be organized under the following categories: *Substance, Status, Splendor,* and *Self.* Honor, in each of these senses, reflects a publicly understood form of value. The discussion will integrate synonymous and antonymous terms for these concepts as well. The accompanying diagram illustrates the intersection of the conceptual spheres of honor as well as the various expressions of public response which each anticipates.

*Substance* is the material nuance of the adjectival form כָּבֵד, following the literal meaning of the root, "weight, heaviness." A famine, for example, could be "heavy" (Gen. 12:10 et al). Quantity or size is in focus (cf. Ex. 12:38). The material emphasis

of the term is extended to various forms of power and strength.[25]
A ruler might, as a result of the excessive use of power, be a
"burden" on his people (I Kgs. 12:11; Isa. 47:6). Power is also
integral to the *kabod* of kings or God (Isa. 8:7; 10:16; 17:14) and
implied in the *niphal* of the verbal form of כבד in Ex. 14:4,18.

Heaviness is metaphorically extended to wealth.[26] This is
clearly the meaning of the root when used as an adjective in
Gen. 13:2 and as a noun in Gen. 31:1.[27] The command to "*Honor*
thy mother and father*" (Ex. 20:12; Deut. 5:16) is a command to
provide financial assistance.[28] "*Honoring* the Lord" is also done
materially, with offerings and sacrifice (cf. Prov. 3:9). In return,
the Lord will *honor* his people with material blessing (Num.
22:12; 24:11). Prosperity, in all its variety, is a sign of honor, and
poverty of all sorts is a mark of shame.[29]

Substance and power are demonstrated in contexts of
conflict, most notably in warfare. כבד in this sense involves the
ability to subdue. But substance also creates expectations in the
context of ongoing patron-client relationships. A wife, child,
vassal or slave is seen as an economic dependent. Honor is
maintained materially by provision, protection and control. For
the subordinate in such a relationship, gifts or sacrifices are
reduced reciprocations of the material bounty bestowed by the
patron, suzerain or deity.[30]

*Status* is the kind of honor associated with the symbols of
authority, prestige and rank (2 Sam. 23:19,23). It is linked to titles

---

[25] כבד is used with עז (strength) in Isa. 25:3. Compare the use of הוד as vigor
in Prov. 5:9.
[26] Wealth in the ANE, as the commentary will demonstrate, included not
only money, clothing and livestock but also the size of one's family.
[27] Another root which shares this materialist nuance with כבד is הדר (Prov.
14:28).
[28] Compare the meaning "to provide food" for k-b-d in Ugaritic and other
forms of Hebrew (J. Naveh 1981; cmp. Greenfield 1982).
[29] Poverty, often depicted as nakedness, is associated with shame in Isa.
20:4; 47:3; Mic. 1:11.
[30] See the helpful comments on "Sacrifice and Sacrificial Offerings" by G.
Anderson (1992:872; cmp. Valeri 1985:66 cited by Anderson).

and formal gestures which confirm social hierarchies.[31] This kind of honor is "contagious"; objects in the temple or court receive it by their association with divinity or royalty (I Sam. 2:8; Hag. 2:9; Ex. 28:2, 40). For example, Hannah mentions a "seat of honor" (I Sam. 2:8). People are "held in honor" (*hiphil*, Jer. 30:19) or "treated as important" (*piel*, I Sam. 15:30) according to position, class, age, gender or, in the *niphal*, special achievement (I Sam. 9:6; 22:14; 2 Sam. 23:19, 23).

This same nuance is also implied by רום ("high") and some forms of גדל ("great"). They share with כבד a "geographical" symbolism; for example, height is a synonym for honor-as-status and the shamed are often described as "low" (שפל; e.g. Prov. 29:23; 2 Sam. 6:22; cmp. ציר in Job 14:21). "It is better to be told, 'Come up here,' than to be put lower in the presence of a noble" (Prov. 25:7). Separation is another way of emphasizing distinction. The Sabbath (or God's name) is "honored" (כבד; Isa. 58:13), that is kept holy by maintaining the boundaries which preserve its "otherness."

Respect for status might take the form of gestures and words of deference or concrete expressions of exclusive loyalty. To ignore someone's status might involve disregard for a symbol (Job. 19:9) or, in the case of God, indifference to ritual law (Josh. 7:19; Mal. 1:6). One might show contempt (חרף, בזה) in a number of symbolic ways, through direct verbal mocking (לעג; e.g. Neh. 2:19) or, indirectly, through false accusation. "To oppress the poor is to insult (לעג) their Maker, but those who are kind to the needy honor (כבד) him" (Prov. 14:31).

*Splendor* is the conceptual sphere most closely associated with sacrality. Lev. 10:3 assumes a parallel between what is treated as holy (קדש) and what is honored (כבד). The earth is "full of your glory" (*kabod*; Isa. 6:3), that is, it is filled with God's radiant presence. The *kabod* was the fiery glory cloud of God's presence, a mobile theophany for Israel in the wilderness and a permanent

---

[31] Gruber (1980) is a useful source on non-verbal gestures in the Bible and ANE. The majority of these are forms of deference to superiors, be they human or divine.

manifestation of God's glory in the tabernacle and temple (Ex. 40:34ff.; Zech. 2:5; 2 Chr. 7:1f.). This kind of glory "appears" or is "revealed" (Isa. 40:5). Ezekiel speaks of the *kabod* "shining" (אור; Ezk. 43:2). It is, thus, most often a *visual* expression of the divine presence. Throughout the ANE, the spectacular *kabod* of deities evoked fear (Weinfeld 1995:29ff.).

Similar in meaning are certain terms derived from the roots צבה, הוד, אדר, יתר, יאה, הדר, and נשא. Many of these terms for (divine) beauty and light similarly call for reverent responses of humility, awe or dread. Job describes the terror of God's שאת (Job 13:11, 23). In a contagious sense these terms may refer to items in the tabernacle (Ex. 28:2,40) or, in a derivative sense, to the glory or beauty of humans (Ps. 8:6[5]; 21:6[5]). When the ultimate source of splendor is despised, terms for glory describe arrogant pride and hubris which are transient and shallow (Isa. 28:1–5).

*Self.* כָּבֵד is also a nominal term for one's liver, the most significant organ of the body according to the ancient's perception. As such, it was often a euphemism for the person. Typically translated "soul" (NRSV: Ps. 7:6[5]; 16:9; 30:13[12]; 57:9[8]; 108:2[1]), this use of the root suggests the interior of a person.

כבד is also closely equated with a person through its connotation of reputation. Reputation, or "name,"[32] has far-reaching significance, according to the Proverbs (and elsewhere). "A good name is more desirable than great riches" (22:1). The ancient writers often described immortality as the perpetuation of the name (e.g., Isa. 56:5).

Honor-as-reputation follows wisdom (Prov. 3:35; 8:18; 12:8), humility[33] (Prov. 15:33; 18:12), and the fear of the Lord (Prov. 22:4). Honor accompanies the patient (Prov. 20:3; cmp. Prov. 25:9,10) and the generous (Ps. 112:9). Only the righteous deserve to be well thought of; those who receive recognition

---

[32] כבד is coupled with שֵׁם in Ps. 79:9f.; Isa. 48:9; Jer. 14:21; Ezk. 39:16; Mal. 1:6.

[33] The positive character quality of humility should not be confused with humiliation, an undesirable state of shame.

without deserving it create a mockery. The good name of a family or patron depends on the good behavior of all the subjects (cf. Prov. 28:7; 30:9; 31:23).

There is a host of terms for the shameful who do not deserve honor-as-reputation. Adulterers, the proud, and those who avoid discipline deserve disgrace (קלון) (Prov. 6:32; 11:2; 13:18); the wicked bring shame (בוש) (Prov. 13:5) and contempt (בוז) (Prov. 18:3); sin is shameful (חסר) (Prov. 14:34); and the foolish are disgraceful (מביש) (Prov. 14:35; 17:2).

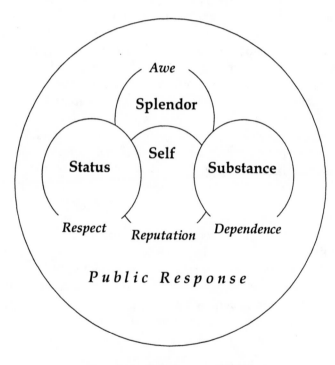

*Conceptual Spheres of* כבד

The preceding diagram illustrates the conceptual spheres or semantic domains of כבד. The italicized terms describe the expected and necessary specific response for each of these kinds of honor (awe for splendor, respect for status, dependence for substance). The large circle surrounding the smaller spheres illustrates the public dimension which all of these domains require. Reputation is not only the specific, expected response for self (or character) but it also stands at the center of all the spheres as the common response to each.

Each of the spheres overlaps the others to a certain extent. The root כבד, as well as other honor roots, can bear more than one of these particular meanings in a given context or deliberately retain an ambiguity for literary and theological purposes. When the psalmist, for example, gives praise and honor to God, he confesses awe, respect and dependence as well as admiration for the character of God and his purposes.[34]

Another important point is emphasized by the expressions of community response associated with each of the inner circles. Terms for honor typically have an objective and subjective dimension to them. Splendor is a quality that can exist without being seen, but the Bible emphasizes the *recognition* of it. Material substance can be calculated in solitude, but it is typically described as a source of bounty for others to share or an oppressive power to bear. Status derives its significance from appropriate formal recognition. And, in terms of the central circle, a distinct separation between self and reputation is impossible to maintain. Honor is only "complete" when it is appropriately recognized.

It is helpful to become acquainted with some of the synonyms for כבד. The conceptual categories for כבד approximate the semantic ranges of other terms for honor (הוד, יקר, תפארת, אבי, הדר etc.), many of which are as fluid in meaning. The most important synonym for our study is the term yᵉqar, the primary term for honor in Esther. The root יקר is a widely attested Aramaic root and is probably a loan word in biblical Hebrew (S. Wagner 1990:279). Its primary meaning of "value" can carry a "material" sense (substance), an "abstract" sense (status and reputation) and a "theological" sense (divine assessments) (ibid., 279–287). Although כבד is attested in every

---

[34] The commentary on Esther 1 will demonstrate these dynamics.

period of Hebrew, there is a preference for its Aramaic cousin in certain post-exilic texts.

A number of terms for shame emerged in the survey which also deserve comment. The primary biblical roots for shame/shaming include the following: חפר, חרף, קלה, כלם, בוש, שפל, נבל, לעג, בוז, בזה, שרק, נאץ, and שמם (see also Bechtel 1991:54–55). There is a greater variability among such terms when related to the category of *Self*. It is no surprise that a person's reputation would be the primary object for shaming. Many of the other shame terms are reciprocally related to various kinds of honor. Wisdom, in the Proverbs, is linked with honor (Prov. 3:35), and foolish behavior is identified as shameful (Prov. 18:13). Loss of wealth, loss of position, loss of beauty, and loss of reputation each create a loss of honor. To be poor, demoted, disfigured or mocked was, by definition, to be shamed (i.e., I Sam. 18:23). These states are shameful as a result of diminished honor but also by their association with death.[35] The antonymous relationship of honor and shame seems to follow a binary opposition not only in the proverbial collection but also in narrative as well.

The preponderance of shame terms in the Bible which are devoted to the issue of exile is quite significant. A sampling should make the point: 13 of 30 total occurrences of כלמה and 47 derivatives of the root שמם[36] are in Ezekiel. Isaiah has 63 uses of כבד, 17 of תפארה, 12 of חרף, 22 of בוש. These terms are concentrated in sections referring to life in the exilic and post-exilic periods. Jeremiah uses בוש 35x, שרק 9x (only 12x elsewhere), חרף 13x, and שמם 27x.

The preceding thematic categorization of biblical terms for honor and shame offers control to the assessment of honor and shame dynamics in texts in which only one or two terms are used. It also brings insight of a more suggestive nature to texts in which specific terms may not occur at all.

---

[35] See the discussion on Esther 4 below.

[36] BDB states that the connection between the two meanings of this root, "desolate" and "appalled," is unclear. The relationship between shame states and shame sentiments should become clear as a result of the following commentary.

## The Rubric of Honor and Shame

### *The Psychology and Anthropology of Shame*

Shame has been a topic of inquiry in the field of psychology since its inception. Freud (1913, 1930) was interested in shame, though he de-emphasized it in comparison with guilt. A more substantial emphasis on shame came later with the classic analysis of Piers and Singer (1953). They identified shame as perceived inadequacy and failure *vis à vis* societal ideals. Guilt, in contrast, was defined as a behavioral transgression of authoritative boundaries and the attendant fear of punishment. Another key study by Lynd (1958) focused on shame as abandonment, rejection, and the loss of social position—together with the fear of each. Feelings of ostracism are triggered by situations of incongruity, inappropriateness and expectation reversal. Shame is both the state and the affect.[37]

A more recent group of studies emphasizes the role of the *seeing other*. Examples include Deigh's (1983) emphasis on shame as covering and C. Schneider's (1992) equation of shame with exposure. Kilborne (1992:231) highlights the element of hiding which is etymologically central to the Indo-European root *skam* or *skem* (from which both "skin" and "hide" derive). His definition of shame centers on being seen and trying not to be seen:

> The concept of shame relates (1) the (internal) experience of disgrace together with fear that (perceived, external) others will see how we have dishonored ourselves; (2) the feeling that others are looking on with contempt and scorn at everything we do or don't do; and (3) a preventative attitude (I must hide or disappear in order not to be disgraced).

---

[37] Fajans (1983:167), following Durkheim, describes this affective dimension as *sentiment*: "Where problems arise in the demarcation of boundaries, or in areas of conflicting interests and expectations, sentiments are found. Sentiments are marked by their appearance in problematic situations." Shame is the sentiment most closely associated with this "disorder of the margins" (ibid., 174).

At the most fundamental level, shame has to do with the identity of *Self* in relation to the *Other* (Balint 1968; Lewis 1971; Wurmser 1981, 1987). The observing other provides the primary cues for self-perception. In the words of M. Zelditch (1968:250), "What matters is not what you really are but what people believe you to be."[38]

Some of the discussion on shame has benefited from cross-cultural comparison. Piers and Singers, for example, built their psychological analysis on anthropological data. One catalyst for the discussion of shame and guilt was Ruth Benedict's (1946) classic work, *The Chrysanthemum and the Sword*. As an anthropologist, she tried to explain the recently defeated Japanese people to the West. Benedict categorized the U.S. as a guilt-oriented culture and Japan as a shame-oriented culture. The book had unprecedented sales in Japan, a fact that subtly reinforced Benedict's assessment. But many *Japanese* scholars of Japanese society hotly disagreed with her cultural categorizations. She had overlooked the presence of guilt in the East. She had also underestimated and undervalued the category of shame in the West (Creighton 1990).

Benedict opened up a discussion that goes on today, especially among the Japanese. The emphasis of many Japanese writers has moved to definitions of the individual. Hamaguchi (Creighton 1990:294) designates the social actor as a "contextual." Rather than viewing oneself as a bounded entity, "Contextuals treat interpersonal relations as a part of oneself" (ibid.). The Japanese word for "myself," *jibun*, means "my part," i.e. of the larger whole. Mori Joji (ibid.) describes the Japanese person as a "shell-less egg." An understanding of the self as an interrelational, interdependent being supports the use of ostracism, contempt and social criticism as social sanctions. It also contributes to a situationally based ethic in which the moral "goal" in Japanese society is to be a "master in life, ... "a person who never errs in judging the right behavior at any particular moment, given the particular situation." (ibid., 297). Shame, from this perspective, results from inappropriate performance of

---

[38] Better still is the statement: "You are neither what you think you are nor what others think you are, but *you are what you think others think you are*."

social obligations and inadequate expressions of relational loyalties.

## Honor and Shame in Mediterranean Studies

The topic of shame as a conceptual antonym for honor emerged in a different quarter of anthropological discussion during the 1960's. Coterminous with the emergence of "Mediterranean anthropology" was a concise description of this pair of master symbols which, in reality, *defined* the Mediterranean as a cultural unit.[39] J. G. Peristiany's edited volume in 1966, entitled *Honor and Shame: The Values of Mediterranean Society*, marks the beginning of a collaborative investigation of these issues on all sides of the Mediterranean. Peristiany and Pitt-Rivers, two British structuralists, were the most influential[40] voices in the construction of a model for interpreting the value systems of Southern Europe, North Africa and the Middle East. Shame came to be interpreted as the absence of honor. Peristiany (1966:10) would say:

> Honour is at the apex of the pyramid of temporal social values and it conditions their hierarchical order. Cutting across all other social classifications it divides social beings into two fundamental categories, those endowed with honour and those deprived of it.

Pitt-Rivers (1966:21) defined honor in terms of both internal and external dimensions, what he would call elsewhere (1968b:503) "sentiment" and "reputation":

> Honour is the value of a person in his own eyes, but also in the eyes of his society. It is his estimation of his own worth, his *claim* to pride, but it is also the acknowledgment of that claim, his excellence recognized by society, his *right* to pride.

---

[39] The historical studies of Adkins (1960aandb; 1971; 1972a and 1972b) and Friedrich (1973, 1977) share a common interest in honor and shame.
[40] Other major figures during this period were John Campbell (1964) and J. Baroja (1966).

Pitt-Rivers (1977:4) explained two modes of honor, one agonistic and the other altruistic, and presented a distinction between the honor of precedence (primarily for elites [1966:55ff.] and vindicated through violence [1977:83]) and the honor of virtue (for all [1966:42]). J. Schneider (1971) and J. Davis (1977) emphasized the historically central *economic* dimension of honor and shame which was inseparable from constructions of gender (cf. Pitt-Rivers 1954:114; Peristiany 1966b:9; Antoun 1968).

There emerged a binary model of honor and shame which followed this primary association between gender and evaluation. The following list combines contributions from a number of sources:[41]

> man:woman :: subject:object
> public:private
> autonomy:dependence
> production:reproduction
> active:passive
> agonistic: passivistic
> strength:weakness
> purity:impurity
> honor:shame

Other scholars further developed this schema.[42] Delaney (1987; cf. 1991) sees the entire pattern generated from a seed:sown polarity. Natural ecology is homologously related to social roles and metaphysical conceptions of the deity. Blok (1981:430,31) illustrates how the model extends itself in the symbolism of rams and billygoats taken on by humans:

> ram:billy goat
> sheep:goat
> virility:cornute

---

[41] M. B. Arthur (1981) describes an analogous conceptual grid in ancient Greece.

[42] The biblical equation of villages with virgins and walled cities with married women who are defiled by invading armies builds on this kind of conceptual framework.

Blok's point is that the ubiquitous shame symbol of the cornute male is a predictable expression of the bipolar Mediterranean world-view. Although criticized for other reasons (Herzfeld 1984), the implication of shame for the qualities to the right of the colon is widely attested (Gilmore 1987aandb) and highly significant.[43]

A second generation of Mediterranean scholars tested the honor and shame model of their forebears in a variety of specific locations. The second landmark volume, *Honor and Shame and the Unity of the Mediterranean* (Gilmore 1987b), prioritized contextual specificity and attention to other related terms and categories. Herzfeld (1987) preferred the more circumscribed topic of hospitality. He had already (1980) voiced concern about a premature reification of honor and shame categories, describing the binary grid as imposed, circular "apriorism" (ibid., 339). Herzfeld's insistence on local, lexical, contextually sensitive studies has been welcomed by most as a necessary warning, but as Gilmore (1987b:7) states, for the most part Mediterraneanists still agree that an "almost universal thread in the literature ... is the organic connection between sexuality and economic criteria in the evaluation of moral character."

Criticism of the honor/shame model has generally invigorated the discussion. Gender studies (i.e., Delaney 1987:35–48; 1991; Giovannini 1987:61–74) confirm the common association between honor and shame and sex roles but have added an appreciation for non-institutional, informal expressions of honor and power, for "more oblique forms of address" (Rosaldo 1989:190) and other "discourses on sentiment" (Abu-Lughod 1986:169). Identification of viewpoint is also a valuable contribution of gender research. *Which community of onlookers attributes honor or shame to an*

---

[43] Antoun (1968:672), describing shame as modesty, mentions many of these related categories: "Modesty, in the present context has three referents: it refers narrowly to patterns of coverage for various parts of the body; more broadly to various character traits—bashfulnes, humility, diffidence, and shyness; and most widely to institutions often associated with the above— the customs and beliefs relating to the chastity, fidelity, purity, seclusion, adultery, animality and inferiority of women, to the superiority of men, to the legitimacy of children, and to the honor of the group."

individual's behavior? (Wikan 1984:649). Many ethnographic studies have presented the viewpoint of the dominant group as if it represented the value-system of the whole society (Lever 1986).

Attention to context and relationship-specific behavior, noted in Japanese society, is now a common concern for Mediterraneanists (Gilmore 1987a:94,100). One contributor (M. Asano-Tamanoi) to the 1987 discussion offered a comparison between Japanese and Spanish views of shame. This comparative venture was itself an important critical step[44] for honor/shame analysis. An understanding of the dynamics of shame and honor in the Mediterranean littoral requires a broader context for comparison.

For some, the reciprocal linkage of honor and shame has misled the whole enterprise of Mediterranean anthropology (Herzfeld 1980, 1984; Kressel 1992). Wikan (1984) calls them a "contestable pair" because in so many cases they do not accurately function as true opposites. The binary grid may be a beguiling form of reductionism. Many societies emphasize one value more than the other. Any ethnographic study which seeks to describe the values of honor and shame cannot begin with this grid as a predetermined formulation.

Fundamental criticism also revolves around the primary terminology. "Honor" is, itself, the problem. Lever (1986) calls it a "red herring." "Honour" is a term with one set of connotations in British parlance and "honor" has another set in the Old South (Wyatt-Brown 1982). The same problem faces students of Greek society today: the concept of honor in ancient Greek society (Adkins 1960b) is expressed in lexical terms still used in modern Greece but with different meanings. The problem is compounded when cross-cultural studies attempt to translate terms, especially if these studies make assumptions about supposedly equivalent conceptual categories.

---

[44] Wyatt-Brown's (1982) discussion of honor in the "Old South" provides more comparative data. As a widely recognized interpretation of the causes of the Civil War, it demonstrates the extent to which psycho-social values can influence political history.

*Honor and Shame and the Bible*

Until recently, the topic of honor and shame received only limited attention in biblical scholarship, primarily through the works of W. R. Smith (1889) and, especially, J. Pedersen (1926). With great respect for the cultural milieu of the ancient Israelites, Pederson devoted 50 pages of his monumental work to the topics of honor, shame and name. Both of these authors are clearly heirs of 19th century thought, of Lévy-Bruhl's and Frazer's "primitive mentality", of Tylor's "survivals," and of Darwin and Hegel's evolutionary scheme.

More recent assessments of ancient Israelite society show an appreciation for tribal patterns and values (De Vaux 1965: 1–15, Gottwald 1979, etc.) but fail to address the topics of honor and shame in detail. Only in the wake of the relatively recent Mediterraneanist discussion did biblical scholars see the potential for reevaluating the concepts of honor and shame. The first efforts were made by B. Malina (1981, 1986) and J. Neyrey (1988) in the field of New Testament. They have been joined by R. Rohrbaugh (Malina and Rohrbaugh 1992) and, most recently, D. A. deSilva (1995).

In Old Testament studies, the first contribution[45] was made by Julian Pitt-Rivers (1977), entitled *The Fate of Shechem or The Politics of Sex.* This was an anthropologist's view of the story of Dinah in Genesis 38. Not until the 1990's did a small group of Bible scholars finally begin to integrate an analysis of honor and shame in the OT with research in the social sciences. "Honor and Shame" was the featured topic in the Social World of the Hebrew Bible Section of the Society of Biblical Literature (SBL) in 1991.[46] L. Bechtel's (1991, 1994) work drew more from the psychological literature with its focus on shame.[47] Stansell (1992, 1995) discussed various honor episodes in the David narratives.

---

[45] Klopfenstein (1971) provided a valuable lexical study of three shame roots in the Hebrew Bible (חפר, כלם, בוש).

[46] The papers presented at the conference by D. Bergant, R. Simkins, G. Stansell, K. C. Hanson, and J. Neyrey were later published in *Semeia* 68 (Matthews and Benjamin 1994).

[47] Bechtel's research on shame began with her dissertation at Drew (L. B. Huber 1983).

Matthews (1991a) and Matthews and Benjamin (1993) provided helpful introductory descriptions in their surveys of history and society. Matthews (1991b) also produced an analysis of Judges 4 and 5 from an anthropological perspective. Stone (1995), following Pitt-Rivers' interests, analyzed sexual politics in Judges 19.

In 1994, the topic of honor and shame was again addressed at SBL, this time specifically in relation to the book of Esther. Lilian Klein (published later in Brenner 1995:149–175), following the work of L. Bechtel and L. Abu-Lughod, took a special interest in sexual politics. The second paper, presented by myself, reached more broadly into the social scientific literature and began to isolate a number of issues that were related to honor and shame. The following thesis builds on these initial interests and investigations.

Research in anthropology and psychology has posed for us several critical questions, some relevant guidelines, and a wide variety of comparative data. The discussion about honor and shame in these other disciplines should receive a serious hearing among scholars who choose to investigate these values in the texts of the Bible. The challenge of lexical and contextual specificity is already an axiom of biblical scholarship. Yet, the temptation to use the honor/shame model as if it were a fixed construct to be "applied" (Chance 1996) is strong. One finds a regrettable neglect of the progress made in anthropology since the functionalist era.

On the other hand, the evidence from the Bible briefly reviewed above suggests a strong polarizing tendency in the biblical languages and texts. Terms for both honor and shame are equally abundant and it appears that they bear reciprocal connotations. In the study that follows it will also become clear that honor and shame are the central values to which other values are subsidiary. Hospitality, generosity, status, obedience, anger, accusation and revenge are the very behaviors and sentiments which are explicitly linked with terms for honor and shame in the text.

To the concern of Lever and Herzfeld that the umbrella term "honor" is too ambiguous, we must contend that the biblical counterpart כבד is even *more* elastic and multivalent. כבד and its Aramaic cousin, יקר, express a wide range of connotations in the book of Esther. Thus, restricting our analysis to the original language does not automatically dissolve ambiguity. At times the context makes it clear that a particular meaning of honor is in mind. In such cases we will refer to "honor-as-status" or "honor-as-substance," etc. In other cases ambiguity (deliberate or otherwise) should be maintained by a similarly ambiguous English translation (i.e., the word "honor"). The very repetition of a given root in different forms supplies important information about the structure and agenda of so many of the Bible's stories. Good translations should avoid concealing these dynamics.

This project, therefore, seeks to be bound neither to the idealistic "apriorism" of a previous generation nor to the specific agendas of any group of contemporary scholars. It seeks to benefit from the research and discussion that has gone on in other fields and to contribute to it as well.[48]

## Method and Format

The book of Esther is structurally organized around the four movements of the socio-literary pattern discussed above. Esther 1-2 provides an introduction to the characters of the story, in particular, to the two Jewish exiles who experience surprising favor in the Persian court. Esther 3-5 constitutes the threat section. Haman falsely accuses the Jews to the king and plots their genocide. The Jews respond to the scheme by various expressions of lament: sackcloth, fasting and mourning—and by a plan to send Esther to the king to seek protection. Esther 6-7 describes the primary reversal of the story: the arrogant, accusing enemy becomes the humiliated, accused enemy. He is condemned to receive the very punishment he had designed for Mordecai. Esther 8-10 continues the reversal with descriptions

---

[48] The use of anthropology in the study of a "dead" society may be unacceptable to some, but restricting ourselves to the tools of traditional historical or literary analysis certainly poses greater interpretive risks.

of the counter-edicts and the battles between the Jews and their enemies. Following their total victory and celebration of rest is the inauguration of Purim, the Jewish holiday that perpetually recalls their vindication. Chapter 10 summarizes life after the conflict as a time of peace and prosperity for the Jews, and honor, in particular, for Mordecai and Ahasuerus.

A chapter of the dissertation is devoted to each of these four movements. At the beginning of each chapter is a plot summary which emphasizes thematic and structural issues in the story's development. This summary will interact primarily with the key scholars who have produced the standard commentaries and monographs on Esther: Paton (1908), Moore (1971), Berg (1979), Clines (1984), Fox (1991a) and Levenson (1997).

A topical commentary follows the consideration of literary issues in each chapter. The terms, motifs and themes which are central in the text and/or most complex will receive sustained attention from a social-scientific point of view. Cross-referencing to similar stories, historical accounts and the psalms of lament will provide the first pool of comparative data. Insights from anthropology and psychology will be evaluated in light of the biblical evidence.

This type of social-science commentary[49] has both advantages and disadvantages. On the negative side, the comprehensiveness of the critical commentary format cannot be maintained. A detailed commentary on each verse is not possible. Similarly, the background issues of dating, historicity, textual history and the history of interpretation all receive scant attention.

On the positive side, the substantial work already done on these critical issues creates a foundation for more lengthy analysis of the issues which dominate the book. The standard commentary cannot provide sustained attention to such topics as revenge, ritual humiliation, covering and shame, etc. These are topics which, of course, receive attention in "manners and

---

[49] A precedent for this approach is provided by Malina and Rohrbaugh (1992) which follows its "Textual Notes" with anthropologically informed "Reading Scenarios."

customs" books, but in such cases the focus on any particular biblical text is lost.

The following venture concerns itself with issues (both emic and etic) which are central to the book of Esther. The text yields a multifaceted description of the dynamics of honor and shame in the exile. These dynamics only become visible when the plot is understood[50] in its larger literary and sociological contexts.

---

[50] With C. Geertz (1976:236,37), I define the anthropological task of *understanding* not as a romantic attempt at "achieving communion" with the "natives," but rather the ability to comprehend a society's symbol systems through open-mindedness and comprehensive exposure to indigenous modes of expression.

# Chapter 1

# CONTEXT
# *UNEXPECTED FAVOR*
# *IN THE GENTILE COURT*

## (ESTHER 1–2)

### Esther 1: The King's Honor Challenged

*Summary of the Narrative*

Esther 1 opens with a royal banquet of hyperbolic proportions. In fact, not one but three court festivals are mentioned in succession. The first affair is held for the king's officials and lasts for 180 days.[1] The second, seven-day feast, is hosted for the general population in the capital. The narrator records in vivid detail the opulence of the palace, the number of guests and the liberality of King Ahasuerus.[2] A third banquet is simultaneously held by Queen Vashti for the women of the palace.

The descriptions of the royal banquets in vv. 1–9 are followed by an account of Vashti's disobedience in vv. 10–22. The literary and thematic links between these two "scenes" are noteworthy.[3] On the final day of the second feast, the inebriated

---

[1] Compare the 120-day celebration of military victory mentioned in Judith 1:16.

[2] Contrary to the understanding of the LXX, Ahasuerus is another name for king Xerxes I (485–465 BC) (See Fox 1991a:14).

[3] Fox (1991a:13–25) places them together as "Act I."

king orders Vashti to be brought before all the guests at his party
(v. 10).

> After he has displayed to them the full splendor of his palace
> and regaled them at the most sumptuous of banquets, he
> takes it into his head to show off the greatest of all his
> treasures—the beautiful queen. But ... she refuses to come,
> thus ruining at one stroke the effect of the whole ostentatious
> exhibition ... (Gaster 1950:381)

Vashti's refusal causes an eruption of the king's anger. The
incident prompts the story's first law-making episode. All of the
king's advisors join in the process of banning any subversive
behavior which might use Vashti's refusal as its precedent.
Vashti herself is excommunicated.

The purpose of the king's banquets becomes increasingly
clear: they are occasions for the king to honor himself.[4] The
Vashti episode describes a *coup de main*, a completely unexpected
blow to the king's honor. The display of Vashti's beauty was
intended to be the culminating moment of the series of feasts,
the final exhibition of the king's royal treasury. Her refusal
(regardless of personal motivation) effectively undermines the
purpose of the half-year celebration and potentially disrupts
social order across the Empire—or at least so it is said. It is
perceived by males in positions of control as a global threat to
their honor. She has publicly disobeyed not only as queen but
also as representative wife. And this in full view of all the
nobles' wives!

The first chapter of Esther skillfully introduces its readers
to the primary themes and literary motifs present throughout the
story. In it one finds the first three of the narrative's ten
banquets. The structure of the entire story chiastically revolves
around feasts,[5] culminating with the festival of Purim in Susa.[6]

---

[4] Moore (1971:6) unnecessarily follows the Vulgate in his translation of 1:4,
conveying a sense of continuation rather than purpose. The context makes
it clear that the purpose of the celebration was royal self-glorification.

[5] Levenson (1997:47) notes the biblical associations of wine and fate in
Daniel 5, I Samuel 25 and 2 Samuel 13.

[6] See Fox (1991a:156–58).

Royalty is introduced as a common denominator of objects both animate and inanimate. In direct association with royalty we find the first notices of power and rank. The themes of control, law[7] and obedience are also introduced as is the characterization of the king as rash and dependent on his council. Gender-based roles are accentuated in a way that foreshadows the entrance of Esther, a superior[8] woman, wife, and queen (cf. 1:19).

Typical stylistic techniques which are used throughout the book also appear in the first chapter. The story of Esther is presented primarily as *history*. Gordis (1981) has made a case that it follows quite closely the conventions of the Persian court annals. The writer demonstrates a great concern for historical detail in the descriptions of the banquets and the official proceedings. The reader is even given an explicit account of the way drinking was handled by the royal host.[9] Specific historical references are especially evident here and, again, during the final chapters when dates, holidays, numbers and ranking are described.

The reader is also aware that this is the beginning of a *story*.[10] There is a sense of extravagance in the numbers of provinces, guests, and days.[11] The opulence of the palace is astounding. There are, especially during the Vashti episode, elements of both tragedy and comedy.[12] At the very climax of the

---

[7] Even drinking, according to 1:8, was done according to דת (law). Actually the law was an exemption from law; there were no guidelines for consumption during the banquet.

[8] Levenson (1997:52) demonstrates a resemblance in the terminology of 1:19 to references to Saul in I Sam. 15:28. Both Vashti and Saul were replaced by someone more worthy for their respective royal positions.

[9] In this regard, Esther can be compared with the accounts of the Persian courts given by Herodotus (Bk. I), Xenophon (*Cyropaedia* VIII) and Strabo (*Geography* 15).

[10] Bickerman (1967:171ff.) compares the opening scenes to those of the *Arabian Nights*.

[11] The symbolic number seven emerges not only in the number of provinces but in the seven day feasts of v. 5 and v. 10, the number of eunuchs in v. 10 and in the number of princes in v. 14.

[12] This satire on a king and his men desperately seeking to protect their honor initiates the reader into the author's characterization of the gentile "powers that be."

king's great feasts he is humiliated by his queen when she refuses to indulge his guests with a display of her beauty. The king clearly has a "dangerously tender ego" (Fox 1991a:26) and, as a result, Vashti is expelled. All the king's advisors promptly devise a law to ensure that such a disgrace will never again be perpetrated by any woman in the kingdom.[13]

The first two sections of chapter 1 share a central focus on the king's honor and on the mechanics by which the king and his men seek to protect it. The first section describes honor as it is *displayed*, the second shows how it is *challenged*. This challenge is met in stages: first, by banning the queen, second, by writing a law, and third, by choosing a new queen (in chapter 2). Throughout the whole process, the narrator consistently employs terms for honor (and shame) to explain the proceedings. Our analysis will explore what social dynamics and values these introductory descriptions represent.

### Status: Honor and Royalty

The introduction to the book of Esther focuses on the accouterments of royal status. The opening verse reads, "In the days of Ahasuerus, *the Ahasuerus who reigned over 127 provinces from India to Ethiopia* ..." This line is more than a means of identifying which of the Persian kings reigned during the life and times of Esther. It is also, more importantly, a statement about sovereignty, one which asserts the virtually universal extent of that sovereignty.[14] Xenophon (*Cyropaedia* VIII. 1)

---

[13] The language of the law, as Gaster (1950:381) shows, uses the very terms of official protocol, even to the point of entitling husbands to the use of their own native tongue!

[14] C. Moore (1971:3,4) suggests that this formula identifies which Xerxes the generic name Ahasuerus (lit., "chief of rulers") refers to. It is true that more than one Xerxes reigned in Persia. There are, however, numerous royal inscriptions which follow the name of a known king with descriptions of the extent of his reign. Moore (ibid.) himself cites a strikingly similar foundation tablet from Persepolis which states, "I am Xerxes, king of kings ... who reigns from India to Cush." The identity of the king is not in question; *the extent of his sovereignty is.* Herodotus (I.134) states that the Persians ascribed national honor according to the geographical extent of an empire's dominion.

similarly describes the "greatness" and "glory" of Cyrus (Xerxes' grandfather) with a delineation of his empire's territories. To emphasize the importance of Ahauserus' realm, the author insists (v. 20) that "his kingdom, it is great." Ahasuerus is the king atop the global social hierarchy without superior and without equal.

Status is marked not only for the king but also for his guests, by reference to their respective ranking.[15] Terms for greatness and height and terms of temporal and spatial priority suggest status. The inclusion of individual titles and the identification of groups by their proximity to the king provide clues to the status system. The first banquet in Esther carefully documents each class of guests (v. 3) and the second banquet describes the invitation to guests, *"from the greatest to the least"* (v. 5).[16] Rank is referenced, in v. 10, with the seven eunuchs and, in v. 14, the seven princes "who sat *first* in the kingdom." It is Vashti's *position* (literally, her "queenship"; מלכותה) which must be transferred to another woman in v. 19.

Descriptions of drinking vessels and court hangings also illustrate the status-marking significance of objects in the court. That gold and silver or purple and white linen are associated with royalty is no coincidence. According to the monistic world-view of many cultures, precious metals and materials form analogous hierarchies to human society.[17] Paradigms which

---

[15] Both Strabo (*Geography* 15.3.20) and Herodotus (ibid.) recount the high degree of status-consciousness among the Persians at each level of society. At every greeting there were gestures (i.e., kisses or bows) to identify superiority or equality. Herodotus interestingly notes that those who lived farthest away were deemed least honorable. In Esther 3 Haman will disparage the Jews as a nameless ethnic group which is "scattered" (מפזר) among the provinces.

[16] Gordis (1976:45–46) comments on the significance of social stratification in Persia and the subtle ways status is emphasized in the guest descriptions of this chapter.

[17] Haran (1985:175–188) demonstrates an association between the ranking of metals and fabrics in the tabernacle with the ranking of its personnel. The gradations and boundary marking, he states earlier (165), is "not merely a matter of externals. They demarcate two graduated spheres..." Haran's emphasis on both the gradations and the parallel spheres of the ritual environment may shed light on the court context which reflects these

conceive of an organic interconnectedness between the spheres of society and nature would consider this correlation essential.

The association of rare and costly materials with royalty is rooted in notions of value. *Yᵉqar*, the common term for honor in Esther, is primarily a value term which might be translated "precious" or "costly." What is valued is what is honored and what is honored is what is valued. Put in verbal form, to honor is to value and to value is to honor. Precious materials are appropriate "status symbols" for the king. This is true, not only because of a perceived homology among corresponding spheres of reality, but also because worth or honor is ascribed to the king as a result of his possession of these valued objects.

Status is visibly evident in the static descriptions of the kingdom, palace, and guests in vv. 1–9 and, more explicitly, in the social dynamics which test that status in vv. 10–22. Social position never exists in a vacuum; it is a dynamic which is exposed and tested in the drama of social intercourse (cf. Turner 1967:278).[18] The simplest test of a superior's status is the obedience of the vassal, client, wife, child or slave who is under authority. The hierarchy which is celebrated through ceremony is easily subverted simply by the refusal of one of the king's subordinates to comply with his demands. When denied, the claim to status "becomes mere vanity [and] an object of ridicule or contempt" (Pitt-Rivers, 1966:22).

In Esther the display and demand sections are linked by language and motif. The display (בהראת) of his riches in the first section is mirrored by the "display" (להראות) of Vashti at the beginning of the second section. So, too, the ranking and totality of the second banquet's guest list (v. 5) is mirrored by the ranking and totality of those affected by Vashti's "wrong" (v. 16) and by the king's new law (v. 20). The *yᵉqar* which the king

---

dynamics as well. As the story of Esther unfolds, the sense of contagious honor (like holiness), of explicit boundary making (and transgressing), the prohibition of approach, and the element of wrath each echo the cultic literature in consistent ways.

[18] Heidegger (1962:133) suggests that the meaning of any object is revealed in a moment of breakdown, when its relationship to a greater whole is demonstrated.

displays in v. 4 is also the *yᵉqar* which every man must enjoy in his own home (v. 20).

In the brief account of Vashti, the concern with status as a symbolic sphere is explicit. The use of the *hiphil* infinitive construct with ראה parallels the king's intention to "show-off" the glory of his wealth in v. 4 and the beauty of his wife and queen in v. 11. She was meant to be on display as his greatest status symbol during the grand finale of his double celebration. The king commanded her to perform, to confirm her role as the obedient, beautiful, "pleasing" queen.[19] This was not a demand to do something difficult or dangerous. The issue at stake was a matter of symbol more than substance. Her performance was designed to enhance his own honor.

Daniel 3 similarly highlights the theme of royal status. This court-conflict story follows the same structural outline of Daniel 6 and the book of Esther. Each begins with a caricature of royal self-absorption. King Nebuchadnezzar constructs an imposing image for the public to worship. It is, predictably, made of gold. The king issues a command that everyone must fall down and worship the statue when the musical signal is given. As in Esther 1, display is coupled with demand. In both accounts, it is a demand for symbolic validation of the king's status. When the three Jewish administrators refused to bow down on command,[20] they were charged with disrespect (literally, "they do not place taste/judgment/discretion" [טעם], v. 12) toward the king. This is a capital offense. Once his honor is challenged, the

---

[19] These are adjectives which come from descriptions of Esther, for whom Vashti is the obvious literary foil.

[20] It is noteworthy that in both of these stories law/command is used to require symbolic gestures of respect, and law/command is used to redress disrespect when it occurs. In both books the reader is led to believe, however, that status is not well maintained by such force. Vashti is banished, to be sure. And the king picks out a more respectful queen. But the Jewish heroes in each of these books eventually show a calculated indifference to the king's laws and yet they are each promoted in rank.

king's anger "justifiably"[21] erupts. A royal decree in each case summarily banishes the offending party.[22]

The two sections which constitute the first chapter of Esther undoubtedly revolve around the theme of honor and, specifically, the honor of the king. This early equation of terms for honor and royalty illuminates a fundamental assumption which runs throughout the book of Esther. Anything royal—that is, associated with the king or with kingship—has honor or is to be honored. To act as a king is to have honor. To be treated like the king is to be honored. And king-honor is the prototypical model for male honor in Esther. This equation between royalty and honor is semantically demonstrated by the uses of the term *yᵉqar* in the first chapter, its numerous uses in the hinge chapter (6), and its final appearance in 8:16 at the end of the story's action.

Another term which signifies royal honor is built on the root מלך. *Malkut,* used twenty-six times altogether in Esther,[23] has the meaning of "kingdom" (9x) as a noun, but it functions more commonly in construct form as an adjective defining an object or person as "royal" (15x).[24] Of its nine uses in the first chapter, seven are adjectival. The throne (v. 2), the wine (v. 7) and the palace (v. 9) are all *malkut.* The queen's crown (v. 11) and position (v. 19) are *malkut* as is the king's edict (v. 19). These items belong to the king or to kingship. Sociologists describe status as a "contagious" phenomenon (Zelditch 1968:255). The status value of an occupation can be communicated almost limitlessly to associated objects.

Interestingly, the first banquet is summarily described as one which displayed the riches of the king's *kᵉbod malkut* (v. 4), a

---

[21] The issue of the king's anger will be addressed shortly.

[22] The Daniel story takes a characteristic turn. Upon finding the three Jews unharmed by his fiery furnace, he commends them for disregarding (literally "changing," v. 28) his words and proceeds to legally prohibit disrespect ("speaking amiss" [יאמר שלה], v. 29) for the God of the Jews.

[23] The term is also common in Daniel, occurring 16x.

[24] The adjectival usage appears in 1:2, 1:4, 1:7, 1:9, 1:11, 1:19 (2x), 2:16, 2:17, 5:1 (3x), 6:8 (2x), 8:15. The noun form, translated "kingdom," appears in 1:14, 1:20, 2:3, 3:6, 3:8, 5:3, 5:6, 7:2, 9:30. The term also expresses the idea of "royalty" in 4:14 and "kingship" in 2:16.

phrase which combines the notions of honor and royalty. This rather unique construct is only found elsewhere in Psalm 145, a hymn of praise to the God of Israel. The basis for praise is the universal extent of his reign. God, addressed as "my King"[25] in the first verse, is the heavenly *Melek*[26] who is above all others. We will return to this psalm shortly.

### Substance: Honor as "Material Capital"

Scholarship on Esther is aware of the prominent role that feasting and banquets play in the plot and structure of the story. Craig's (1995) thesis that Esther is an early version of the "carnivalesque" novel is built on the centrality of the party motif. The many banquets in Esther cleverly foreshadow the festival of Purim, which many claim is the *raison d'être* of the book. But beyond the literary function of the banquet motif, the banquets in Esther also reflect certain social values current in the world of the narrator.

According to ethnographic analysis of various societies, generosity is frequently viewed as an expression of a person's honor, especially in the context of hospitality.[27] In Mediterranean anthropology, the image of the generous host is a classic example of the man of honor. The Bedouin who feeds well even his enemy, once inside his tent, illustrates the extent to which one's honor can be defined in terms of open-ended hospitality.[28] A

---

[25] Various translations for אלוהי המלך are permissible. Our translation understands the possessive suffix distributively: "my God and [my] King."

[26] The term *melek* (king) is used nearly 200x in the small book of Esther. Ahasuerus is constantly identified by his title. Interestingly, Vashti is referred to as "Queen Vashti" six times (vv. 9, 11, 12, 15, 16, 17), once as "the queen" (v. 18) and then, in the context of the edict to banish her, she is simply "Vashti" (v. 19). When her title is removed, she exits the plot.

[27] This topic has precipitated a vast secondary literature. One useful article from a Mediterranean scholar is M. Herzfeld's (1987) "'As in Your Own House': Hospitality, Ethnography, and the Stereotype of Mediterranean Society." Mauss' (1990:37) classic piece on this topic describes the North American Indian potlatches as occasions which mix honor and gift-giving in extreme ways.

[28] Outside observers are often shocked to learn that in some places in the Middle East women of the household are offered sexually to guests as a form of hospitality. See R. Patai (1959:138–44).

closer look at the descriptions of the king's parties in chapter 1 suggests that in providing liberally for his guests, Ahasuerus is demonstrating his own honor and making efforts to secure it.[29]

Analyses of social honor typically follow a distinction drawn between the concepts of material and nonmaterial "capital."[30] Nonmaterial capital refers to intangible assets which a person inherits or acquires, assets which grant a person prestige.[31] When these assets are human qualities, a person is considered "honorable." Material capital refers to tangible, economic assets such as cattle or money. For social scientists of an exclusively materialist orientation, tangible capital alone constitutes honor (cf. J. Davis 1977). Biblical terminology, as illustrated in our introductory semantic analysis, resists such reductionism. There are terms for honor, however, that do refer to wealth[32] and there is evidence of these material associations in Esther 1.

Est. 1:4 uses terminology which demonstrates what we have called honor-as-substance. There are two sets of double constructs which could be translated literally, "the riches of the glory of his kingship" and "the honor of the beauty of his greatness." A more accurate translation of the constructs would be: "the riches of his glorious kingship" and "the honor of his beautiful greatness." There are many attempts to translate these phrases still more dynamically. Important to each attempt is the pairing of two different kinds of "objects" on display.[33] The first

---

[29] Provisioning, we will shortly see, also subtly obligates guests and clients to the host. For the reciprocal nature of gifts and giving see Mauss (1990) and Bailey (1971).

[30] Pierre Bourdieu (1984) contributed to this formulation using the categories of "economic" and "cultural" capital.

[31] Two significant examples of nonmaterialist approaches are George Homans (1961) and William Goode (1978).

[32] In Ps. 49: 16 and Isa. 61:6, wealth and honor are synonyms. In Gen. 31:1 כבד is a root used unambiguously for wealth.

[33] The LXX makes the distinction between the two phrases in this verse but assumes that the king's wealth is the common object on display: "The king showed them the wealth of his kingdom and the abundant glory of his wealth ..." Josephus follows the LXX describing simply a "public demonstration of his riches."

clause refers to wealth while the second suggests splendor or beauty. Fox (1991a:14) properly maintains the difference with his translation: "displaying the opulent wealth of his kingdom and the splendid honor of his greatness ..."

The description of the second banquet in Esther pictures a liberal king lavishly entertaining his citizenry. Like the kings of ancient Hawaii (Valeri 1985), Ahasuerus is the archetypical provisioner. His resources are not only a "feast for the eyes" to be viewed but also a feast for the stomach to be *shared*. The narrator notes in v. 7 that there was a lot (רב) of wine according to the king's "bounty" (lit., "hand"). There was to be no restraint in the guest's drinking; they were to drink according to their own desires (v. 8).[34] In the words of J. Campbell (1964:259), "The role of the patron is to give benefits; that of the client is to honour the patron by accepting dependence."

Xenophon (VIII. 1) similarly describes Cyrus as both international sovereign and domestic provider:

> And although [the empire] was of such magnitude, it was governed by the single will of Cyrus; and he honored his subjects and cared for them as if they were his own children; and they, on their part reverenced Cyrus as a father.

This brief statement suggests several dynamics of honor which our discussion will explore. Honor for Cyrus is defined in terms of the extent of his empire *and* the material provisioning of his subjects *and* their resulting "reverence" for him. Honor is a pivotal concern in both the giving and receiving of material goods.

The image of the king as generous host subtly conveys another important point. The frequent use of *malkut* reveals not only a narratological and historical concern for status (discussed above), but it also marks various items as the king's personal possessions. What he offers is *his*. The narrator wants the reader to notice this obvious fact for there is constant identification of

---

[34] Ancient historians often comment on the abundance of wine in the Persian court. See, for example, the comments of Herodotus (I. 133) and Xenophon (*Cyropaedia* VIII.10,12).

the king's possessions as *malkut* throughout the first chapter.
When Vashti hosts a banquet for the women, it is in the
בית המלכות אשר למלך אחשורוש, "the royal house *which belonged to
King Ahasuerus*" (v. 9).

We find, in the Vashti episode, the reason for this
redundant emphasis on the obvious. The queen herself was only
a participant in the royal drama by virtue of what the king
provided for her. In v. 11 she is commanded to wear the royal
crown, literally, the "crown of kingship" (כתר מלכות). While
early commentators wondered whether or not this was *all* she
was asked to wear, a better question might be why this was all
the narrator chose to mention. In v. 19 her *malkut*, her royal
position, is to be taken away because she does not understand
the obligations incumbent on subjects of the king.[35] Better stated,
she does not understand that she is one of the *objects* of the king.
The quality of royalty is reserved for those items which the king
can display at will as his own possessions. All things *malkut* are
material capital for the king's honor.

### Splendor: Visual Assets

While the first phrase in v. 4 refers to a material quality of
the king's honor, the second phrase identifies the visible
qualities of glory and splendor. Material assets create
dependence but splendor, a "visual asset," elicits awe. We have
examined this sphere of meaning in our introductory discussion
of the root כבד. In Esther 1 this visually directed connotation
appears first in the word תפארה in v. 4.

תפארה is found in the Bible together with terms for glory,
beauty, and light. The sacred vestments in Ex. 28:2 and 40, the
"house" in Isa. 60:7, and the finery of the anklets in Isa. 3:18 are
all תפארה, something visually extraordinary. In Isaiah, it is found
in parallel with צבי, a word which refers to an object's beauty.[36]
Finally, as a term for light, תפארה is used to describe the light of

---

[35] Vashti is not only a subject but one recently provisioned by the king. Her
indifference to him is underscored by this disparity.

[36] Isa. 13:19, 28:1, 28:4.

God which will make unnecessary the light of the sun and moon (Isa. 60:19).

The concept of splendor, introduced by the term תפארה, is also conveyed by the unusual style of v. 6. The author leaves a gap at the end of v. 5, giving the reader the impression of speechless awe. Most translations create a proper sentence such as: "There were white cotton curtains and blue hangings..." (NRSV). This effort diminishes the intended effect. Without narrative introduction, the rough syntax conveys the sensory experience of the guests and the "visuality" of the descriptions. We, as readers, are positioned in full view of the regalia and expected to feel the intensity of the visual sensation.[37]

While, strictly speaking, תפארה refers to visual attractiveness and resultant awe, its metaphorical connotation suggests pride and arrogance. The "proud crown of the drunkards of Ephraim" are compared in Isaiah 28 with the "glorious beauty" (צבי תפארתו) of the fading flower (v. 1). But the Lord, in v. 5, will become a beautiful crown and be as a glorious diadem (לצפירת תפארה) to his remnant. The arrogant possess a fleeting beauty; their glory is both shallow and temporary compared to the glory of God. The תפארה given to the orphan (= Israel) in Ezekiel 16:12 becomes a sham when used without respect for the patron who provided it (vv 17, 39).

The complex semantic world of תפארה simultaneously stimulates a sense of wonder and the possibility of shame. In the words of M. Fox (1991a:17):

> ... the long exclamatory listing creates a mass of images that overwhelm the sensory imagination and suggest both a sybaritic delight in opulence and an awareness of its excess.

---

[37] Paton (1908:138–39) insightfully points out that the description of the king's palace draws on vocabulary used for the Tabernacle (Exodus 26–27) and Temple (I Kings 7 and I Chr. 29:2). The common ANE association of royalty and divinity reinforces the equation of honor and sacrality.

The pomp of the king is an affective, awe-inspiring reality. But the exaggeration of it serves, as it does in Daniel,[38] a "hermeneutics of suspicion."[39]

## *Sentiment: Honor and Perception*

In our introductory discussion on the semantics of honor we noted that each conceptual sphere of honor requires a particular, predictable, public response in order for it to be complete. This two-sided dynamic trades on a distinction often made between honor as an objective reality (whether it be material or non-material) and honor as a perceived, subjective reality. Pitt-Rivers (1968b:503–11) labels these dimensions "fact" and "sentiment." The king is identified with symbols of status and splendor. He has also displayed his material wealth and shared his resources. But, in vv. 10 ff. a public incident undermines the success of the whole display. Is the zealous reaction of the king and his courtiers slap-stick or does it reflect, instead, a cohesive social code which is hinged on symbolic gesture?

Comparative research encourages a thorough examination of the king's reaction. If honor is incomplete until it is recognized, if it is a tenuous commodity, subject to constant testing, then the person who has the most to lose at any given point in time is the one who assumes the highest position on the social or moral ladder. The sword of Damocles hangs over the

---

[38] In the stories of Daniel, the enormous statue and grandiose banquets of the king are similarly described with the precision of court annals. The reader is drawn into such scenes in all of their visuality and attendant emotion. But each episode ironically concludes with the pagan king praising the God of the Jews. In Daniel 4, the king loses his own splendor and glory in order to understand that the God Most High is the true King. The temporary, contingent, human experience of glory is allowed again only after this eternal perspective is internalized (4:36).

[39] I borrow this Ricoeurean phrase with Clines (1984:33). An interesting comparison could be made between this outsider's view of Persian history and that of Xenophon. His *Cyropaedia* VIII gives an account of Persian customs in later generations and compares them negatively with the great days of Cyrus. In the decades that followed Cyrus the great virtues of honor (VIII.4), honesty (VIII.6) and valour (VIII.12) were given up for wine (VIII.10,12) and "effeminacy" (to which he gives great detail in VIII.16f.).

head of the king perilously because the prerogatives of his kingship are no more secure than a human hair.

The author's insistence on honor-as-perception has already been demonstrated in the preceding discussion. The visual display of things and persons, the generous provisioning of guests, and the explicitly stated need for public respect reinforce the narrative's focus on the public validation of the king *qua* king. The public nature of the activities in the first chapter is also emphasized by the Hebrew word for "face," פנה, typically found as a plural with attached preposition (לפני), meaning "before" or "in the presence of." The concept of "face," often associated with Chinese shame, is important in the Bible as well (S. Funaki 1953). The human face is basic to human presence, that is, to humans in relation to other humans (Levinas 1979).

Although common and idiomatic in LBH, the frequency of this term in Esther 1 makes it conspicuous. Of the 35 times פני is used in the book, 9 of its occurrences are here. The first banquet is given by the king for all the princes and nobles *before him* (v. 3). The seven eunuchs of v. 10 served *before* King Ahasuerus. In v. 11 Vashti was summoned to appear *before* the king (cf. v. 17). The king speaks in v. 13 *before* those who knew the laws. They were the advisors who, literally, saw the *face* of the king (v. 14). Memucan speaks *before* the king in v. 16 to prohibit Vashti from coming *before* the king (v. 19). The word that goes out in v. 19 is sent from *before* the king. The concept of presence in this chapter explains the serious implications of any activity which takes place in the royal court. It also reinforces the vulnerability of the king, noted above. Presence implies visibility, exposure, and accountability.

Another helpful vein of insight regarding the dynamic of honor-as-perception comes from a different biblical context which utilizes many of the terms and phrases found in Esther 1. Psalm 145, noted above, is an acrostic hymn of praise which braids various terms for glory, honor, and greatness (כבד, גדולה, הוד, הדר) with the term *malkut*. It specifically uses *kᵉbod malkut* twice. This psalm is the only other passage in the Bible where the phrase is used. Honor is closely associated with royalty as it is in

Esther. Royalty in the psalm, however, is *divine* royalty. God, "my King," becomes the standard for honor.

Praise is given to God for the extent of his kingdom, an indication of his "status" (discussed above). He is great (גדל, v. 3) and his kingdom is everlasting (v. 13). His "splendor" is described with visual terms for light and glory (הוד, כבוד, הדר in v. 5, הדר, כבוד in v. 12). His "substance" is described in terms of what he offers his dependent subjects: he is the source of protection and provision to those in need (v. 9, 14–20). But within this description of God's honor as fact is the awareness that it must be recognized and received as sentiment.

The statements, "I will extol," "I will tell," "I will bless," etc. are statements which give honor to God. Recitation of a psalm is a declaration of honor. All "the generations" are called upon to offer honor to God, to join in the celebration of his fame. In the words of James Kugel (1986:127), public praise is:

> a kind of *prise de position*, a formal setting up of the worshiper as subject to God (one might almost say, in the royal sense, a subject of God, dependent, indebted), in every sense a devotee...[40]

One might venture to say that Est. 1:1–9 contains hymnic sentiments for it aggrandizes the king through descriptions of his glory and provision.

### Honor and Hierarchies: Social Roles and Rules

> *A virtuous wife is the crown of her husband,*
> *but she who brings shame is like rottenness in his bones.*
> Prov. 12:4

Mediterranean anthropologists have observed an intrinsic linkage between the values of honor and shame and social role obligations (e.g. Davis 1977:99; Gilmore 1987a). There is an honor of "blood" and an honor of "name" among families (Bella

---

[40] Kugel's comments are inspired by the insights of H. L. Ginzberg (1945) who compares the psalms of Israel to the king-honoring inscriptions of her Near Eastern neighbors.

1992:151–166). There is, more specifically, father-honor and mother-honor. There is also host-honor and guest-honor. Each of these roles—and a myriad of others—has community-driven assumptions about what constitutes proper, or honorable, conduct.

In a cross-cultural comparison between sample villages in Spain and Japan, Mariko Asano-Tamanoi (1987) explains this dynamic in two, otherwise different, societies. In the Mediterranean context, role expectations are crystallized along gender lines. There are certain absolutes or laws which have become universal principles[41] for the society and internalized guidelines for its members. In Japan individuals "perform" many roles simultaneously and each situation provides a unique set of variables in which the "actor" chooses the proper behavior (112; cmp. Paine 1989). To achieve and/or maintain honor is to successfully navigate one's way through countless "social dilemmas" (116).

This distinction is important on two levels. First of all, the association of honor with social role is evident in two different cultures. Consequently, its presence in the biblical context deserves clarification. Secondly, the nuanced discussion of Asano-Tamanoi reminds us of a *situational* quality which is also discernible in Esther. Certain behavior may bring honor in one social context , or before one set of viewers, but dishonor in another.[42] We must look for indications from the immediate "community" to assess the perception of a particular behavior in a discreet context. The meaning of honor is determined not only by the social location of a given individual, but also by the circumstances and perceptions surrounding a specific situation.

The account of Vashti describes a transgression of role expectations which is explicitly identified as a form of dishonor

---

[41] Delaney explores the way these universal principles are understood in terms of the dynamics of nature (1987, 1991).

[42] Stansell's (1992:105–9) excellent discussion of David's dishonor before Michal is pertinent here. She "despises him in her heart" (2 Sam. 6:16) because he "honored himself" (6:20), a sarcastic reference to exposing himself before the slave girls. His behavior would have been acceptable for one of the local men without status (הרקים), but not *a king*.

and shame. Ahasuerus and all of his advisors are enraged as a result of Vashti's refusal to obey the king. The summons to appear before the king and his all-male party was probably unexpected and may have been unusual. Josephus (Bk. XI VI. 1) comments that "she was mindful of the laws of the Persians, which do not permit strangers to look upon wives." Whether or not such a law existed, the king's command would have taken precedence.[43] She did "wrong" by disobeying the king, not by a misstep in her daily, routine performance but by a blatant refusal to perform "extemporaneously." Because she has not lived up to the expectations associated with her role, she will no longer be able to fill that role legitimately.

The clues about role expectations are embedded in the discussion by the royal advisors which follows. Memucan's argument presupposes a well-known standard by which her behavior should be judged:

> "Vashti has wronged not only the king but all the princes, and all the peoples who are in all the provinces of King Ahasuerus. For the queen's conduct will become known to all the women causing them to despise their husbands, by saying ... King Ahasuerus commanded ... but she did not come ... and there will be plenty of contempt and anger." (1:16-18)

The first term which deserves attention is the verb usually translated, "wronged." Est. 1:16 employs one of several (late) denominative uses of עוה (BDB, root #2), derived from the common term for iniquity עָוֹן. In Daniel's prayer of repentance, the verbal form is found in parallel with the common Hebrew term for sinning: "We have sinned (חטאנו) and we have done wrong (עוינו)..." (Dan. 9:5).

Verbs with these same three radicals in Hebrew presumably represent another, distinct Semitic root which literally means, "to bend or twist" (BDB, root #1). Often used metaphorically in reference to unacceptable behavior, this verb carries the connotations of shame. Saul calls his son Jonathan

---

43 The emphasis in the LXX is clearly on the king's will (θέλημα in 1:12,13) which Vashti disregarded.

"the son of a *perverse* woman" (I Sam. 20:30), surely an epithet of disgrace. The Proverbs tell us, "A man will be praised according to his insight, but one of *perverse* mind will be despised (לבוז)" (Prov. 12:8). Both of these adjectives are *niphal* participles of עוה. Job describes a man saying, "I have sinned (חטאתי) and *perverted* (העויתי; *hiphil* perfect) what is right. And it is not proper (שוה) for me." (Job 33:27). שוה is a term which designates suitability and propriety. Impropriety results when expectations are ignored. This term will surface again in our discussion when it appears in Est. 3:8 and 7:4.

It seems likely that these two Semitic roots (if they were, in fact, distinct) merged meanings in the history of the language. The *hiphil* of עוה in Job 33:27, noted above, recalls a similar form used when Shimei confesses to wronging (העוה) King David in 2 Sam. 19:19. His "wrong" was the public ridicule of the king during his retreat from Jerusalem. Shimei had taken advantage of the king's vulnerability on an occasion during which his loyalty should have been demonstrated.[44] Vashti similarly "wronged" king Ahasuerus by disgracing him at a crisis moment of royal vulnerability.[45]

The purpose of Memucan's proposed law was to rectify the anticipated fall-out from this precedent-setting misbehavior. The law would presumably guarantee that "every woman would give honor to her husband" (1:20). Though situations might vary across the empire, the principle of honor *qua* obedience would be upheld.

### Honor and Shame: Reciprocal Categories

Recent anthropological debate considers the extent to which the values of honor and shame are perfectly antonymous. As a result of her research in Cairo and Oman, and in reaction to current categorizations, Uni Wikan (1984:649) insists that, "the apparently binary nature of 'honour' and 'shame' is deceptive ...

---

[44] The same dynamic is evident in the sin of Ham, recorded in Gen. 9:20ff. The subordinate shames his patron during a moment of vulnerability. Like Shimei, Ham (and his descendants) is punished for his behavior.

[45] Vashti's insult is especially grave since the king has just provided her with a lavish banquet.

[and] poorly matched on a conceptual level." Wikan follows others in this critique of a perfectly matched honor vs. shame value system. M. Herzfeld (1980, 1984, 1985, 1987) has been a consistent voice for a particularist approach which pays close attention to the specific words and contexts in which honor or shame is evident. S. Brandes (1987:122) calls this separation the most significant contribution of the second generation of research on the topic.

Our introduction demonstrated a binary opposition among biblical terms for shame and honor. In Esther 1 we find our first opportunity to clarify the nature of this reciprocal relationship. The shame term is found in 1:17 where the queen's conduct threatens to cause all women to *look with contempt* on their husbands. The phrase בעיניהן להבזות בעליהן literally translates, "to despise their husbands in their eyes." The root בזה implies value judgment in status contexts like Esther 1. Michal, noted above, "despised in her heart" (ותבז לו בלבה ;2 Sam. 6:16) her husband the king as he danced among the commoners "just like one of the commoners." He was not worthy of respect because he did not maintain the boundaries of his position. The result was, in the words of Est. 1:18, "plenty of contempt (בזיון)[46] and anger." Inanimate objects can also be *despised* as a result of similar value judgments. In I Sam. 15:9, Saul saved "all that was good" after the defeat of Agag, but he destroyed everything "despised and worthless" (נמבזה ונמס). בזה represents a category of things devalued or denied status recognition.

Vashti's contempt may be further illuminated by a comparison with one of Israel's dishonorable priests. When Eli showed more honor for his own sons than for the sacrifices of the Tent, God broke his covenant with Eli's line. The explanation given in I Sam. 2:30 is simply a variation on the code of honor so often repeated in Mediterranean cultures today: "Those who honor (כבד) me I will honor; but those who despise (בזה) me will be lightly esteemed (קלל)." The covenant was publicly broken by God because it was already publicly broken by Eli's dishonoring

---

[46] The meaning of this *hapax legomenon* clearly follows the meaning of the verbal forms.

and despising behavior.[47] Thus, when Vashti is expelled it is neither indiscriminate punishment nor unthinking retaliation. It is the publicly demonstrated, logical consequence of her disobedient (= dishonoring)[48] behavior. What is *de facto* becomes *de jure*.

The banishing of Vashti is the first step in redressing her wrong. The next step is a law which would prevent the snowballing effect of her act. The purpose of the proposed edict, stated quite clearly in v. 20, is that "all women will give honor (*yᵉqar*) to their husbands." This phrase provides a definitive answer to the anthropological question posed above. בזה, contextually defined as contempt-via-disobedience,[49] is rectified by *yᵉqar*, its opposite.[50] The nuance of honor=obedience is confirmed again in v. 22, where each husband is given the authoritative position of "ruler" (שרר) in his own home.[51]

The utilization of בזה in prophetic imagery will clarify its connotations still further. In Jer. 49:15 the prophet quotes the Lord as saying to Israel, "I made you small among the nations, despised (בזוי) among men." This description is found almost

---

[47] The same terminology and social dynamic is evident in Mal. 1:6–12; 2:9.

[48] The specific equation of בזה with disobedience is not unique to Esther. To disobey God is to *despise* him (Prov. 14:2). So also, to disobey one's parents is to *despise* them (Prov. 15:20).

[49] The LXX not only insists that Vashti had disregarded the king's will (noted above) but that she (literally) "knocked down" (κυρόω) his counsel (1:14). This sense of cavalier independence contributes to the king's public humiliation.

[50] The opposition of בזה and יקר has apparently replaced the standard juxtaposition of בזה and כבד, noted in I Sam. 2:30 and in Malachi 1 and 2.

[51] This proposal reflects an analogical relationship among various social slots. For example, children respect their parents the way wives respect their husbands. Fathers act honorably over their families as chiefs do over tribes or as elders over kin-groups. Kings become the archetypal human head, *Man-writ-large*, in this analogical system and "king-honor" functions as the archetype of father-honor or husband-honor. In Esther, the king's edict is sent out to ensure that every man will be "ruler over his own house" (v. 22), or, in contemporary idiom, "king of his own castle." In applying the language of royalty to its God in other contexts, the Hebrew Scriptures regularly assert that God is the King of kings, and, thus, the ultimate archetype for all heads and head-honor.

word for word again in Ob. 1:2.[52] Israel bore the contempt of the
nations[53] because she had, in the words of the prophets, despised
a covenant with her King. Like Eli of old, Israel's leaders had
shown more honor to themselves than to God. And this was
precisely the wrong Vashti had committed against her king.

## Honor and Anger: A Divine Association

Many commentators maintain that the wrath which Vashti
provoked was a result of the king's drunkenness and his general
lack of emotional control.[54] While inviting a certain degree of
suspicion about the king's character, the text does provide a
reasonable explanation for his response.[55] The western reader
needs to appreciate the fact that the king's most valued
possession was jeopardized. In honor-based societies, shaming
constitutes a grave offense which regularly produces the most
extreme responses. In contexts of *status anxiety* one is likely to
find just this kind of anger (Zelditch 1968:253).

To support the suggestion that we take a second look at the
reaction of the king, we need only look at the biblical uses of
terms for anger. The majority of the words translated "anger" or
"wrath" have God as their subject, not a human. And it is
precisely in contexts analogous to Esther 1 where God is so
frequently angry.

---

[52] The same parallel of smallness and contempt is also found in the petition
of the lamenter in Ps. 119:141.

[53] These same sentiments are expressed in regard to the suffering servant in
Isaiah. The servant of rulers is "the despised one" (לבזה נפש) in Isa. 49:7.
Twice in Isa. 53:3 he is called the "despised one" (נבזה). God's chosen
servant was unrecognized, disrespected, and disdained by the nations.

[54] Moore's (1971:17,25) reflections on 2:1 are representative: Once he
sobered up, Xerxes was filled with "morning after" regrets over his rash
decision. This interpretation finds support in Josephus' *Antiquities* XI. 195
and in the Targums.

[55] Strabo (*Geography* 15.20) tells his readers that the Persians "carry on their
most important deliberations when drinking wine; and they regard
decisions then made as more lasting than those made when they are sober."
Herodotus (I. 133) also mentions drunken deliberations over the gravest
matters, though he states that decisions might be reconsidered when sober.

There are two terms for anger used in the Esther account. These are the two primary BH words for anger. In 1:18 Memucan warns that, without his proposed law, there will be "plenty of contempt and anger (קֶצֶף)." This קֶצֶף is an extension of the king's anger expressed in v. 12: וַיִּקְצֹף הַמֶּלֶךְ מְאֹד ("The king became very angry"). The anger is emphasized with a synonymous clause, וַחֲמָתוֹ בָּעֲרָה בוֹ ("and his anger burned within him"),[56] חֵמָה being in parallel with קֶצֶף.

In the Bible, the root קֶצֶף is used of God almost exclusively, except in late books like Esther and Daniel. Often the term is used without designating the divine subject. In Leviticus and Numbers, for example, it is simply "wrath" which "goes out" on the community because of sin.[57] In Deuteronomy, Isaiah, and Jeremiah there is frequent reference to the wrath of God which Israel provoked by her disobedience.[58] And herein lies the first important observation: God is angry *because he has been disobeyed*. As we noted above, disobedience is viewed as an affront to one's honor. According to many of the writing prophets, unrighteousness was viewed as an expression of personal disloyalty to God. It was a breach of the covenantal stipulations which God had personally created for Israel.[59] The automatic, *expected* response to a breach in the covenant was divine wrath.[60]

---

[56] As the next scene opens in chapter 2 this חֵמָה of the king has abated (שָׁכַךְ). This verb is also used in Gen. 8:1 of the flood waters once the rain stopped. The king's anger seems similarly comprehensive not only in terms of its effect on him but also on the whole court.

[57] This is true also in 2 Chron. 29:8.

[58] This anger results from what Heschel (1955:198) calls "God's stake in human history."

[59] For the relationship of honor and shame to ANE covenants, see the recent article by S. Olyan (1996:201-218) and further comments by Hobbs (1997).

[60] According to Pentateuchal history the broken covenant with Eli began as a covenant with Phinehas. In Numbers 25 God creates this covenant of a perpetual priesthood because Phinehas had "turned away my wrath from the children of Israel, in that he was jealous with my jealousy..." (v.11) He had expressed his loyalty to God so intimately (when he speared the adulterous couple) that his very emotions and actions were equated with those of God. The covenant was nullified when Eli demonstrated the lack of these emotions and actions on behalf of God and his house some generations later.

The fact that God is so often the source of anger in the Bible has at least two implications. First of all, judgment of the emotion should be suspended until contextual information clarifies the author's perspective. Anger was more than likely the culturally expected and morally sanctioned response to challenge in that society. In ancient Israel, surprise would surely surface in the *absence* of volatile reaction.

Secondly, there may be a subtle association here between Ahasuerus and Israel's God. Descriptions of the king's glory earlier in chapter 1 reflected hymnic sentiments from the Bible.[61] The drama of vv. 10 ff. faintly echoes a common scenario described by Israel's prophets. Vashti is the literary counterpart to Esther, antitypically foreshadowing Esther's "better" behavior. Could it be that Vashti also represents Israel's historical role as disobedient subject-wife, the one who dishonored her God and King by disobedience and was, as a result, sent into exile? Might the image of the Israel who angered God stand behind the description of a queen who angered King Ahasuerus?

This equation is only suggestive and not comprehensively appropriate. Ahasuerus is impulsive, capricious and relatively impotent. But Ahasuerus is the king.[62] And he is the spurned provider. The pattern of defiance and exile illustrated in the introduction is certainly evident with respect to Vashti's banishment. When Esther emerges as the new and better queen,

---

[61] We also noted above that the king's palace shares common features with Israel's Temple and Tabernacle.

[62] The possibility of this faint comparison is supported by the way in which rabbinic and NT parables refer indirectly to God with images of kings and masters who are also unlikely representatives. The point of the parable of the persistent widow (Lk. 18:1–8), for example, is not that a cajoled judge is exactly like God. Rather, the story suggests that if a self-interested, human judge can be moved to take up the cause of a persistent petitioner, *how much more* would God in heaven respond to the supplications of his children. (This style of reasoning "from the lesser to the greater" (*Kal wahomer*) became Hillel's first of seven hermeneutical principles) In Esther 1, a similar sentiment might be evident: If a human king has the right to banish any subject guilty of disrespect, *how much more* would God, the King of the Universe!

it seems likely that she is also a more fitting symbol for a renewed Israel.

## Esther 2: The Jews in the Court of Ahasuerus

*Summary of the Narrative*

Chapter 1 concludes with the formation of a plan designed to restore the king's honor and to protect male honor throughout the empire. The plan initially involves the exile of Vashti and the proclamation of an edict. Vashti's excommunication is a punishment that fits her crime: if she will not come into the king's presence when he calls, then she will never come into his presence again. But her absence creates a vacuum in the king's court and in his heart as well.[63] The king's honor cannot be fully restored until she is replaced. To meet this need, a contest[64] is organized which will give the king his choice among all the virgins of the land. He will find one "better than Vashti" (1:19).

Esther is, on all accounts, an unlikely candidate to replace Vashti. She is an exiled Jew, a non-Persian by birth and, therefore, viewed as an outsider in the Persian kingdom.[65] In terms of status, Esther could not be lower; she was a *female-Jewish-exile-orphan*. Esther had one quality, however, which unlocked the doors of opportunity: her beauty.[66] And this is the

---

[63] In 2:1, the king remembers (זכר) Vashti and what was decreed against her. Levenson (1997:54) notes the sense of fondness in this verb as well as a hint of remorse.

[64] The beauty contest which follows is more accurately described as a sex contest (Fox 1991a:28).

[65] Ancient historians insist that Persian queens were chosen from select royal families. According to Herodotus (III. 84) Amestris was the queen at this time. She was the daughter of an influential Persian general (cmp VII. 61 and Ctesias 68b). For exceptions to this practice see Yamauchi (1990:233).

[66] While Niditch (1995:36) mentions a number of folk parallels to Esther's beauty and the king's contest, the attractiveness of this Jewish figure is best viewed as a common *biblical* motif. יפה is used of women: Sarah (Gen. 12:11,14), Rachel (Gen. 29:17), Tamar (2 Sam. 13:1; 14:27) and Abishag (I Kgs. 1:3,4); and of men: David (I Sam. 16:12; 25:3) and Absalom (2 Sam. 14:25). The specific coupling of תאר with יפה is found with reference to Joseph (Gen. 39:6), Abigail (I Sam. 25:3) and the community of Israel (Jer.

quality which explains Esther's placement among Vashti's potential replacements. She soon becomes the recipient of unexpected and undeserved favor at the hands of the king's eunuch and, finally, at the hand of the king himself. Esther becomes the next queen of Persia after winning the heart of the king and the approval of the members of his court. Another banquet follows at her crowning and the provinces enjoy more gifts (tax relief)[67] from the king (2:18).

The Jewish protagonists are each introduced in this second chapter in two ways. There is, first, a biographical note (with genealogy) which identifies ethnic history and social status. Secondly, there is an episode which demonstrates significant character qualities. Esther's cousin Mordecai is given a lineage in the royal line of Saul. He was one of the nobles, a Benjaminite from the royal line of Kish taken into exile by the Babylonians. More personally, he is the adoptive father of his cousin, having taken Esther in as his own daughter when her parents died. The episode which brings this chapter to a close reveals Mordecai to be a faithful courtier, who dutifully exposes an assassination attempt on the king.

From a literary point of view, several elements are strategically added to the narrative through the final incident in chapter 2. Mordecai's place in the court is established. He is one of the courtiers or ministers (Fox 1991a:38,39).[68] "Sitting at the gate" (v. 21) is a phrase similarly used of Daniel when he was promoted to prime minister in Babylon (Dan. 2:49).

This chapter also illustrates a style of relationship Esther accepts with her superiors. She *obeys* her patron-cousin after she is removed from him and placed under the protective care of the

---

11:16). The other phrase for beauty used for Esther (מראה טבה) in 2:7 is also used for Vashti in 1:11 and Daniel (Dan. 1:4). The descriptions of Esther's beauty in the LXX (5:1ff.) are more expansive. One should also compare the attractiveness of Susanna and Judith mentioned, respectively, in Sus. 2 and Judith 8:7.

[67] Fox (1991a:38) remarks that, as in the story of Joseph, "when things go well with the Jews, others benefit too."

[68] The A-Text explicitly identifies Mordecai as a courtier.

eunuchs, "just as she had always done" (v. 20).[69] Her deference to Mordecai is mirrored by her passive acquiescence to the procedures of the royal contest. Though Esther will eventually become an independently authoritative figure later in the story, her style of public deference never subsides.

In chapter 2, the Jewish identity of the two protagonists is provided for the readers but it is a secret in the court. Further on it will become apparent how dangerous it is to be Jewish.[70] At the conclusion of the story, a complete reversal will take place with many Gentiles joining the Jews (8:17).

This chapter also introduces the topos of hanging (or impaling) which reappears with the hanging of Haman and his sons at the end of the story. Hanging is, in both cases, a punishment for treason and disloyalty, a punishment which visibly exposes private realities to the public. Death with dishonor is required of those who seek their own ends at the risk of the king's life and honor.

### Esther: Liminal Status

Esther enters the story as an archetypal *dependent*. As a female symbol of disenfranchisement and dependence, and an outsider in need of protection, she resembles Ruth. Dependence, as Lilian Abu-Lughod (1986) has demonstrated, defines the state of shame in contemporary, traditional Middle Eastern communities. In Israelite society, orphans (like widows and strangers) were often objects of injustice because of their liminal status outside the normal kinship structure. They were helpless and easily oppressed, requiring legal and personal protection for their very survival.

The God of Israel is frequently described as the one who defends and supports the cause of the orphan (along with the weak, the stranger, the oppressed and/or the widow).[71] This

---

[69] Levenson (1997:61) explains the way in which the structure of chapter 2 reinforces Esther's loyalty to her family.

[70] The root יהד is used 94x in the Bible, with 57 of these occurrences in Esther. It is used as a term for Jews generally (rather than for Judahites) only in the later literature.

[71] Examples in the Psalms include Ps. 10:14; 10:18; 82:3; 146:9.

divine protection is a result of more than universal pity. The history of Israel is prophetically depicted in both pre-monarchical and exilic images as the story of a particular, *chosen* orphan under divine care. The parable of Ezekiel 16 poignantly illustrates God's covenantal love for Israel first expressed when she was an "orphan" among the nations. God had nurtured her as a helpless baby. He became her adoptive father and, later, her husband. The cry of the exiles in Lam. 5:3 is that history had brought Israel full circle: "We have become orphans, fatherless...[again]." Israel, in prophetic imagery, had returned to her original, unprotected state as a form of divine punishment.

As a female Jewish orphan, Esther is a living metaphor for Jewish life in the Diaspora. Her particular circumstances mirror the plight of the entire community:

> As they have lost their king and their land and taken up residence in a foreign country, so has she lost her father and her mother, become adopted by her cousin, and taken a foreign name (v. 7). (Levenson 1997:56)

The harsh realities of Jewish exile are set in contrast to the royal pomp of the Persian court in chapter 1:

> While the Persians are aristocrats living amid legendary opulence, exercising power worldwide, and partying with abandon, the Jews are kingless and in exile, where they have been driven by a foreign conqueror. In fact, v. 6 employs the root of the word for exile (*glh*) in four distinct constructions, lest the full measure of the Jewish plight be overlooked. (ibid.)

### Esther: Deferential Female

A collection of all the beautiful virgins is organized for the king's selection of a new queen, one (lit.) "good in his eyes" (2:4). In chapter 1 the advisors had already proposed replacing Vashti with another woman, "better than she" (1:19). These two verses trade on the related Hebrew terms for "good" and "to be good" (טוב, יטב). In both cases there are two references to what seems "good" to the king. In 1:19 the proposal begins with the phrase, "If it seems good to the king" (אם־על־המלך טוב). The king's response to the plan is described in 1:21: "And the idea was good in the eyes of the king" (וייטב הדבר בעיני המלך). With exactly the same wording, the beauty contest proposed in 2:1ff. receives the king's approval (2:4).

Esther, unlike Vashti, meets the expectations of the king. The author presents Esther's acceptability and approval as a pattern in her career in the court. As soon as the king's decree went into effect, Esther was chosen along with numerous other virgins and placed under the care of Hegai. "And the young girl [Esther] *was good in his eyes*" (2:9).

To be "good in the eyes of" implies a value judgment. The common translation, she (or it) "pleased the king" might convey too easily a spontaneous, emotional effect. But the context implies worth, that is relative worth. Esther is better *in the eyes of the king*. This is, of course, an idiom, but a very descriptive one indeed. It is the king's eyes, so to speak, which matter. *His* viewpoint, *his* valuation, *his* standard, *his* expectations must be met in the court. And his criteria constitute the informal counterpart to his laws: they are (at least theoretically) immutable.

### Esther: Object of Grace

אשת־חן תתמך כבוד

*A woman of grace attains honor*
(Prov. 11:16)

Another phrase draws our attention to the surprising effect Esther has on members of the court. When Hegai took Esther under his custody she was (lit.) "good in his eyes and she elicited his kindness" (2:9). Kindness, חסד,[72] is usually "done/shown" (עשה) to someone and, thus, something received. Favor, חן, is usually "found" (מצא), an idiomatic expression

---

[72] The root חסד has a range of meanings which have been exhaustively debated, especially in regard to covenantal associations (see, for example, K. D. Sakenfeld 1978). Patron/client relationships provide a broader, more defensible context in which to place the term (Lemche 1995). It is in such arrangements that חסד conveys the attitude of a superior to an inferior (Fox 1991a:31; for an exception, see Ruth 3:10).

which emphasizes passivity and respect. Three times in Esther 2, the queen-to-be actively acquires the benevolence of her male superiors. She literally "takes" (נשא) or, better, "elicits" or "wins" kindness (חסד) and favor (חן). In 2:9 she wins חסד from Hegai, in 2:15 she wins חן from "all who saw her," and in 2:17 she wins חן and חסד from the king.

Like Joseph and Daniel, Esther's rise in status is marked by gaining חן and חסד in the eyes of her patrons and before the general population as a whole. Daniel was given חסד before Ashpenaz, the literary counterpart to Hegai (Dan. 1:9). Joseph found חן in the eyes of Potiphar (Gen. 39:4) and חן, again, in the eyes of the chief jailer (Gen. 39:21).

In the stories of both Joseph and Daniel, God is explicitly given credit for the increase in favor. God "gives" (נתן) Daniel his חסד before Ashpenaz, and Joseph's חן before the jailer is explicitly attributed to God's חסד in Gen. 39:21. Early readers of Esther would undoubtedly make assumptions about the hand of God behind the coincidences of Esther's rise to prominence. In fact, only in Genesis[73] and in Esther is the pairing of these two terms found.

These stories of Jews in a state of vulnerability, away from home, and subject to reproach, share a common emphasis on unexpected favor. This favor is more than a positive feeling; it is concrete support. Ashpenaz risks his own reputation by giving Daniel and his friends a 10-day trial on kosher foods. Because of Hegai's regard for Esther, he quickly provides her with the necessary cosmetics, foods and servants to "give her an advantage" (Levenson 1997:59) in the king's contest (Est. 2:9). Similarly, Joseph is given extra responsibility and privilege by Potiphar (Gen. 39:4) and by the jail keeper (Gen. 39:21f.) as an expression of their favor and kindness. In each case, favor from a direct superior is the agency of status advancement (honor) for the Jewish protagonist.

---

[73] There are two places in Genesis where the terms are found together, Gen. 19:19 and 39:21. In Gen. 19:19, Lot is the recipient of חן and חסד from the angels who are sent to destroy Sodom.

Current anthropological analysis posits an essential connection between honor and grace (or favor). In *Honor and Grace and Anthropology* (Peristiany and Pitt-Rivers 1992) essays from a number of European and Middle Eastern anthropologists explicate the intrinsic connection between these two cultural themes. Pitt-Rivers (ibid., 231) emphasizes the common notion of grace as:

> something over and above what is due, economically, legally, or morally; it is neither foreseeable, predictable by reasoning, nor subject to guarantee.

To receive favor or grace, as Esther does, is an unexpected boon, a stroke of luck or the blessing of God.[74] "[Grace] belongs on the register of the extraordinary (hence its association with the sacred)" (ibid., 217).

The connection between the concepts of honor and grace in this cross-cultural collection expresses itself in many forms. In each case grace is a process which *honors* the recipient (ibid., 234). To show favor is to confer honor or dignity; to "be disgraced" is to be dishonored (ibid., 240). Vashti is dis-graced, removed from the king's presence (= favor), because she had not honored his favor.[75] Esther is a worthy recipient of grace and, consequently, becomes the recipient of honor. To maintain her honor, Esther will have to maintain her respect for the king's honor.

### Mordecai: Jewish Nobility

Mordecai's name seems to enter the plot of Esther almost incidentally as the narrator provides background information on the virgin who will win the contest in chapter 2. The biographical note about the two Jews provides a bridge between the suggested contest of vv. 2–4 and the gathering of Esther along with numerous other maidens in v. 8. On closer inspection,

---

[74] To "elicit" such favor is not unusual. It is the normal desire for any dependent person vis-à-vis his/her superior. Pitt-Rivers (223) reminds us that the Catholic sacrament constitute an institutional means of "obtaining grace."

[75] Haman is characterized the same way in LXX Add. E.

however, the information provided about Mordecai is as
revealing about his role in this story as is the information about
Esther.

Mordecai is one of the noble[76] Jews exiled from Jerusalem
by Nebuchadnezzar (v. 6). He was the "son of Jair, the son of
Shimei, the son of Kish, a Benjamite" (v. 5). Mordecai came from
the royal family of Saul (Kish's son), from the independent tribe
of Benjamin (cf. Gen. 49:27; Jud. 3:21; 20:16; 2 Sam. 2:9; 16:11, 20).
The narrator positions the genealogy here by way of
introduction, but explicit reference to the Saulide line (and
Benjamin) is extremely important background for the
confrontation between Mordecai and Haman ("the Agagite")
which follows in chapter 3.[77] Beside this foreshadowing function,
the royal heritage posits an *acquired status* for Mordecai; he has a
certain honor-by-birth.

Mordecai is, thus, introduced as a person who bears a
royal pedigree and enjoys a prestigious position, albeit, in a
liminal state (exile). It is a precarious mix of honor and shame.
Like Esther, he becomes an appropriate symbol for Israel in exile,
but for different reasons. Esther is first presented as the
vulnerable, female *object* of grace—the recipient of unwarranted
(though attracted)—favor of kin and court alike. Mordecai, in
contrast, is male *subject*. He is born with honor, he acts with
honor and he will soon defend his honor. He represents not
Israel the protected orphan, but Israel the chosen, loyal,
proactive man of character.

### Mordecai: Faithful Patron, Loyal Client

Our discussion of Esther's status as female Jewish orphan
suggested certain theological assumptions regarding YHWH's
protective responsibilities. Her status also serves to underscore
the honorable character of her cousin, Mordecai. Embedded
within the same biographical note which introduces Esther is a

---

[76] See Bickerman's (1967:209) note on the constituency of the 597
deportation.
[77] See Levenson's (1997:56) comments on the subtle connections with the
Saul narrative.

description of the one who became her patron, "[taking] her as his own daughter" (2:7).

Mordecai is a good man, by biblical definition, because he cared for his kin. He is called an *'omen*, the participial form of אמן, a designation which suggests intimate support and protection. In Isa. 60:4 the feminine participle of the same root describes "*nurses*" who "carry your daughters on their arms." Moses' complaint to God about the Israelites uses the same root: "Did I conceive them and *nurse* them?" (Num. 11:12). Mordecai, we read in 2:20, had taken Esther "*under his care*" (באמנה). As an *'omen* for one of Israel's weak and defenseless, he was a man of honor who acted like the God of Israel.

This positive valuation of Mordecai provides a check on criticism which has called into question his character, accusing him of arrogance and cowardice at later points in the story. On both biblical and anthropological grounds the characterization of Mordecai is quite the opposite. Loyalty to one's family and ethnic community is a moral absolute in honor/shame societies.[78] It is precisely this kind of loyalty which Mordecai exhibits here and to which he later calls Esther (4:14). If anything, this Jewish protagonist is described as one who goes beyond the letter of the law in his expression of Jewish morality.[79]

Mordecai's sense of loyalty extends beyond his family to the king. By exposing a secret assassination plot, Mordecai saved the life of the king. This act of loyalty stands in contrast to the

---

[78] This "law" explains the anger Saul holds for his own son. Jonathan's loyalty to Saul's (and, indirectly, Jonathan's) rival, David, is treason. For such disloyalty Saul calls his preferred successor a "son of a whore" (following Stansell 1992:99) and tries to murder him in the palace (I Sam. 20:30-33). Holy's (1989) work on kinship provides a stimulating commentary on the nature of the relationship between Mordecai and Esther. His responsibility to her was quite visibly demonstrated in a way comparable to the marriage of Boaz and Ruth.

[79] Mordecai's loyalties to his people (in contrast to Haman's loyalties to himself) are evident throughout the story. The final line of the book underscores this paternal concern for his kin.

great *dis*honoring act of treason. For that crime the two plotting eunuchs, Bigthan and Teresh, are hanged.[80]

The incident of the eunuchs provides another insight into the character of Mordecai. Not only does he show the king honor by saving his life,[81] he does so without getting (or seeking) a reward. If historical characterizations of the Persian kings are accurate, there is, here, a jarring gap in the narrative. "It was a point of honor with the Persian kings to reward promptly and magnificently those who conferred benefits upon them" (Paton 1908:245).[82] Yet, nothing was done for Mordecai. The silence is deafening. The king's own question later in 6:3 confirms the surprise of the reader here: "What honor (יקר) or dignity (גדולה) has been bestowed upon Mordecai for this?" The Persian king has a debt of honor to pay to his Jewish savior.

---

[80] The root תלה may refer to hanging, impaling or crucifixion. The Greek terms for these procedures are equally ambiguous without contextual explanation. Because Haman's sons are hanged (same verb) *after* they are dead, it would seem that there is more here than a description of execution. These are occasions for public shame. Haman built an enormous gallows for Mordecai, the height of which can only be explained by the desire for humiliating exposure. Similar sentiments are involved in the account of Saul's dead body which was hung on the city walls at Bethshan by his gloating enemies (I Sam. 31:10).

[81] The assumption that saving the king's life was a form of honoring him is made explicit in the Latin version in chapter 6: "What is to be done for the man *who honors the king* whom the king longs to honor?"

[82] See Herodotus III 139–41, 153; VII; IX 107.

# Chapter 2

# *THREAT*
# *THE PLOT TO KILL THE JEWS*

## *(ESTHER 3–5)*

### Esther 3: Haman's Honor Challenged

*Summary of the Narrative*

Following the stage-setting and introduction of characters in the first two chapters of the book, chapters 3–5 comprise the threat section of the story. The status and very lives of the two Jews in the court are jeopardized, as are the lives of all the Jews in the empire. The threat begins with an accusation which escalates into a royal edict aimed at Jewish annihilation.

The apparent lack of connectedness between this act and the final episode of chapter 2 begs for an explanation. Mordecai has just saved the king's life by exposing an assassination plot. But "after these things," the king promotes[1] *Haman* above all the other ministers. One wonders, "Who is this Haman, and why is

---

[1] Haman is literally "made great" (גדל, *piel*) by the king who "advanced him" (from נשא) over all the other nobles (v. 1). The use of גדל here recalls the various forms of the same root in Esther 1 used with reference to the greatness of the king. By promoting Haman, the king is, in a sense, sharing his גדולה (1:4). In the LXX A text, the king "glorifies" (ἐδόξασεν) Haman.

*he* promoted?" and "Why not Mordecai?"[2] Is the author simply
moving chronologically to a later moment in time, or is the
juxtaposition of these events[3] designed to stimulate a sense of
irony and curiosity? Certainly, the details which follow suggest a
great deal of intentionality behind the structuring of the account.
The stage is being carefully set for the central rivalry of the story.

Haman's promotion to prime minister is accompanied by a
royal command for the other members of the court to bow[4]
before him (v. 2). Mordecai, to the great interest of the other
ministers (and the reader), is the only one of the king's servants
who refuses to bow (vv. 2 and 3).[5] After persistent questioning,[6]
he finally explains his behavior in terms of ethnicity: "... he told
them that he was a Jew" (v. 4).[7] Haman is enraged when he sees
what Mordecai is doing—or rather, what he is *not* doing. He
decides to seek royal permission for nothing less than an empire-
wide purging of all Jewry (vv. 5 and 6).

---

[2] Moore's (1971:35) assessment is the same: "This verse sets up a sharp
contrast between the unrewarded merit of Mordecai and Haman's
unmerited rewards." See also Bickerman (1967), who explains Mordecai's
behavior in the following verses to be a result of *not* being honored.

[3] The same sense of discontinuity is evident between Daniel chapters 2 and
3.

[4] Bowing, according to Herodotus (I 134), was an excessive practice in the
Persian court.

[5] Refusal to bow is a motif shared with Daniel (3:12; 6:10). An analogous
form of resistance is found in the Jewish disregard for Nebuchadnezzar's
summons in Judith 1:11, an act which precipitates the king's anger and
revenge.

[6] Levenson (1997:68) points out the parallels in wording between
Mordecai's refusal and Joseph's (to Potiphar's wife) in Gen. 39:10. In both
cases the authenticity of the Jew is preserved, but not without serious
consequences.

[7] That Mordecai's response *explains* his non-conformist behavior is clear
from the context and also from the structure of the language in the text
itself (See Fox 1991a: 45,46). Of course, Mordecai's answer is not completely
self-explanatory. Jews did bow down to high ranking officials (See Gen.
23:7, 27:29, 33:3; I Sam 24:9[8]; 2 Sam. 14:4; I Kings 1:16). The issue is not
that as a Jew he will refuse to bow down to anyone. Rather, Mordecai, the
*Jew*, will not bow down to Haman, *the Agagite*.

Before going to the king, Haman seeks providence by casting lots to set a date for the slaughter. Then he confidently brings an accusation against the Jews to the king.[8] With ambiguity and innuendo, Haman craftily describes this unnamed community as a threat to the whole empire (v. 8). And, he offers to subsidize their executions with his own money (v. 9).[9] The king carelessly[10] grants permission to destroy a people whose identity is still unrevealed (v. 11). As the king and his prime minister sit down to drink (v. 15; cf. Gen. 37:25) Haman already tastes the sweetness of revenge.

Esther chapter 3 parallels chapter 1 both structurally and thematically, strategically placing Haman in a position analogous to that of the king. It was the king's honor which was displayed in the opening scene. It was also the king's honor which was challenged by one whose role required her to demonstrate deference in public. Now it is Haman whose honor is on display.[11] The objective fact of promotion is acknowledged by the visual gestures of respect required of the members of the court. Mordecai threatens Haman's status as prime minister as

---

[8] Haman acts like the "enemy" in the Psalms who "conceives evil" (7:14), "utters slander" (27:1) and schemes to snatch away the life of the righteous (31:13).

[9] The amount of money Haman offers in 3:9 is an outrageous sum. Fox (1991a:52) estimates it's value at 58%–68% of the annual revenue of the whole empire. This *bakshish* reveals Haman's resolve to get the job done, but it also provides a window into what motivates the king. Recall Haman's argument in the preceding verse, that it is not "worth it" for the king to let them remain. Later, in 7:4, Esther will cry out that her people were "sold" to destruction.

It is also possible that Haman's offer (and Esther's plea in 7:4) is actually a way of shaming the king into acting. In effect, Haman may be saying, "If money is the problem, let me take care of it." Pitt-Rivers (1966:60) tells of a man who stabbed his guest for a similar insinuation!

[10] Fox (1991a:173) describes how dangerous the king is because of his laziness. His random unpredictability and malleable abdication to the advice of others makes him a loose canon in the court.

[11] In Fox's (1991a:56) words, Act I (chapter 1) was the "king's moment of 'greatness'"; Act III (chapter 3) is the "moment of Haman's 'greatness'."

Vashti had threatened Ahasuerus' status as king.[12] A single subject holds the power to challenge the honor of his/her superior.[13] Both challenges are met with anger and subsequently countered by a comprehensive legal decree.

The edict of 3:12,[14] like the letter in 1:22, is sent by royal couriers to "every people according to its language." An unwieldy administrative system is put to the task of rectifying personal grievances on a global scale. The emotions of rage and insecurity and the strategy of totalitarian repression combine to produce a ghastly "final solution" to the "problem" of the Jews. Haman, like the king himself, finds no sense of respite until this administrative solution is initiated. In both cases, however, the solution is unexpectedly less than final.[15]

Chapter 3 also includes the structurally central banquet image. As the couriers ride off to all the king's provinces, "the king and Haman sat down to drink" (v. 15). "But" the verse continues, "the city of Susa was in confusion." The opening banquets of Esther (1:3; 1:5–8; 1:9; 2:18), we recall, were public displays of power and wealth. The strategic, private "middle banquets" of Esther (3:15; 5:4–8; 7:1–2), Craig (1995:64) notes, are marked by curiosity and suspense.[16] When the common root for feasting in Esther, שׁתח, appears in 3:15, it is a signal only that order is *officially* restored. Those whose honor have been challenged have *formally* retained it. For the king and Haman the control of threat prompts a celebration. But, while the two powerful men dine within the insulated walls of the castle and the legal protection of its bureaucratic system, the population

---

[12] Again, in the words of M. Fox (ibid.), "In Act I, an independent-minded woman defies the king and fills him with wrath. In Act III, an independent-minded Jew defies Haman and fills him with wrath."

[13] Levenson (1997:68) highlights the parallels between Mordecai and Vashti.

[14] This edict of annihilation is written, ironically, the day before the Jewish Passover.

[15] Vashti's replacement, we will soon discover, is not merely the passive female puppet required by the edict of chapter 1. Esther eventually wields more power than the prime minister himself.

[16] The victory celebrations of 8:17 and 9:18 and the permanent festival (Purim) banquets of chapter 9 are yet other types of banquets featured in the story.

outside is aware that all is not well in the world. What bespeaks order for the court creates chaos for the city.

Chapter 3 also introduces motifs which will become central to the story. Closely tied to the banqueting theme is the casting of the *pur* (lot) in 3:7. The story of Esther will eventually become the annually re-read story of *Purim*. This holiday is named after the device by which Haman selected a date for the extermination of the Jews.

The casting of the *pur* is more than a variation on the banqueting theme, however. It is also one of several indications of providence in the story. Providence is present in the unlikely coincidences of Esther's rise to queenship and Mordecai's discovery of the assassination plot. But providence is also the source of direction for Haman. He will follow the lead of the New Year (Nisan) lots to fix the date for his plan.[17] Mordecai, the Jews, and Esther will soon fast as they too seek from providence a way our of their predicament. Haman confidently, yet unwittingly, submits to the decrees of fate which have nothing but his own ultimate defeat in store. He unknowingly casts lots which determine the timing of his own death! The name Purim conjures up the unpredictable, often ironic, nature of fate.

Accusation is another motif introduced in chapter 3 (v. 8), and one which is common to the court stories. A jealous plot against the loyal Jew follows Daniel's promotion in Dan. 6:4. In the story of Esther it is *Haman* — not Mordecai the Jew — who has just been promoted. Yet Haman is obsessed with anger over his *unpromoted* rival. His accusation constitutes the beginning of the central threat in the plot. Resolution will only occur after a series of suspenseful episodes.

### Tribal Feud

Haman is given no other introduction in 3:1 than "son of Hammedatha, the Agagite." His previous loyalty to the king or

---

[17] Moore (1971:38) reminds us that "The beginning of the New Year was an especially appropriate time for Haman to resort to divination because, according to the Babylonian religion, at that time the gods also come together to fix the fate of men." See also Haupt (1906). Nisan was also, as mentioned above, the month of the Jewish Passover.

meritorious behavior are matters about which the narrator is silent. But there is one piece of essential information which explains the rivalry which surfaces: Haman was a descendent of Agag. By this, the reader understands that he was an Amalekite. The history of antagonism between Israel and her arch-rival Amalek spans from the wilderness period to the days of Hezekiah. This corporate history of tribal feuding lies just beneath the surface of our later story about two rival ministers (McKane 1961).

Feuding has certain universal characteristics which are described in ethnographic detail by Black-Michaud (1975) and conceptually summarized by Pospisil (1968). Common to all tribal feuds is a *relationship* between the two groups (Black-Michaud 1975:24; Pospisil 1968:392). Black-Michaud (209ff.) describes feuds as "rituals of social relations." A protracted sequence of violence between rival groups is usually tolerated under the umbrella of a central political structure. Black-Michaud (209) further describes this style of relationship as "eternal." There is an indefiniteness and lack of closure to these conflicts, which more often subside into "cease-fire" rather than end in "peace."

The Amalekites, descendants of Esau (Gen. 36:11-16) in the land of Edom, were among the earliest enemies of Israel who opposed them on their journey to the Promised Land (Ex. 17:8-16). This conflict with Israel's ethnic cousins took on "Alamo" proportions in Israelite literature. In Deut. 25:17-19 Israel is commanded to remember the mistreatment they received in the wilderness and to "blot out the remembrance of Amalek from under heaven. *Do not forget!*" The Amalekites had assumed the role of archetypal wilderness enemies of Israel[18] and were destined to live under the sacred ban.

During the early days of the monarchy the armies of King Saul again faced the tribe of Amalek, and the issue of their absolute obliteration is emphasized once more. In fact, the Lord took the throne away from Saul (I Sam. 15:15, 23 ff.) precisely because he allowed the Amalekite king Agag (and "the best of

---

[18] In rabbinic literature, the Amalekites become a trope for absolute evil (Cf. *Pesikta Rabbati* 12:47; *Pesikta de-Rav Kahana* 27; *Mekhilta*, 181).

the sheep and cattle") to live. Saul's life ends ironically on the spear of an Amalekite (2 Sam. 1:1–10).

This historical/biblical background provides a rationale for Mordecai's refusal to bow down to a hated Amalekite.[19] It also explains Haman's instantaneous plan for genocide. Resolution to this ancient feud will only be achieved, according to the book of Esther, with the extermination of Haman and his kin who bear the legacy of the ancient "Agagites."

## Corporate Personality, Representative Responsibility

> *The second relevant feature of social structure is the social solidarity of the family, and the categorical nature of obligations between its members. This solidarity is both active and passive. Whatever is done or suffered by one member equally affects the honour and shame of the others. No actor stands in isolation without reference to his membership in a family. He carries always a weight of representative responsibility when his actions are observed or even speculated on by others.* J. K. Campbell (1964:319)

> *The longer I remained in the field, the clearer it became to me that, in the evaluation of conduct, the individual actor was conceived as the protagonist of a family and that the village was commenting upon and evaluating every action.* J. G. Peristiany (1966a:179)

The rivalry between Mordecai and Haman is not only a late chapter in the story of an ancient tribal conflict. It

---

[19] A useful survey of all the standard interpretations of Mordecai's refusal is provided by Fox (1991a:43–46. See also Paton (1908:196,97). Along with Ehrlich, Moore, Meinhold, and Bardtke, Fox (ibid.) agrees that tribal enmity is at the root of the conflict.

Bickerman (1967:179–181) prefers to understand Mordecai's behavior in light of the tales of the *Arabian Nights*: Mordecai should have been promoted because he had just saved the king's life. Thus, to bow before Haman would only acquiesce to injustice and disgrace. Mordecai's honor was at stake. This thesis fits nicely into the categories of honor and shame, but the reason Mordecai gives for not bowing should not be ignored.

Both Bickerman (ibid.) and Fox (ibid.) see these motivations as petty. Herr (1981) helpfully reminds us that ancient Near Eastern law assumes the significance of injured honor and disgrace in cases dealing with vengeance and retribution.

specifically pits the *representative heads* of each community against each other. The biographical notes about Mordecai (2:5) and Haman (3:1) are linear genealogies[20] which identify both individuals as descendants of ancient kings (Haman explicitly, Mordecai implicitly). Both ministers are royal representatives of rival groups, each with a genealogically based claim to rule (=ascribed status).

Ongoing rivalry between group representatives is consistent with the notion of *corporate personality*. H. Wheeler Robinson (1964),[21] following the views of Lévy-Bruhl (1923) (cmp. Durkheim 1961 and Evans-Pritchard 1965),[22] employed this concept in his study of ancient Israel. Anthropologists today question the categorization of a "primitive mentality" which stands behind Robinson's psychology. And biblical scholars prefer the notion of corporate *responsibility*.[23] Yet, some of Robinson's insights are applicable.

The representation of a group by an individual takes on many forms in the Bible. Along with those texts which imply corporate guilt and punishment,[24] there are others which assume that representative figures can stand in the place of the whole community. We know this to be true in the case of kings and other military figures.[25] Goliath, for example, challenged the Israelites with the words:

---

[20] The purpose of a linear genealogy is to "ground a claim to power, status, rank, office... in an earlier ancestor" (R. Wilson 1992:931). In contrast to linear genealogies are the more common "segmented" genealogies which define family relationships and provide a basis for marriage and inheritance and a host of other social rights and obligations. For a fuller treatment of genealogies in the Bible see Wilson (1977).

[21] Robinson's insights were originally presented at conferences and printed as articles during the 1930's. He represents a generation of Israelite religion scholars including J. Pederson, W. R. Smith and J. Frazer.

[22] This school of thought is also exemplified in Lévi-Strauss' (1966) *The Savage Mind*.

[23] See the critiques offered by J. R. Porter (1965:361–80), and J. W. Rogerson (1970:1–16) as well as G. M. Tucker's (1980:11–13) comments in Fortress Press' revised edition of Robinson's article.

[24] The story of Achan in Joshua 7 is a prime example.

[25] Pitt-Rivers (1966:36) finds this dynamic to be true at all levels in contemporary Mediterranean societies: "In both the family and the

"Choose a man for yourselves and let him come down to me. If he is able to fight me and kill me, then we will be your servants. But if I prevail against him and kill him, then you shall be our servants and serve us." (I Sam. 17: 8b–9 NRSV).

*"Choose a man..."* the challenge begins. Goliath was disgraced and enraged when Israel did choose. David was not, in his eyes, Israel's best (and, thus, a true) rival nor was he even a man! (17:42).

There are other examples of representative figures in biblical literature. The Servant Songs of Isaiah unwittingly initiated centuries of interpretive dispute because of the grammatical ambiguity between corporate and individual identities.[26] The "I" of the Psalms is also a representative figure, whether royal or not.[27] Robinson (1964:29) also points out the frequent use of female figures to represent Israel (i.e., Ezekiel 16

---

monarchy a single person symbolizes the group whose collective honour is vested in his person." Klinger (1987:364) describes the same orientation as typical to kinship societies, where "... each represents the right and duties of his group and acts in its name." This "principle of representation," as he calls it, "... accounts for the phenomenon of sequential vengeance... The result is feuds and wars." In such societies, he explains, "personal existence and collective existence are regarded as interchangeable. The group is the vital sphere for the individual and the individual is a quantity in the vital capital of the group" (363)

Similarly, Black-Michaud (1975:27), following S. Nadel (1947), summarizes the theoretical basis for feuding in terms of the "collective responsibility of all members of a group for the behavior of one of its members" and the "collective duty of all members of the injured group to avenge this injury." (See also his comments on pp. 38–54 regarding the solidarity of the vengeance group).

[26] Isa. 49:1–6 provides an exemplary case of the ambiguity, referring to the Servant in the singular in vv. 1 and 2 and then changing to the plural in v. 3.

[27] The identification of "I" laments as royal psalms was promoted by Birkeland (1933; cf. 1955) and later accepted by Mowinckel (1962), A. R. Johnson (1976) and Eaton (1986). Johnson's (1961, 1964) concept of "personality extension" is similar to Robinson's corporate personality and also traces its roots to Lévy-Bruhl.

and Isaiah 54), and the single figure of Dan. 7:13, 27, who represents all the saints.

If corporate personality is defined as the symbolic investment of an individual representative with the attributes and responsibilities of the group, then there is substantial evidence that ancient Israel shared such a view. An appreciation of this perspective suggests that Mordecai and Haman are more than *literary* archetypes. Mordecai[28] is a socio-historical hero who embodies the aspirations of the entire community in the context of tribal feud.

Underneath this passages—and numerous other battle stories—is a notion of holy war which assumes that battles between two nations are simultaneously battles between their respective deities.[29] This understanding is explicit in the encounter between Israel and the Philistines in I Samuel 7. Insulted by David's appearance, Goliath curses David by his gods in v. 43. David, in vs. 45, challenges the Philistine in the name of the God of Israel, "whom you have defied." The conflict between Mordecai and Haman is presumably not only between their respective peoples but also between their respective gods.[30] Other evidence for holy war imagery in Esther will follow in our analysis of Esther 8-10.

### Honor as a "Limited Commodity"

Anthropologists routinely refer to honor as a "limited commodity" (e.g. Foster 1967). The phrase emphasizes the nature of honor as something more than an ideal or value. It is perceived as an entity, a finite substance which must be shared

---

[28] In 4:13,14, Mordecai appeals to Esther's solidarity with her people and specifically warns her that if she does not respond, she and her "father's family" will perish. In this sense, she too represents her kin in the escalating conflict.

[29] For one standard summary of holy war theology which emphasizes divine/human synergy, see P. Miller (1973). The point of departure for this topic is G. von Rad (1958).

[30] The pattern of conflict between the gods in ANE myth mirrors the geo-political rivalries among states on earth.

by all (i.e. male) participants.[31] A zero-sum equation is always in effect: When one person's status goes up, the status of other persons *automatically* and *necessarily* goes down. For agonistic societies with these assumptions, competitive rivalry is endemic.

Haman's promotion is described by the verb גדל and also by the phrase וינשאהו וישם את־כסאו מעל כל־השרים אשר אתו (3:1). Haman was "advanced" (נשא) and "his seat was set over all the nobles that were with him." In 5:11 Haman uses the same language when he recounts to his wife and friends how the king had promoted him (גדל), and advanced him above the other servants of the king (נשאו השרים ועבדי המלך). The emphasis is not only on being exalted but on being exalted *over* the other ministers. The hierarchy shifts for all the ministers when Haman is exalted. And this shift is in full view of all the ministers.[32]

Honor is granted to Haman in the currency of public promotion. It is reinforced by the command that others bow in his presence. The gestures of obeisance in Esther 3 are tokens of respect. In prescribed situations these tokens must be given in order for the status of a superior to be confirmed.

> The ritual and ceremonial aspects of honour assure not only
> the opportunity for those who feel respect to pay it, but they
> commit those who pay it even if they do not feel it.
> (Pitt-Rivers 1966:38)

When Mordecai refuses to comply, he diminishes the honor given by the promotion. Furthermore, the honor which he denies Haman is honor which he is implicitly reserving for himself. Hence, the court interrogation (vv. 3,4), Haman's anger (v. 5) and Haman's plot (v. 6 ff.) follow.

In Daniel 3 the king requires a comparable display of homage when his statue is put on parade. When the three Jewish boys refuse to pay respect to the statue, the comparable cycle of

---

[31] Black-Michaud (1975:121–22, 160ff.) describes honor, like material resources, within a system of "total scarcity." This reality creates interminable conflict.

[32] The connotation of גדל (*piel*) elsewhere in the Bible is *publicly viewed* promotion. In Josh. 3:7 and 4:14 God exalts Joshua "in the eyes of the people." Solomon is, likewise, exalted "in the sight of Israel" (I Chr. 29:25).

interrogation (vv. 13–15), anger (vv. 13, 19) and death-sentence (vv. 19–21) is put into motion.

In Esther 3 the gestures of honor are taken from the roots כרע and חוה. These gestures, like those in Daniel 3,[33] usually refer to behaviors associated with the worship of a deity.[34] But they are also positions of respect used to display deference to a human superior. In Gruber's (1980) analysis of nonverbal communication in the Ancient Near East he carefully analyzes comparative and contextual clues to identify designated gestures. His translation of the two terms in Esther 3 is "to stoop and bend" (199,200). כרע, by far the least common of the two terms,[35] is used most often by itself as a term for crouching, bending the knee, or sinking before humans. The symbolic valence is unmistakably clear: one person is *lower* than another. The act of lowering oneself is an act of humbling oneself. In the economy and geography of honor and shame, the symbolic affirmation of one's own subservient position simultaneously maintains the exalted position of the other.

### The "Laws" of Challenge and Response

> *"We should conceive shame not as a reaction to a loss, but as a reaction to a threat, specifically the threat of demeaning treatment..."* (Deigh 1983:242)

Once the outside observer is aware that honor is viewed as a limited resource, patterns of social behavior can be predicted in the inevitable conflicts that arise. A Mediterranean pattern of "challenge and riposte" has been documented from Homeric

---

[33] The comparable Aramaic verbs in Daniel 3 are from the roots פלח and סוד.

[34] Although the text gives us no reason to suspect that Mordecai felt compelled to worship Haman (which is the assumption of LXX Add. C 7 and the Targums), it is interesting to note that of the 14 occurrences of כרע and חוה together, only in Esther is the compound term a symbolic gesture of reverence for a human; in all other places, it is directed toward a deity.

[35] Verbs from the root, כרע, number 36. There are 200+ occurrences of verbal forms from חוה.

times to the present.[36] A male seeks to gain honor at the expense
of another male through verbal jousting. In the Bible there is
some evidence for this pattern,[37] but an analogous physical
challenge and response model is more prevalent.

Pitt-Rivers (1966:57) insists that an honor challenge is
"something which can only be given by a conceptual equal."[38]
This is especially true among members of a royal court:

> The honour of the aristocracy is such that they are appreciated
> by their dependents and admired by the populace, but their
> reputation looks to their equals for validation, not to their
> inferiors... He is dishonored only by being ostracized by his
> social equals."(ibid., 62)

The relative equality assumed in tribal feuds is mirrored at the
highest levels of society.

While it may be true that "equality invites rivalry" (Pitt-
Rivers 1968a:21), the book of Esther portrays both inter-class and
intra-class challenges. Vashti's disregard for the command of the
king in chapter 1 is clearly a challenge from a subordinate.
Mordecai also disregards the king's command, but his challenge
is directed mostly at Haman, an equal-turned-superior. The fact
that a challenge has been made is apparent to both the
challenged and the onlookers. When a challenge is registered in
the social life of a given community it will eventuate in a
quantitative change in honor for both parties. Mordecai's
challenge[39] to Haman's honor is a witnessed fact in the court.
Peristiany (1966:14) describes this typically agonistic scenario as

---

[36] Adkins (1960a and b, et al) provides examples from the ancient Greek
context. Bourdieu (1966:211-15) reflects on the pattern in modern Kabyle
society.

[37] Malina (1993) and various contributors in Neyrey (1991) build an analysis
of New Testament texts on an understanding of this pattern. See also
Neyrey (1995).

[38] Recall here the angry reaction of Goliath who felt ridiculed by the
appearance of David as his rival.

[39] At a similar point in the Daniel stories, Daniel finds himself in a conflict
not provoked by his own sense of honor but as a result of his own religious
convictions. It is not so clear that Mordecai (in the MT) is operating on such
convictions. See the comments of Collins (1993:272).

"a contest before a chorus, a commenting and evaluating audience."[40] The other ministers simply must find out whether or not Mordecai's challenge will "stand" (עמד; 3:4).

Once a challenge is made, it must be "answered." Response may take different forms, each of which must conform to publicly acknowledged standards. Pitt-Rivers (1966:22) states that:

> ... the claimant to honour must get himself accepted at his own evaluation, must be granted reputation, or else the claim becomes mere vanity, an object of ridicule or contempt.

He further observes that the "honour of the affronted person is in jeopardy and requires "satisfaction" if it is to return to its normal condition" (24).

The language of debt and satisfaction which is central to tribal understandings of feud and retaliation[41] represents the criteria for establishing a successful response to challenges of honor. Haman has to "repay" Mordecai. While he is planning his response, his honor is in a liminal state, as was the king's in Esther 1. Just as possession is said to be nine-tenths of the law, so the *de facto* achievement of honour depends upon the ability to silence anyone who would dispute the title.

The use of the root בזה[42] in Est. 3:6 emphasizes shame dynamics familiar to Haman and Mordecai. Paton (1908:200)[43] partially understands the sense when he comments, "It seemed to him *beneath his dignity* to lay hands on Mordecai alone." The connotation of this verb is not, however, limited to feelings of indignity. בזה was used in the argument of Memucan in 1:17: All

---

[40] The scene in Est. 3:1-6 *necessarily* emphasizes the public awareness and discussion of the other ministers. Compare the remarks of Malina (1993:34–37) on the stages of challenge >> public perception >> response.

[41] Black-Michaud (1975:85) describes the feud as "an unending process whereby the satisfaction of debts simultaneously creates new ones. Feud is an eternal relationship between groups who by the manipulation of debt constantly endeavor to swing the pendulum of political dominance in their favor." (Cmp. Klinger 1987:363)

[42] The phrase ויבז בעיניו literally reads, "he despised in his eyes."

[43] This sense is also found in Fox (1991a:42) and in the NRSV translation.

the women of the kingdom would *despise* their husbands if Vashti's conduct went unchecked. This kind of contempt implies a value judgment *which extends into behaviors of disrespect*. Haman's disdain of Mordecai leads directly to the plot to slaughter his kin. His honor demands that he shame the one who shamed him.

## The Spiral of Revenge

Haman's anger over Mordecai's insolence leads to a dramatic escalation of violence. What begins with gesture may end in genocide. This cycle of increasing retaliation is especially apparent in the kind of feud relationships between Israel and the Philistines and Amalekites. Insults and private squabbles stand on a continuum with warfare.[44] Black-Michaud (1975:32) notes that:

> ... the homicidal stage of vengeance killing and feud cannot be conceptually divorced from the succession of illegitimate acts or torts which in most instances preceded recourse to violence.

"Retribution," in the words of Klinger (1987:368), "is not only a response to action, but it surpasses it."

The tendency to take more than "an eye for an eye" from one's enemy — *with YHWH's blessing* — was part of Israel's code of honor and world-view. Certain accounts give us reason to believe that zealous revenge on one's external enemies was viewed as divinely condoned "just recompense" and not subject to the laws of the community.[45] The story of Samson (Judges 13–

---

[44] Samson's many conflicts with the Philistines illustrate the perceived connection between his own private conflicts with individual Philistines and the relationship between the two tribal nations in general. The best example is the story of Samson's near marriage to a woman from Timnah in Judges 14–15.

[45] As an institution typical to kinship societies, revenge is a law which, by definition, governs behavior with *other* groups. Klinger (1987:363) defines revenge generally as an "act of self-assertion by a group against an outside attacker, *an outward directed act of solidarity*." (italics added)

16), for example, climaxes as Samson is "avenged"[46] for his *two*[47] eyes when he kills 3,000 Philistines. And this was accomplished by the Spirit of the Lord.[48]

Haman's desire to seek revenge on all of Mordecai's kin may have a certain culturally-accepted rationale. But it also, by the same standard, raises the stakes for the Jews when they decide what constitutes the terms of "just recompense."

### Accusation and Slander

> *They lay crafty plans against your people;*
> > *They consult together against those you protect.*
> *They say, "Come, let us wipe them out as a nation;*
> > *Let the name of Israel be remembered no more."*
>
> Ps. 83:4–5 [3–4]

> *One of these more generic problems is that of the corporeal and psychic integrity of the individual, and the threats posed to it by injury and death, destructive mockery and social defeat. A second such problem is that of the terrible conflict when one's reaction to offense and one's ability to retaliate are inhibited by social and political factors.*        P. F. Friedrich (1973:125)

We have noted that the crisis of the story, from a literary point of view, begins with the accusation Haman makes to the king about *a certain people* (3:8):

> There is a certain people scattered and separated among all the peoples in all the provinces of your kingdom; their laws are different from those of all other people and they do not

---

[46] The primary verb for vengeance is נקם, a root about which our discussion will reflect when it appears in Est. 8:13.

[47] The literal translation of Judg. 16:28 actually reads, "... that I might be avenged for *one* of my two eyes..."

[48] Samson prays in Judg. 16:28 that God would strengthen him this one last time. The reader has every reason to believe that the super-human strength which he did receive in the following verses was an answer to that prayer: he was empowered by the same Spirit of God which had filled him from the very beginning (13:25, 14:19, 15:14).

observe the laws of the king. It doesn't pay[49] the king to let them remain.[50]

The key words in this accusation are "certain" (אֶחָד; lit., "one"), "scattered" (פֻּזָר), "separated" (פָּרֵד) and "different" (שֹׁנֶה). Haman creates a threat by reconstructing a nameless people whose pervasive presence, cultural peculiarities and treasonous behavior set them apart from "all other people." Haman's strategy effectively isolates the Jews and thereby shames them before the king. In biblical terms, this strategy is called "slander."[51]

To slander is to malign verbally, to construct an unfavorable representation of another person or group. It is a cousin of the lie (Prov. 10:18) because it involves a distortion of truth. Both require a third party. Although slander is something done with the tongue (Ps. 50:20), it is a form of violence nonetheless (Ps. 140:11).[52] For an exiled people, to be an object of slander and mockery was to suffer insult with injury (Ezk. 36:3). In the case of the Jews in the story of Esther, it is the insult which initiates the process of a global injury.

In this context אֶחָד evokes an image of threatening solidarity and also one of peculiarity. This is a certain, particular,

---

[49] A discussion of the root שׁוה will follow below. An accurate translation might be, "It's not worth it to the king..." but the monetary nuance present in Esther in all three uses of the term could be missed with this idiom.

[50] Fox (1991a:51) makes the observation that the consonantal text in this verse (לחניח)) could as easily mean "to leave alone" as "to give rest." This deliberate ambiguity cleverly foreshadows the "rest" which the Jews will finally receive in 9:17, 18, 22.

[51] Prov. 16:28 says "a slanderer separates (פרד) close friends." Mordecai might legitimately be considered one of the king's "friends" for saving his life.

[52] The cycle of violence often begins with some word or gesture which is understood to be a form of attack. The old adage, "Sticks and stones may break my bones but names will never hurt me," is not a truism but an attempt to circumvent the substantial effects of insult. Words are verbal sticks and stones and when they are thrown indirectly by a rival through a listening third party they may do even more damage than physical violence. One Japanese informer told Ruth Benedict (1946:160,161) that a public "sneer" was considered an "assassination of the soul and heart."

*distinct* people.[53] Being unnamed subtly makes the Jews even
more threatening. The slander continues by isolating (lit.,
"separating"; פרד) the Jews from all other ethnic groups.[54] They
are different and their laws are different.[55] Shame, we have
noted, results from isolation (both physical and emotional) from
one's group. To be isolated in any sense is to suffer
vulnerability[56] and disgrace.

The Jews, according to Haman, are also "scattered"
(מפזר).[57] Scattered is the shame state of defeated enemies (Ps.
53:5, 89:10, 141:7).[58] It can imply homelessness, uprootedness and
decentralization. Moore (1971:39) suggests that the term here
implies self-imposed separateness or exclusiveness: They are
"scattered, yet unassimilated." Haman is suggesting that their
ubiquitous presence, coupled with their exclusivistic and
rebellious ways, insidiously threatens the empire.

Similar sentiments are found in Ezra 4:12-16. The rivals of
the Jews in Palestine describe the early Jewish movement to
restore the city of Jerusalem as a threat to the Persian empire:

> Let it be known to the king that the Jews who came up ... will
> not pay tribute, custom or toll and it will damage the revenue
> of the kings. Now because we are in the service of the palace,
> and it is not fitting for us to see the king's dishonor, therefore
> we have sent and informed the king ...

The monetary dimension explicit here is inherent in Haman's
request and in Esther's later charge (7:4). The king's potential
dishonor is a constant theme in the book of Esther and it is
central to the accusations in Dan. 3:12 and 6:13 as well. The self-

---

[53] Being unique can, of course, be a good thing. God, as declared in the
great *Shema* of Israel, is אחד (Deut. 6:4). The distinction of Israel as God's
elect is at the heart of the covenant.

[54] Note the use of פרד in the reference to Israel's boundaries in Deut. 32:8.

[55] The uniqueness of Israel's laws was meant to be a source of positive
distinction among the nations, not shame (Deut. 4:5-8).

[56] Compare Neh. 4:19 where physical vulnerability is a consequence of
physical separation.

[57] There are 10 forms of פור in the MT.

[58] Israel is described as a "scattered flock" in Jer. 50:17.

aggrandizing statements of loyalty to the king which supposedly motivate such accusations are also implicit in Haman's speech.

Daniel's accusers in Dan. 6:13 are, literally, those who "ate his pieces" (אכלו קרצוהי). This ancient idiom[59] illustrates the seriousness of slander (cmp. Gal. 5:15). It also serves the irony of the conclusion as Daniel's accusers are literally eaten to pieces by the lions (Dan. 6:24). Poetic justice is similarly expressed when Haman hangs on the gallows he erects for Mordecai. Haman had taken the king aside to verbally isolate the Jews. As providential justice will have it, Haman's turn for isolation and exposure is next.

### Esther 4 –5: The Jewish Response to Haman's Edict

#### *Summary of the Narrative*

Esther 4 and 5 describes the Jewish response to Haman's scheme. Chapter 4 recounts the fasting of the whole Jewish community with Mordecai as its head. In this symbolic parallel to Haman casting the *pur*, the Jews seek divine intervention for their cause.[60] Once Mordecai gains Esther's attention[61] — and cooperation — they begin to construct a plan to subvert Haman's edict. As the chapter concludes, the Jews, now with Esther as their symbolic representative, fast again for three days. These fasts form a literary antithesis to the banqueting of the king and Haman.

---

[59] This phrase is found in all dialects of Akkadian in the Amarna texts.

[60] The religious nature of fasting in Esther will be discussed below.

[61] When Esther hears of Mordecai's public behavior, she is "very disturbed," or, with Moore (1971:48), "shocked." The *hithpalpal* of חיל appears only here in the MT. The Greek uses the same verb (ταράσσω) for Esther's response in 4:4 as is does for the "confusion" (נבוכה) of the city in 3:15 and Haman's terrified response in 7:6. This linguistic connection in Greek reflects the social and literary see-saw in the story. When Haman is in control, there is confusion and terror for both the city and the Jews. When Haman is challenged, he is terrified but the Jews and the city return to order and peace.

The plan which unfolds as we move into chapter 5 begins with faith[62] but its execution will involve a combination of composure and cunning.[63] Esther decides to risk her life[64] and seek an audience with the king. When the king sees her dressed in royalty (*malkut*), "she obtained favor in his sight" (5:2).[65] The king's favor is expressed by granting her acceptance into the court and by offering her virtually whatever she wants.[66] To the surprise of the reader (and most likely the king), she simply invites him to a banquet along with his premier. At the banquet the king's offer is repeated and Esther, more surprisingly, invites

---

[62] Esther's statement, "If I perish, I perish," at the close of chapter 4 (v. 16) is reminiscent not only of Jacob's response to the news of Joseph's death in Gen. 43:14 (Fox 1991a:64) but also of the sentiments of Shadrach, Meshach and Abednego in Dan. 3:17,18: "If our God is able to deliver us ... let it be so. But if not ... we will not serve your gods..."

[63] Esther's interceding and saving role is very much like that of Abigail (I Sam. 25:24–31) and the woman of Tekoa (2 Sam. 14:4–17). As she removes her sackcloth and puts on her royal attire for the task ahead, one is also reminded of Judith (Judith 10:1–5). Esther and Judith are both known already for their beauty (cf. Est. 2:7; Judith 8:7) but as they each emerge from fasting, they consciously clothe themselves with a sense of purpose and destiny. They literally "dress to kill."

[64] Josephus vividly describes Artaxerxes' throne encircled by men with axes who would chop to pieces any intruders (*Antiquities* XI 6.3).

[65] See the discussion above concerning favor and grace in Esther 2. Also compare the vivid sentiments expressed in the LXX rendering of this account.

[66] This offer is often compared with Xerxes' offer to his daughter-in-law, Artaynte (Herodotus IX 109–11) and to Herod's offer to Salome (Mark 6:23). In all three cases, a grandiose gesture is taken literally by a female who has something very specific in mind. In the other two accounts, the request satisfies personal jealousy and animosity with the result that the king is chagrined. In Esther, as we will see, the request is one that similarly surprises the king but it is one which represents self-sacrificing loyalty to kin.

The king's offer is also another example of his generosity. In chapter 1 he offered his guests drink without restraint. His magnanimity takes on perverse dimensions when he allows his prime minister to do what he wishes with an unidentified constituency in his empire.

the king and Haman to yet another banquet. Only then will she make her request known.[67]

Haman sets off homeward "happy and in good spirits"[68] (5:9), but his self-satisfaction is drained the moment he experiences Mordecai's indifference[69] to him. *Status anxiety* returns. When he recounts all of his wealth[70] and honors to his family and friends, he admits that none of this can compensate (שׁוֹה) for Mordecai's refusal to pay him respect (v. 13). Zeresh, his wife, revives his self-centered happiness when she suggests a personal gallows tailored for Mordecai.

Chapter 5 is the scene in which the narrative generates the most suspense. The delays and detailed descriptions arouse the reader's curiosity at the very moment during which the narrative is poised for the most critical action (Fox 1991a:66). Plot-retardation gives the reader an opportunity to ask the unanswerable questions: Why does Esther hesitate to ask for the king's favor? Is she, in fact, out of the king's favor (v. 11)? What if

---

[67] Compare the "banquet" Joseph prepares for his brothers in Gen. 43:16–34 during which he keeps his purposes and identity secret. Only at a later occasion (45:3) does he reveal himself and his intentions.

[68] Haman was "happy" (שׂמח; a term to which we will return) and, literally, "good of heart" (טוב לב). This second phrase is one often (though not always) used to describe a state of inebriation (as it was in Est. 1:10; cmp. Judg. 16:25, I Sam. 25:36, 2 Sam. 13:28). It is a phrase explicitly connected with feasting not only here in Esther but also in Prov. 15:15. The scene at Haman's house is, thus, a continuation of the feasting which concludes chapter 3. He can happily banquet with the king as long as there are plans underway to restore his injured dignity.

[69] Not only does Haman want Mordecai to bow, as the king commanded, but also to rise in his presence and "tremble" (זוע). This little used term for shaking describes the subjects response to the awesome presence of a king in Dan. 5:19 and the living God in Dan. 6:27[26]. With characteristic irony, the author will describe Haman in a terrified (בעת) state before Esther in Est. 7:6.

[70] The number of one's sons was a sign of wealth in ancient Persia (*Herodotus* I. 136). For similar sentiments regarding modern Mediterranean societies, see the comments of J. K. Campbell (1964:297). The words of Ps. 127:4,5 represent this biblical equation between sons and honor:

Like arrows in the hand of a warrior are the sons of one's youth.

Happy is the man who has his quiver full of them.

He shall not be put to shame when he speaks with his enemies at the gate.

king's favor? Is she, in fact, out of the king's favor (v. 11)? What if his mood changes and his magnanimous offer disappears? What if Mordecai is hanged before the next banquet? This is that critical moment, the *kairos*,[71] for which Esther was brought to the throne (cf. 4:14). When Haman goes off to his home to boast, there is no way to know in which direction the scales will tip. It is this tension which creates the anticipation that chapter 6 will answer with such characteristic irony.

Chapters 4 and 5 are pivotal for the development of Esther's character. Fox (1991a:66) calls 4:13-17 *the* turning point in Esther's development:[72]

> She moves from being a dependent of others (all of them men) to an independent operator ... who will manipulate one man and break another.

She was passive in the previous chapters, being "taken" from place to place and "admired" (ibid. 197-9). Her obedience to Mordecai was noted more than once. Now, in this dramatic scene, Esther emerges as the one who chooses (though hesitatingly at first)[73] the call of duty and honor. Her independence begins with her resistance to Mordecai's challenge in 4:11. Although she eventually agrees, it is she who gives orders, even to Mordecai (4:16). The plan she then executes is one of her own devising.

Esther continues to exhibit deference to the males in positions of control throughout this section; even her final banquet request in 5:8 is framed as a response to the king's

---

[71] The use of the term καιρός, in the LXX, both here and in Est. 2:12, underscores the sense of timing and serendipity at these points in the story. Her courageous resolve at this point signals her as a true heroine. A Japanese proverb is *apropos*: "The reputation of a thousand years may be decided by the conduct of a single hour."

[72] I agree with Fox (1991a:66), contrary to Berg (1979:110), that the turning point in Esther's development is not the turning point of the story. The turning point of the story is built on the tensions of chapters 4 and 5 and lies ahead in the next section.

[73] Gerleman (1973:18) notes the comparable hesitancy of Esther and Moses before they seek deliverance from the hand of the king (cmp. Est. 4:11ff with Ex. 3:11; 4:10, 13; 6:12, 30).

command (Fox 1991a:73). But Esther is now a person using the formalities of honor and shame to accomplish the deliverance of her people. Through a style of "subversive submission" (cf. Herzfeld 1991) she will remain in control[74] from this point onward.

### Ritual Mourning, Ritual Humiliation

The Jewish response to Haman's edict includes a series of ritual gestures commonly practiced throughout the Near East:

> "Mordecai *tore his clothes* and *put on sackcloth and ashes* and *paraded through the city, wailing with a loud and bitter cry;* ... In every province ... there was a *great mourning* among the Jews by means of *fasting* and *weeping* and *breast-beating,* and most of them *lay in sackcloth and dust.*[75] (Est. 4:1-3)

These gestures are typical lamentation rituals enacted in the wake of death or calamity.[76] On occasion — as in Esther 4 — they are also behaviors which *precede* an anticipated disaster. In such cases, they seek to move the hand of God to prevent it.[77] Rituals and words of laments may be, ultimately, expressions of hope.

---

[74] Esther's capacity to wait bespeaks her self-control. It should be pointed out that Haman also "refrains" (אפק) from doing anything rash with Mordecai in 5:10. Like the king, Haman seeks comprehensive legal action as the more effective response to challenge. According to L. Abu-Lughod (1986:90-92), self-mastery is a form of autonomy which characterizes honor in the Middle East today.

[75] I follow Gruber's (1980:418) translation of these terms as well as his understanding that all of these actions were ritual components of the "great mourning."

[76] DeVaux's (1965:59) summary gives ample biblical citations. Gruber (ibid.) provides comparative (ANE) evidence and gives detailed descriptions of each behavior (see especially pp. 412, 417-18, 446, 457, 460 for those mentioned in Esther 4).

[77] A comparable example of "preventive fasting" is found in the third chapter of the story of Jonah. After the prophet warns Nineveh of its imminent overthrow, the king "removed his robe, covered himself with sackcloth, and sat in ashes" (v. 6). He proclaimed a city-wide fast (no food or water) for human and beast, ordering that every living thing should be covered with sackcloth and that every person should "cry mightily to God" (v. 8). "Who knows?" he asks, "God may relent...so that we do not perish."

The specifically detailed behavioral descriptions of Esther 4 deserve careful attention. Position is emphasized as Mordecai *parades*[78] through the city wearing sackcloth and wailing. The Jews are depicted *laying* in sackcloth and dust. Clothing is powerfully symbolic. Mordecai rips his clothes and then puts on sackcloth and ashes. This common movement of public undressing and then redressing in the clothing of death (dust, ashes) symbolizes a change in status and state.[79] Mordecai is humbling himself by voluntarily wearing the clothing of the poor. He is also dramatically presenting himself as a dead person, for that is his sentence. Wailing, crying and mourning are also emphasized. Mordecai's cry in v. 1 is *loud* (lit., "great") and *bitter*. Throughout all the provinces there was *great mourning* (v. 3). All of these ritual behaviors are accompanied by fasting, a

---

(v. 9). In another story with similar sentiments, David explains, "I fasted and wept; for I said, 'Who knows whether the Lord will be gracious to me, that the child may live.'" (2 Sam. 12:22). When God did not heal his son, David anointed himself and began eating again.

To make the claim that the Jews in Esther are clearly seeking help *from God* is controversial. In a book in which religious sentiment is so persistently avoided, some wonder whether this kind of fast was not rather a natural human response to tragedy. Job's friends, one recalls, wept aloud and tore their robes and threw dust on their heads just from the sight of him (Job 2:12). Similarly, Tamar tears her clothes, covers herself with ashes and mourns as a "natural" (though ritualized) response to tragedy (2 Sam. 13:19). It is outside the scope of our discussion to enter directly into this debate but the combination of these ritual forms of mourning with community fasting is suggestive of a religious fast. The LXX and Targums clearly understand these actions to be directed toward God. This is also the point in the court story pattern where Daniel seeks God in prayer (Dan. 6:10).

[78] This translation of אצי captures the sense that Mordecai desires to be seen in this state.

[79] The anthropology of clothing is a fascinating and relevant topic to which we will devote our attention in the analysis of chapter 6. The link between clothing and status is evident in this section not only in terms of mourning rituals but also when Esther emerges from the fast in 5:1. She then dons royal apparel, or literally, "queenship" (*malkut*). *Malkut*, in Mordecai's argument, is a position Esther had been granted by providence for just such a critical moment (4:14).

practice on which Esther will insist for her assistants as well (v. 16).

Gestures of mourning are multivalent. At the heart of mourning ritual is the theme of death.[80] G. Anderson (1991:89) points out that, in the ANE, mourning is not merely a means of expressing grief. It is also, more symbolically, a *ritual identification with the dead*.[81] Death is symbolized by the dust and ashes. When mourners lie in them and sprinkle them on their heads they are dramatizing the state of death. Fasting is a similar life-denying mourning ritual (cf. 2 Samuel 1 and 3).

Death is, however, also a metaphorical state into which one enters through disaster and calamity.[82] The laments illustrate this perception quite profoundly. When one is separated from God and friends; when one is under attack by sickness and enemies; when one suffers the death of one's reputation (= shame); in these moments the language of the mourner is engaged (Anderson, ibid.). In fact, ancient Israelite conceptions of death and disaster may best be understood as end points on a shared continuum. Disaster and disgrace are versions of death.[83]

The symbols of death were also, necessarily, associated with impurity.[84] To wear these symbols and to engage in

---

[80] Turner (1969:95; cf. 108–113) notes that death is frequently associated with liminal states and entities. Lament and mourning mark the crucial moment of liminality for the Jews in the Esther story.

[81] Vogelzang and van Bekkum (1986:269ff.) support this thesis with parallels from mythic texts.

[82] In C. Barth's (1947) classic examination of Israel's views on death he explains the role of Sheol in the experience of the living.

[83] G. Anderson (1991:87) defines the ancient view of death as a "process that can culminate in the complete termination of life but does not have to." The Jews in Esther 4, like the lamenters of the Psalms, entered Sheol on the day their sentence was signed by the king. They mark their absence from God by ritual impurity (see ahead) and the rites of mourning. In so doing they also "state their case," with the hope that God will deliver them from their virtual death.

[84] The impurity laws in ancient Israel—most of which are concerned with death or sex—have often been compared with taboos in other cultures (see Neusner 1973:22). Ritual uncleanness of any kind is often associated with death in the Bible. Laws regarding leprosy, bodily discharges and sexual activity each bear an association with death (Andre and Ringgren 1986; G.

mourning was to put oneself outside the state of purity. Friedrich (1973:121) describes ancient Greek mourning rituals as "homeopathic self pollution." Mordecai was probably forbidden entrance into the king's gate (v. 2) because of his unclean state.[85]

Mourning rites are also self-shaming rituals: "I put on sackcloth and *humbled myself* with fasting" (Ps. 35:13). Esther's actions are described in the AT[86] with vivid terms for shame:

> And Esther the queen, seized with deathly anxiety, fled to the Lord; she took off her splendid apparel and every sign of her glorious rank, and clothed herself with distress and mourning, and instead of costly perfumes she covered her head with ashes and dung, and she utterly humbled her body, and every sign of her adornment and delight on her lovely head she covered with humiliation.

The public ripping of outer clothing and exposure of inner clothing is virtual nakedness.[87] Sackcloth, the inner garment, is a synonym for nakedness in Mic. 1:8. Mourners at times would also shave their hair and beard.[88] These rituals of nakedness are rites of self-degradation, self-humiliation, and self-shaming (Vogelzang and van Bekkum 1986:272ff.). When an individual or

---

Anderson 1991:87 n.81). The seven day mourning period in ancient Israel required a ritual purification at its termination (Num. 19:1–22). For more discussion on the relation of mourning and uncleanness see Feldman (1977).

[85] Purity is a central feature in many stories of this period (cf. Daniel 1). Perhaps it is in this scene of ritual mourning that the issue is raised in Esther.

[86] The following translation is taken from Clines (1984:229).

[87] In some cases shoes and headdresses were also removed (e.g. Ezk. 24:17,23). Note the clear contrast set up between the shame rituals of mourning and the clothing of honor which Esther puts on in 5:1. The LXX describes her clothing there as "garments of glory."

[88] A story in 2 Samuel 10 illustrates the link between various forms of nakedness and shame. Mistrusting David's gesture of kindness, Hanun cuts off the beards and half of the skirts of David's servants. The Ammonites immediately prepare for war for they knew that they had "greatly dishonored" David (v. 5). For a thorough discussion of the dynamics of honor and shame in this story, see Stansell (1992:109) and, more recently, Olyan (1996:212,213).

group lies in the dust, the act is not only a ritual identification with the dead, it is also a means of deliberately lowering one's status in the eyes of the community.[89]

In much of the social scientific literature on the topic of shame there is a consistent emphasis on shame as *exposure*.[90] Because honor is often expressed in deliberate self-display, one must further qualify shame as *undesirable* exposure. Involuntary nakedness is the archetypal shame state. Only in the exceptional context of mourning would a person voluntarily make a public display of shame. In the story of Esther, this ritual dramatizes the impending disaster from which the Jews seek deliverance.

The deliberate self-shaming of the Jews subtly corresponds to the state of exposure already induced by Haman's slander. Exposure can be as much a matter of misrepresentation as a state of undress. Through slander, entire ethnic groups can lose control over the perceptions of on-lookers. Their perceived status and worth as a collective—in short, their reputation—can be stripped by a simple insinuation. In the case of mourning rituals, that same group "owns" their naked state and turns it into a lament for divine deliverance.

## Primary Loyalties

> The conceptual framework of the field of obligations of honour is that of the family and of families linked together by common obligations to honour — in reality by a common honour to defend.
>
> J. G. Peristiany (1966a:188)

Esther maintains her loyalty to Mordecai through continual obedience even after she moves into the king's household. The ethnic identity which she keeps secret in the court is the very identity which constitutes her greater sphere of loyalty. The crux of Mordecai's argument (4:14) centers on this assumption: She must not remain silent any longer. If she fails to

---

[89] In certain rituals of traditional societies the symbolism of death illustrates the liminal position of a person during a rite of passage (see Turner 1967:93–111; 151–279, esp. pp. 200ff.)

[90] The title of a recent volume by M. Lewis (1992) illustrates the point: *Shame, The Exposed Self*.

speak up for her people at this critical moment, both she and her "father's house" will perish (4:14).

As is typical for kin-based communities, societies in the circum-Mediterranean assume the primary loyalty of individuals to the family. This is especially true for females who often maintain distinct ties to the family of their fathers even after marriage (Campbell 964:257,263; Peristiany 1968:87; Antoun 1968:691–92; Gilmore 1987a:99–100; R. and N. Tapper 1992–3).

Anthropologists define primary loyalty as one that is not only central among other relationships but as one which regulates all the others. A family member is first of all, and more than anything else, a family member. This tautological datum automatically makes one's individual identity secondary.

Loyalty to kin also precedes and informs all ethical decisions. Anthropological discussions of deception, for example, follow the lines of family honor and loyalties. Jean du Boulay (1976:406, 393) observes that:

> Deceit ... [is] intimately connected with the structure of the value system and as part of the legitimate means by which the honour of a family is preserved ... [T]he defense of the family ... is seen not only as a necessity but also as a moral good.

The ancient reader's assessment of Esther's behavior would have followed the issue of her family loyalty more than the subtle ethical issues surrounding her previous silences and potential deceptions. In fact, her performance would undoubtedly be judged by the cleverness with which she outwitted her opponent for the cause of family preservation.[91] In contrast to Haman, Esther is concerned with more than her own life and honor. She is a model of loyalty to her people.

### The Rejoicing Enemy

In the story of Esther there is a duel of sorts going on between two enemies. The author sides with the Jews, naming

---

[91] Compare here the comments of Phillips (1986) on the dynamics of deception in the book of Ruth.

Haman, "the Enemy of the Jews" (3:10). The title will be with him till the end (8:1; 9:10, 24). When Esther does finally identify Haman's plot to the king, she calls him, "A foe and enemy, this wicked Haman" (7:6). The festival of Purim celebrates relief the Jews finally received from "their enemies" (9:22).

The stereotyped role of the enemy in the laments provides insight into the role of "The Enemy" in Esther. G. Anderson (1991:93) notes numerous prayers, psalms and oracles throughout the Bible which refer to the enemy as one who "rejoices over" his victim. The lamenter of Psalm 35, for example, seeks relief from those who "gather in glee" (v. 15), "impiously mock" (v. 16), "wink the eye" (v. 19) and "rejoice over me" (vv. 19, 24, 26). Joy and happiness are unmistakable marks of the winners in war, and they are emotions which drive the participants in conflict. The lamenter desperately seeks escape from the gloating eye[92] of his assailant (cmp. Widengren 1937:205,219 ff.). Haman is most poignantly represented as this rejoicing enemy at the end of Esther 5.

The sentiment of joy described by various biblical terms (primarily from the root שׂמח; cf. Est. 5:9, 14) is one closely associated with shame and honor (cf. Isa. 61:7; 66:5). As the psalmist brings his case to a close in Psalm 35, his prayer is that those who rejoice at his calamity "... be put to *shame and confusion*; [and]... be clothed with *shame and dishonor*" (Ps. 35:26). In contrast, he wants those who seek his vindication to "shout for *joy* and be *glad*" (v. 27). This is precisely the response of the population in the story of Esther when the Jews are vindicated.

The context of enmity creates roles for both participants and onlookers.[93] To be sure, the defeat of one's enemies may satisfy a number of interests (i.e., monetary, agricultural, etc.) which require no "audience." But the prevalence of the rejoicing enemy motif in the Bible suggests that public shame was one of

---

[92] The enemy is sometimes pictured as one who eats after sealing the fate of the Jewish hero. Haman sits down with the king to dine in 3:15. Joseph's brothers also feast once they have him in the pit (Gen. 37:25; cmp. Ps. 23:5).

[93] Anderson (ibid.) emphasizes the tension in the laments where friends of the lamenter chose either the role of comforter or enemy. "To rejoice while a neighbor was in mourning was to declare oneself an enemy..." (94).

the *primary* goals of conflict, and one which assumed a community of onlookers. Being "laughed at" was a dreaded prospect. In David's lament for Saul and Jonathan, he implores silence over creation, lest "the daughters of the Philistines rejoice, the daughters of the uncircumcised exult" (I Sam. 1:20). In so many of the prophetic descriptions of exile there is this dreaded refrain, that Israel will become a laughingstock of the nations.[94] It is precisely Haman's goal to make of Israel such a laughingstock.[95]

In face-to-face societies, continual public scrutiny controls one's social identity. Because "the observing other is ubiquitous" (E. Hatch 1989:349), the concern over *how* one is seen is constant. In biblical terms, a person's "look" may be a watching over in a protective sense. But, more often, to look is to judge or gloat. The constant fear of the lamenter in the Psalms is failure or defeat "before (lit., the face of; לִפְנֵי) my enemies." "Social prestige," observes J. K. Campbell (1964:264,5; cf. 317), "depends overwhelmingly on the opinions of enemies."[96] As this section of Esther comes to a close, the "enemy of the Jews" is "happy" for he assumes that their imminent demise will translate into his own enhanced honor.

---

[94] According to Ezk. 25:3ff., God will exterminate those nations who say "Aha" and "clap their hands" and "rejoice with malice" over the destruction of Israel (See also Ezk. 35:12–13). See the discussion of comparable ANE treaty curses discussed in Hillers (1964:76ff.).

[95] Joy is not only a sentiment ascribed to Haman. The Jews will rejoice at his death and create an annual holiday to re-rejoice over his demise. Rejoicing over one's enemies is usually not condemned (but cmp. Prov. 24:17); it is the enemies who rejoice over God's elect who are condemned (See I Sam. 2:1, 2 Chr. 20:27). The hope of the psalmist is that he will, in the end, look with joy over the punishment of his enemies: "The righteous will rejoice when they see vengeance done; they will bathe their feet in the blood of the wicked" (Ps. 58:11[10]). This topic will receive further attention in the analysis of Esther 8–10 below.

[96] Interestingly, one term for enemy in the Psalms is שׁוֹרֵר, a participial form derived from one of the Hebrew verbs of seeing (שׁוּר). My enemies are, in effect, my *watchers*, those who look at me with evil intent. They watch for me to fail, and when they see me fail they are quick to rejoice (see Ps. 5:9, 27:11, 54:7, 56:3, 59:11, 92:12).

# Chapter 3

# *REVERSAL*
## *THE "FALL" OF THE JEWISH ENEMY*

## ESTHER 6–7

### Esther 6: Mordecai Honored and Haman Disgraced

*Summary of the Narrative*

Chapter 6 is the hinge of the story of Esther; the key reversals around which the plot revolves begin here (Fox 1991a: 82). Haman had first plotted the complete annihilation of the Jews and, upon the urging of his family and friends, an immediate execution of Mordecai. In chapter 6 he unwittingly prescribes honor for the man he sought to humiliate on a stake. Thus begins the reversal of honor for the two men which will lead to Haman's execution, not Mordecai's, and to the death of Haman's kin and supporters, not the Jews.

The episode begins with a remarkable series of circumstances which mark the plot's pivot:

> By coincidence the king could not sleep that night,[1] by coincidence he wiled away the time listening to a reading of the royal annals, and by coincidence the reader hit upon the mention of Mordecai's discovery of the assassination plot.
> (ibid., 75–6)

---

[1] The motif of the king's insomnia is also found in Dan. 6:19[18E] and in 3 Esdras 3:3.

The king asked how Mordecai was honored for this benefaction.
When he found out nothing had been done, he asked that
whoever was in the outer court be brought in so that a suitable
honor might be discussed. By coincidence, Haman happened to
be just outside. By coincidence, the king did not mention the
benefactor's name when he posed the question. By coincidence,
Haman made the calculated assumption that the king wished to
honor him and not anyone else. Consequently, he suggests a
royal parade "to honor one whom the king desires to honor"
(6:7–9).

While the peripety of chapter 6 serves distinct literary
purposes, it also hints at divine intervention. Virtually all of the
ancient interpreters describe these events as the result of
providence. As Josephus (Bk. XI. VI. 10; cmp. LXX Est. 6:1)
recounts the episode, "God laughed to scorn the wicked
expectations of Haman ... [and] that night he took away the
king's sleep." The Latin and Aramaic versions concur. While the
role of God in MT Esther is often debated as a *theological* topic,
the notion of fate must be granted at least the status of a literary
theme for it courses throughout the entire story (cf. Levenson
1997:95).

When Haman is asked what should be done for one the
king "desires to honor," he can imagine no one more deserving
than himself. His suggestions—each of which assumes an
equation between honor and royalty—reveal all too clearly his
pretensions of hubris.

> Haman rolls the phrase 'the man whom the king desires to
> honor' around in his mouth four times, beginning and ending
> his little speech with it. But in the end he will have to use it of
> Mordecai, and do so loudly and repeatedly ... and in the city
> square no less. It is easy to imagine how the words Haman
> once savored will then fill his mouth with gall. (Fox 1991a:76)

The disjointed syntax in 6:7 reveals Haman's overanxiousness to
promote himself. At just the point in his answer when it would
have been appropriate to show formal deference to the king
(cmp. 5:7) he eagerly seeks to "exploit his unexpected
opportunity" (ibid., 76).

Haman is greedy for the symbols of royalty. He asks for a robe which the king has worn, a crowned horse which the king has ridden and a noble to lead him through the streets proclaiming, "this is what is done for the man whom the king desires to honor" (v. 9). Irony borders on slapstick as Haman creates an elaborate public ceremony to honor himself only to find himself the humiliated escort of his decorated enemy.

Several scholars[2] have compared Haman's desired rewards with those involved in Joseph's promotion by the Pharaoh in Gen. 41:38–44.[3] The public honoring of the Jewish courtier is also found in the Daniel stories (2:48,49; 3:30; 5:29). The unique expression of this motif in Esther is provided by Haman's hubris: he impetuously defines the details of the occasion *for himself.*

Royal boundaries are transgressed in other, more subtle ways. Joseph wore a garment of fine linen. Haman wanted one of the king's own robes.[4] Joseph rode in the chariot of the prime minister. Haman wanted one of the king's own horses. Some scholars wonder whether there is behind Haman's prescription not only a desire to be *like* the king, but a treasonous intention to *be* king.[5] When David has Solomon ride on his own mule in I Kgs. 1:33, he is thereby creating a public ceremony of *succession.* The MT of Esther does not explicitly state that this was Haman's intention, but certain ancient versions do (LXX Add. E 16:12–14; cf. Josephus Bk. XI. VI. 12).

---

[2] See, in particular, the works of Rosenthal (1895, 1897), Gan (1961), and Berg (1979).

[3] The Greek versions use items from the Joseph material (Gen. 41:42) not found in MT Esther: the LXX adds "linens" in v. 8 and Josephus adds a "gold necklace."

[4] In Est. 6:8 Haman specifically states that the robes must be ones the king had actually worn. The account in Plutarch (*Artaxerxes* 5) of Teribazus' similar request of Artaxerxes II reveals the near-magical associations of royal clothing in ancient Persia. He was given the robe but forbidden to wear it. Herodotus (III 84, IX 110-111) and Xenophon (*Cyropeadia* VIII 2,8) also infer such associations. These sources are discussed in more detail by S. K. Eddy (1961:45–47) who is cited by Fox (1991a:77).

[5] See the reflections of Levenson (1997:97–98) on this scene and his reference to the ancient Mesopotamian institution of the substitute king.

After Haman endures the painful ordeal, he returns home humiliated. He "hurried to his home, mourning and with his head covered" (6:12). The terms for shame from chapter 4 are revisited with a different subject. Mordecai was previously the one who wore the clothing of humiliation and offered the cries of mourning. For him, and for the Jews who accompanied him, these were gestures and symbols which accompanied the news of their death sentence. Haman, in chapter 6, is now "bewailing the death of his own honor" (Fox 1991a:79).

Looking for words of comfort, Haman hears only the ominous prediction of ultimate demise: "If Mordecai, before whom you have begun to fall, is of the seed of the Jews, you will not prevail over him, but will surely fall before him." (6:13) These sentiments likely refer to the biblical predictions of Amalekite annihilation (Ex. 17:16; Num. 24:20; Deut. 25:17-19; I Samuel 15), discussed above. The awareness of divine support for the Jews *by Gentiles* is, itself, an important biblical motif (cf. Numbers 22-24; Josh. 2:9-14: cf. Dan. 2:46-47; 3:28-33; 4:34). Similarly, in Judith 5:5ff., Achior the Ammonite tries to convince General Holofernes to avoid battle with the Jews. He argues that the Jews are invincible as long as they keep themselves from sin, "... for their Lord and God will defend them, and we will become the laughingstock of the whole world" (v. 21). Haman becomes just this kind of fool not only in the story of Esther once written but also in the drama of Purim annually retold.

The two vignettes at Haman's home serve to frame the episode in chapter 6. In both accounts Haman arrives humiliated. In 5:9-14 he cannot bear to witness Mordecai's indifference to his presence at the gate. In 6:12-14 he unwittingly heaped honor on this very person who denied him honor. In the first vignette Haman's wife and friends are able to encourage him with a concrete plan for revenge. The second vignette reveals how much has changed in the ensuing episode. The encouraging words of "friends" (אהבין) are replaced by the ominous words of "wise men" (חכמיו).

The reversal that chapter 6 details is marked in a variety of ways, some of which we have already highlighted. The annals that are opened are those mentioned in 2:23. The חפץ (desire) of the king to honor in chapter 6 recalls his desire for any of the virgins in 2:14. The symbolism of gestures and clothing has been noted. Mordecai was dressed in sack cloth and mourning in chapter 4. In chapter 6, Haman is covered in shame and mourning.[6] While Haman was previously the one enjoying royal prerogatives, יקר and גדולה are royal terms from chapter 1 now used for Mordecai. Haman's happiness over the advice of his friends turns to profound sorrow at the words of his wise men.

Along with these terms and motifs, other structural clues define the reversals. The framing of the Haman-at-home scenes is actually part of a wider frame provided by the queen's parties. All of the activity in this episode takes place (as providence would have it) between Esther's first banquet (5:5-8), which is characterized by suspense, and the final, climactic banquet (7:1ff.), which brings about Haman's fall. Chapter 6 stands at the center of the chiastic structure of the whole story. The elements which follow reflect a systematic, patterned reversal of the elements of the first five chapters.

Although a reversal is undeniably underway, it should be emphasized that it has only begun. The momentum of Haman's schemes has been checked, but more in terms of his subjective overconfidence than in the concrete laws of public policy. Haman is still officially at the center of the court as prime minister and Mordecai is still on the periphery as one of the nobles at the gate. The threat to the Jews which began with Haman's accusation and edict is effectively neutralized only after Esther enlists the king's support in the following chapter. And even then, all of the activity of chapters 8 and 9 is required to complete the process. Before turning to these events, however, a closer look at some of the terms and interactions of this section is in order.

---

[6] In both Josephus and the Latin version of Esther, it is explicitly stated that Haman found Mordecai still wearing his sackcloth.

### Reward: Gaining Honor by Granting Honor

In Esther 6 the king is disturbed by his own forgetfulness to reward the loyal deeds of a courtier who saved[7] his life. He asks what honor (יקר) or greatness/promotion (גדולה)[8] was granted Mordecai (6:3). Just as the act of disloyalty required public punishment, so the act of loyalty which exposed it must receive public reward.[9]

In recounting the scene of Esther 6, Josephus (Bk. XI. VI, 10) clarifies the nature of the king's reward. Haman goes through the streets proclaiming, "This shall be the reward which the king will bestow on every one whom he loves, and *esteems worthy of honor.*" Mordecai's reward—whether it would be in the currency of money, land or rank—would be a form of honor.

The ancient Greek histories of Persia contain several stories which illustrate rewards for royal benefactors. On one occasion Darius offered "any reward he might desire" to one who rescued his shipwrecked crew from slavery (Herodotus III 138).[10] Theomestor and Phylacus were two officials given power and property as a result of their loyal service to the king (Herodotus VIII 85). With their names recorded among the king's

---

[7] LXX Add. E 16:13, the AT and the Latin use the term "savior" for Mordecai.

[8] The translation, "promotion," for גדולה is suggested by some (see Levenson 1997:96; cmp. Fox 1991a:75). After Mordecai's exposure of the assassination plot in chapter 2, the king had "promoted" (גדל, *piel*) Haman, "setting his seat over all the other ministers" (3:1). Mordecai is similarly promoted (גדל, *piel*) in 10:2. It should be noted, however, that the identical form, גדולה, was used in 1:4 in the more general sense of "greatness," specifically, the king's greatness. This connotation of royal honor will also emerge in the lines that follow. Although Mordecai is honored here, no promotion, *per se*, is granted to him in chapter 6. This is a symbolic ritual of honor after which he "returns to the gate" (v. 12). A substantial change in status will only occur in chapter 8 following another parade.

[9] The MT's use of the verb חפץ to express the king's *longing* to reward his benefactor recalls the king's sexual desire in 2:14, this root's only other usage in Esther. The reader is meant to associate the compulsion to reward Mordecai with the desire for a new queen.

[10] Another case of non-monetary reward for a benefactor follows in Herodutus III 140, 141. Compare also the accounts in Herodotus IX 107 and Xenophon's *Hellenics* III 1,6,7.

benefactors, they were "called in the Persian language, *orosaggai*." The etymology of this term refers either to those who "guard the king" or, quite appropriately, to those "worthy of praise" (Godley 1982:83 n.1).

The historian's reference to a royal register of benefactors underscores the public nature of such an honor and the impact royal reward would have on one's status. These men (and sometimes women) often inherited minor kingdoms as well as gold or private estates.[11]

Paton (1908:245) tells us that it was "a point of honour with the Persian kings to reward promptly and magnificently those who conferred benefits upon them." An honorable deed which was not properly recognized put the honor of both subject *and sovereign* at risk. Moore's (1971:64) assessment concurs:

> That Mordecai had gone unrewarded for saving the king's life was a reflection on the Persian king, for whom it was a point of honor to reward his benefactors.

There is good reason to believe that Ahasuerus was, in fact, more concerned about his own honor than Mordecai's. Josephus renders the king's question: "How may I honor one ... after a manner suitable to *my* magnificence?" (Bk. XI. VI,10). The king's predicament was to find a way to restore his own honor by publicly restoring his benefactor's.[12]

The dilemma which Ahasuerus faces in Esther 6 was a common one for ancient kings. The self-honoring implicit in

---

[11] The *kudurru* stones from the Kassite period represent an earlier public register for royal land grants. These were boundary stones which served a very practical purpose but were, nonetheless, a public record of royal favor. For a standard collection of texts in translation, see L. W. King (1912). (It should be noted that not all *kudurrus* represented grants as a result of loyal service; some of them, for example, record a sale for money)

[12] The capacity of honor to be both granted and gained may seem to contradict the limited commodity model of honor described above. Some of the hierarchical relationships in Esther (i.e., between Vashti or Haman and the king) do participate in the "zero-sum" dynamic which is more typical in rivalries between equals. However, when the hierarchical relationship is not under threat, honor exhibits an elastic quality.

rewards for benefactors is clearly evidenced in the epigraphy of Greece during the 5th–2nd centuries (Mott 1975; Danker 1982; B. W. Winter 1988:88–90). Regarding such formal ceremonies, Demosthenes said that they "applaud the exhibition of gratitude rather than praising the one who is crowned" (Winter 1988:92). Public focus was not only directed toward the good deed but toward the *appropriate honor* considered commensurate with the benefaction. "It was not simply that honours were given, but that honours were seen by all to have been given..." (ibid. 90). Esther 6 reflects an analogous arrangement.

The Greeks also, apparently, viewed such rewards very much in terms of quasi-legal obligations. "This obligation was not seen simply as a cultural convention, but some saw it as a 'law.' Benefactions could be called 'loans'" (ibid. 91).[13] Seneca (*De beneficiis* 1.1.3, 4–8, 13) could say, "He who does not return a benefit sins ..." Cicero considered no duty more important than returning gratitude (*De officiis* 1.47). Ahasuerus may very well have violated a similar code of public etiquette in Persia.

Reward is another side of provision,[14] an important honor theme in Esther. The king is not only the source of periodic bounty for his subjects, he is also the one who must carefully (and promptly) respond to their acts of loyalty. His generosity is publicly evaluated in both spheres. The king's immediate intention to reward Mordecai in chapter 6 proves the reader correct who found the end of chapter 2 strangely silent[15] about this very issue.

The narrator's choice of יקר as a synonym for reward is illuminating. Most of the 70+ appearances of this root in the Bible are adjectival, with an unambiguous connotation of value or worth. Stones, names, words, lives and kings might all have יקר. Of the 10 times the root occurs in Esther, 5 of its uses are

---

[13] Winter notes that monetary compensation could be claimed if a publicly recognized deed was not properly acknowledged.

[14] The offer of Darius, mentioned above, reminds us that the magnanimity which Esther was offered for apparently no reason (except her "favor" with the king) was the same magnanimity offered to a benefactor as a reward.

[15] The text is, in fact, more than silent. The promotion of Haman *instead of Mordecai* (chapter 3) creates an injustice which chapter 6 will finally redress.

nominal. The leitmotif (Fox 1991a:76) of this portion of chapter 6, "the man whom the king desires to honor," uses the least attested, infinitival form of the verb. The language of vv. 3 and 6 makes it clear that by honoring (lit., "doing" honor) there is a substantial, public conferral of worth or value. By wearing the king's garments, Mordecai is, in the words of the AT, wearing "garments of honor."[16]

Haman understands that to be honored is to share in the *king's* honor. Hence his insistence on the *king's* robe, the *king's* horse, and the *king's* nobleman. Haman's prescription cements the narrative's already established association between יקר and royalty.[17]

## Esther 7: Esther's Public Challenge to Haman (and the King)

### *Summary of the Narrative*

> *The act of hospitality can thus become a means of expressing and reversing a pattern of domination at one and the same time.*
> (Herzfeld 1987:77)

After the ironic turn of events in Esther 6, the story maintains its suspense. Esther has not yet asked the king to intervene for the Jews. She and Mordecai and all the Jews in Persia still face an unalterable edict of death. The final banquet of the queen will determine the fate of the Jews and their enemies.

This scene, no less than the previous one, is filled with coincidence and irony. It begins with Esther fully resolved to

---

[16] The LXX consistently uses forms of δόξα (glory) where the MT has יקר (6:3,6,11 et al). In 6:3, the king asks what δόξα or χάρις (favor) was done for Mordecai.

[17] יקר is a root featured in the stories of Daniel 1-6, appearing 6 times as a noun or adjective (2:6, 37; 4:30, 36; 5:18, 20). In these accounts the term bears a strong equation with royalty, but also with divinity. When, like Haman, the kings of Daniel forget that their honor is derivative, they are bound to lose it.

intercede boldly — yet, graciously — with the king on behalf of her people. She describes her "petition and request" only after following the standard etiquette of respect, and calling upon her personal "favor" with the king. Esther adds a phrase of intimacy to the litany of formalities she had previously used: "If I have found[18] favor in your[19] eyes, O King..." (v. 3). This is the king's "favor" (חן) of which Esther had been assured in chapter 2 but which she doubted in chapter 4. She is risking her request on that favor in the petition which follows.

Levenson (1997:101) compares this scene with Exodus 33 in which Moses, like Esther, pleads with God for the life of his people. The basis of his appeal is stated similarly, "that I have found favor in your eyes" (v. 16). It is explicitly upon this basis that God agrees to change his plans in the following verse.

> Like Esther, Moses is the sovereign's darling, and like her, he pleads not simply for himself but for his people, boldly risking the favor that he has won in hopes of having it extended to the entire nation of Israel. And in each case the gamble works. (ibid.)

Esther asks for her life and the life of her people (v. 3). They have, she explains, been sold for annihilation (v. 4a). If they had been merely sold as slaves she would have kept silent (v. 4b).[20] The king is upset and asks who has presumed to do such a thing (v. 5). Esther replies, "A foe and enemy, this wicked Haman!" (v. 6a).

Haman's demise was foreshadowed in the parade of chapter 6 and in the predictions heard in his home just prior to

---

[18] Notice that Esther uses the typical verb מצא with "favor" and not the unusual verb נשא, which was used to describe her appeal in chapter 2.

[19] Levenson (1997:101) notes that the subtle shift in referent from "the king" (in the appeal of 5:4,8) to the second personal form, "your" (in 6:3) reflects more directness and personal intimacy.

[20] Moore (1971:70) remarks that v. 4 contains "undoubtedly the most difficult clause to translate in all of Esther, primarily because the meanings of three of the six words in it are uncertain." Paton (1908:262-2) summarizes various interpretations. In the section below entitled, "Esther's Appeal to the King's Honor," several of these terms will receive attention.

the banquet. Now, as Esther makes her impassioned speech, the author subtly reveals the shift in power among the three. In v. 5, the text reads, "King Ahasuerus said to Queen Esther..." The use of titles was effectively used to mark Vashti's rise and fall from grace. Here the conversation between the royal couple *as royal couple* suggests a boundary which Haman cannot transgress. The boundary is underscored again in v. 6 when Haman is terrified[21] before "the king and queen." Another reversal is effectively established in regard to the king's personal loyalties. In chapter 3, Haman had confidently made his request to the king and then dined with him in private. Esther, at that time, was concerned about having fallen out of grace with the king (4:11). In chapter 7 the king will clearly side with his queen over against his prime minister.

This intensely compact scene further demonstrates the strength of Esther's character. She is no longer passive or hesitant; she is truly courageous:

> Once she revealed her ethnic and religious origins to the king, not to mention her opposition to the king's most powerful official, her future was most uncertain.     (Moore 1971:73)

The risk involved not only challenging the prime minister but, in so doing, she was identifying herself as a Jew. The secrecy of her identity, which had been dutifully kept since her entry into the palace, was essential to her personal security. "By identifying Haman she had unmasked the villain, but she had also unmasked herself." (ibid., 74)

But Esther is more than courageous; she is extremely clever as well.[22] Her line of reasoning with the king protects him

---

[21] The reader of Esther remembers at this point another of the story's ironies. Haman was upset in 5:9 because, in spite of all the honors the king had bestowed on him, Mordecai would not tremble before him. He was infuriated in 3:5 that Mordecai would not bow before him. As Haman slips toward his own demise, he trembles (7:6) and falls (7:8) before those from whom he sought the same response.

[22] In the words of M. Fox (1991a:89), "She is now on her own, faced with a self-centered fickle man she must manipulate and an evil, clever, and determined man she must overcome. Her wit and charms alone must

from blame and, through a suggestion of astounding deference, challenges the king to protect his honor by protecting her from a foe. As it turns out, Haman unknowingly plays the role of challenger to the king in the lines which follow.

Upon hearing this accusation, Ahasuerus "left the banquet in wrath" (v. 7) and, upon returning, finds Haman begging mercy from Esther. The king sees not a suppliant, however, but a rapist, threatening to assault (לכבוש) his wife "in my presence, in my own house!" (v. 8). One of the eunuchs immediately points out the gallows which Haman had prepared for Mordecai.[23] With perfect poetic and moral justice, the king orders Haman's execution on it. Then his anger abates.

There are numerous theories about the king's departure at this crucial moment in the story, but they are all conjectural (cf. Paton 1908:262). The narrator does have a discernible structural purpose, however. The use of חמה (wrath) in v. 7 recalls the king's same response to Vashti's insubordination in 1:12 (and the projected response of all men to any such contempt in 1:18) and to Haman's response to Mordecai's insubordination (3:5; 5:9) (Levenson 1997:104). The clue that this motif is deliberately reused is found in 7:10 where the king's anger "abated" (שכך) just as it had in 2:1. Haman's execution had the same emotional effect on the king that the banishment of Vashti had. The pattern will be completely reconstructed when a plan goes into effect to replace the insolent subject with a more worthy successor.[24] The

---

suffice for the task." To this articulate assessment one must add the role of providence which contributes as much (if not more) to Haman's demise as Esther's "wit and charms."

[23] Harbona's mention of the gallows to the king may serve not only as one more example of a king who needs direction. Herodotus I. 137 refers to a Persian law which requires two offenses before an official can be executed without a trial. The possibility that Harbona is providing evidence of a separate offense (besides attempted rape) lies in his description of Mordecai as the one "whose word saved the king" (7:9). Haman is thereby indicted for plotting the execution of one of the king's benefactors. This was, itself, a form of treason (see LXX Add. E 16:12,13).

[24] Compare the installation of Esther in 2:15–18 with that of Mordecai in 8:15–17.

chiastic movement of the story back to its original motifs and themes is evident in both structure and language.

The coincidences of this dramatic scene satisfy the need for poetic as well as moral justice. Freedman[25] remarks, "But that he should appeal to a Jewess to save him, when he had condemned them all to death is ironic." Fox (1991a:87) similarly notes:

> It is a satisfying irony that the proud Agagite, obsessed with a Jew's refusal to bow, now falls groveling before a Jew to plead for his life. The same word "fall" is used of his predicted downfall before Mordecai in 6:13.

The irony nearly bursts into farce when the execution of Haman follows a misinterpretation of his pleading with the queen. The king's hasty response to Esther's request is not the result of Esther's stratagem but is, rather, a consequence of Haman's unintended impropriety. Here, again, the serendipitous turn of events hints at a divine hand.

As the plot comes to the climax in activity in Esther 6 and 7, the true qualities of the main characters become vividly clear. Haman is the transparently narcissistic biblical "fool" in many respects (cf. Prov. 12:19-28).[26] He is anxious[27] for his own honor but in so doing he sows the seeds of his own humiliation. Mordecai, in contrast, is "wise." He is patient for personal honor yet active for the great cause of vindication and deliverance for his people. We will see more of his character in the final scene. Esther has become an initiating queen. Her early hesitations are overcome by a noble resolve to put family over personal safety. Ahasuerus is a king incapable of making his own decisions. Whether in moments of personal slight or in the creation of

---

[25] Quoted in Moore (1971:71).

[26] Fox (1991a:81) argues convincingly (*contra* Talmon 1963) that Haman is not the archetypal fool of wisdom literature. The antagonist does, however, exhibit many typical characteristics to which our attention will shortly turn (cf. Prov. 11:28; 13:3; 14:16; 16:5; 27:1; 28:11; 29:20 and Levenson's [1997:92-3] comments).

[27] Haman's impatience in getting to the palace, his impulsive response to the king's question, and the way in which he is hurried or hurries in 5:5a; 6:10,12 all together portray a man without real control. (See Fox 1991a:80)

edicts with drastic implications, he depends embarrassingly on his advisors for direction and advice.

### The Queen's Appeal to the King's Honor

Esther's strategically phrased request to the king has a number of important dimensions. Her petition is couched in the formalities of deference which call upon his grace and also subtly call upon his duty and honor.

Esther repeatedly uses the term "sold" (מכר) to describe the threat to herself and her people in 7:4. She is undoubtedly describing the "sale" of the Jews by Haman recounted in chapter 3:9-11 (cf. Neh. 5:8).[28] Although we cannot be sure what kind of monetary transaction actually took place,[29] this reference in chapter 7 implies that the king had accepted the money offered by Haman. The exact sum was known to Mordecai who specifically refers to it in 4:7 when he describes the emergency to the queen. The use of נזק later in 7:4 confirms the fiscal nuance of Esther's argument.

The queen's line of reasoning deftly exempts the king from blame by stirring his anger at the still unknown perpetrator of this heinous crime. Even though Ahasuerus approved the "sale," Haman bears responsibility for a transaction which had left the king unaware that his queen, benefactor, and their kin were slated for annihilation. It is precisely for this reason that the king must see the plot as an act of treason against himself. Fox (1991a:83) shares this interpretation: "[Esther] stokes his indignation by saying she has been 'sold' — *a disgraceful fate which shames her husband no less.*" (italics added)

---

[28] מכר itself can mean as often "hand over" as "sell." In Jud. 2:14; 3:8; 4:2,9; 10:7 God hands over his people to their enemies (cmp. Deut. 32:30). This meaning is often implied when a person or people are sold for money as well. Esther is describing a sale which not only involves a monetary transaction, but one which also implies that a new "owner" can do with her as he wills. Is this, she asks, what the king really wants to do, or has he been betrayed unknowingly?

[29] The language at this point in chapter 3 is ambiguous. See the discussion above.

Esther continues her appeal to the king's personal sense of honor. She makes the remarkable claim that, were she and her people [merely] sold off as slaves, she would have kept silent (v. 4). For, she continues, (and this is where the Hebrew is most difficult) the adversary/adversity (הצר) would not be commensurate/equal to/worth (שׁוה) the trouble/loss (נזק) to the king. The "loss" is, no doubt, a monetary one (cmp. Dan. 6:3; Ezra 4:13, 22; cf. Levenson 1997:102 and Fox 1991a:84,85).[30] Her line of reasoning is not that she resisted "bothering" the king but that she would have understood his need to consider the financial benefits of such a transaction.

Here Esther is perhaps at her best as a skillful diplomat. She portrays herself as one willing to embrace silently the shame state of slavery. Though possessing great honor and prestige herself as the queen, she understands (unlike Vashti) that her honor is, ultimately, the king's honor. She is one of his subjects to do with as he pleases. Of course, she knows the king wouldn't really sell off his favored queen into slavery as she suggests. Her logic is designed to simultaneously stir his deepest sentiments for her — and himself.

Esther reveals an understanding of her own honor as contingent upon her patron's. She subtly appeals to his honor which is at stake in the destiny of his subject. It is the implied suggestion that he would be willing to dishonor her for a price which especially challenges his honor. "Do you really need the money that much?!" she insinuates. Because her honor is cleverly, respectfully and publicly placed in his hands, *he* must maintain it. Certainly it would be a disgraceful thing for *him* if she were sold into slavery. But, she humbly states, she would bear that. How much more is it a shame for the king if she is sold

---

[30] שׁוה (used in Est. 3:8; 5:13; 7:4) is an uncommon word in BH and one which is difficult to translate with any uniformity. The use of the English word, "worth," here is useful because it can imply strictly monetary value or it can convey a sense of the relative value of a deed *vis-à-vis* the king and his time and resources. In places where this Hebrew root occurs the LXX uses forms of ἄξιος, a term which has the same general range of connotations. In 7:4, however, the notion of valuation is explicit: "The accuser is not *worthy* of the king's court."

off for death! The king's question in the AT (at 8:5) demonstrates this perception: "Who would dare humiliate the sign of my reign...?!"

By humbly reminding the king that she is his subject, Esther has posed a challenge to his honor as her patron. Will his grace continue? Can she expect his protection at least as a husband, if not the king? Esther has insinuated that the threat on her life is one directed at her *as his wife*. Framed this way, her words are, at the very least, a challenge to Ahasuerus *as a man*.

For clients, protection is as basic an expectation as provision. Esther, like the psalmist, describes the threats on her own life as ones which her master should take personally. This dynamic is especially evident in the psalms of lament where threats on the lives and honor of God's chosen ones are central. The accusation that the Lord of the suffering servant has been negligent is just beneath the surface. "Where is your God?!" (Ps. 42:3, 10) is the common, defiant question. It is in just such moments of threat, the reasoning goes, that you must demonstrate that I am one of your own. Esther's plea echoes the lament of Psalm 17: "Guard me as the apple of [your] eye; hide me in the shadow of your wings, from the wicked who despoil me, my deadly enemies who surround me" (vv. 7,8). If our relationship means anything, she implies, now is the time to save me. Her words might have been those of the lament in Psalm 31:

> ...you are my refuge. Into your hand I commit my spirit. ...
> Do not let me be put to shame, O Lord, for I call upon you.
> (vv. 4b, 5a,17a).[31]

Petitions for protection and deliverance invoke the honor of the one who called the relationship into being. When Moses made his appeal to God in Exodus 33, it was not only by reminding God of his own personal favor. In vs. 13, he continues, "Consider also that this nation is *your people*." Esther

---

[31] In the LXX Add. C Esther does express these sentiments but they are, as in the laments, directed toward God. In MT Esther she is appealing to the king on a similar basis.

likewise asks the king to consider his favor for her, but then reminds him that she is, more fundamentally, *his.*

This discussion takes an unexpected turn when Haman inadvertently acts the part of the challenging male before the king's very eyes. What Esther has hinted at, Haman now demonstrates. She has refocused the king's attention on an edict which she represents as an act of treason. When the king returns to find Haman kneeling[32] at Esther's side, her point is fully illustrated: Haman had brazenly manipulated the king into the slaughter of his queen and now, without concern for the king's own presence in the room, he seeks to assault her![33]

Although this turn of events is unexpected, Esther's speech (as providence, again, would have it) has prepared the king well. Now he sees Haman clearly as the threat she has described. Haman's execution is a result of the king's perception that he has been challenged as both husband and king. "Xerxes' concern is not for the endangered people, and not even primarily for Esther's safety, but for the royal honor" (Fox 1991a:86). The attempted rape[34] confronts Ahasuerus as a male. To be "cuckolded,"[35] in the language of traditional Mediterranean

---

[32] Haman, like Esther, is appealing to a superior for mercy in a position typical in countless Mesopotamian reliefs (Cmp. I Sam. 25:24: 2 Kgs. 4:27). He is not, however, similarly deserving of favor. Paton (1908:264) criticizes Esther's lack of compassion toward Haman in this scene. Moore's (1971:74) analysis is much more realistic in light of the decree which is still in effect. In any case, the king's reaction overrides any response Esther may have attempted, and whatever her emotional disposition toward Haman might have been.

[33] It is another of the story's delicious ironies that Haman will be executed as a result of a false accusation (by the king). It was, the reader recalls, a false accusation of the Jews which led to their death sentence.

[34] Uses of the term for assault (כבשׁ) suggest a homology in Israel's understanding among various acts of subjugation in both domestic and military spheres. In Neh. 5:5, this root is used of sons and daughters becoming slaves and also of daughters being raped. In each case the verb entails (1) being forced into a change in status to a lower shame state and (2) taking on a new patron. This transference of ownership is also inherent in the root, מכר, discussed above.

[35] This is the image most often attributed to a man shamed when another man takes advantage of his wife (A. Blok 1981:427–40). J. Pitt-Rivers

societies, is the greatest shame for a man. And to violate Esther *the queen* is tantamount to tyranny against the king.[36] Haman must face the same kind of death as the conspirators of chapter 2.[37]

## Honor and Clothing; Shame and Covering

ילבשו־בשת וכלמה המגדילים עלי

*Let those who exalt themselves against me
Be clothed with shame and dishonor.*
(Ps. 35:26)

The "rising" and "falling" of the main characters which constitutes the plot of Esther is intentionally marked by dress indicators. After learning of Haman's plot in chapter 3, Mordecai—together with and as representative of the community of the Jews—removes his garments and puts on sackcloth (chapter 4). Esther apparently wears mourning cloth as well, for, as chapter 5 begins, she finishes her fast by putting on her robes of royalty. In chapter 6, Mordecai is given the clothes of royalty. He no longer wears the garb of mourning but neither does he dress in his regular clothes. He is symbolically granted a higher status than he had before. The parade of chapter 6 foreshadows Mordecai's real promotion in chapter 8 during

---

(1977:127–171) provides insight on this topic by way of his analysis of Genesis 34.

[36] Sleeping with a king's wives and concubines has, throughout the ANE, been a symbolic gesture of attempted succession. When Absalom took over Jerusalem in 2 Samuel 16, one of the first moves recommended by Ahithophel was to sleep with David's concubines. This was a symbolic gesture that reinforced his claim to the throne. It was also, as Ahithophel noted, a gesture guaranteed to make him "odious" to his father (v. 21). The verb, "to stink" (באש), used in this phrase is found together with the common root for shame (בוש) in Prov. 13:5.

[37] In Josephus Bk. XI. 6.12 the king ultimately sees a conspiratorial pattern in Haman's behavior. This assessment is built on the LXX Add. A 12:6 which presumes an association between Haman and the two eunuchs. The same view appears in both Targums.

which he will again wear the royal robes. Honor is cleverly articulated in the language of dress and ornamentation.

Shame and dishonor are also marked by clothing or covering.[38] Haman's response to his public humiliation in chapter 6 was a form of symbolic self-humiliation akin to mourning sackcloth: He covers his head and runs home. This covering, the details of which are unknown, apparently foreshadows the final covering of Haman in the following scene when the king accuses him of rape. Head covering punctuates his death sentence. He is led off to be hung out for public shame on the pole he had erected for his rival.

Clothing is a literary device found throughout Hebrew narrative. In an essay on the Joseph cycle V. Matthews (1995) has examined the manner in which clothing marks not only the status of the characters but their *transitions* in status and the respective social roles which follow. O. H. Prouser's (1996) similar discussion of the David and Saul stories follows David's rise to power through its descriptions of robing, giving clothes, disrobing, nakedness, etc. The "narratological" use of clothing in these stories is widespread.

This socio-literary device is widely used in a variety of other ANE texts. In the story of Gilgamesh,[39] for example, both nudity and clothing (clean and dirty) communicate status changes. In another myth, "Ishtar's Descent to the Netherworld," clothing is transparently associated with the structure of the plot (cf. Vogelzang and van Bekkum [ibid., 268] and D. Freedman [1972:91–95]). Ishtar removes one piece of clothing at each of the gates of the Netherworld, finally taking off her "robe of splendor" at the seventh gate. As she reemerges

---

[38] Shame is, in common biblical idiom, a covering of its own (Isa. 42:17; Jer. 51:51; Ps. 35:26; 132:18; and Job 8:22). The rabbis (b. Shabbat 77b.) provided a popular explanation of the verb לבֹשׁ ("to dress") by repointing it as לא בוֹשׁ ("without shame"). The biblical association between shame and covering appears first in the garden of Eden (Gen. 3:21; cf. Sasson 1985).

[39] See relevant discussions of clothing in this story in W. L. Moran (1987:557–60) and Vogelzang and van Bekkum (1986:265–284). For a general discussion of the structure and themes of Gilgamesh, see T. Jacobsen (1976:193–219).

from the world of the dead, she is systematically robed with the clothes of the living. A homologous symmetry counterpoises life-power-honor-clothing with death-impotence-shame-nakedness.[40]

The usefulness of clothing as symbol in story is rooted in its multivalence in real life. Clothing is defined by anthropologists Roach and Eicher (1979:20,21) as a "part of a total system of communication within a culture." It is:

> ... a crucial, functional, communicative symbol. ... It can be used to indicate social roles, to establish social worth, as a symbol of economic status, as an emblem of political power or ideological inclination, as a reflection of a magico-religious condition, as a facility in social rituals, and as a reinforcement of beliefs,[41] custom, and values. (ibid.)[42]

Vogelzang and van Bekkum (1986:266) and Matthews (ibid., 27–28) remind us that in the Ancient Near East clothing served a legal function as well.

When Mordecai is bedecked in royal attire, a number of these dimensions come into play. The public nature of the parade ensured that his social worth was recognized by the population of the city. The response of Haman's family suggests that political power was in transition as well. There is, after all, room for only one *prime* minister. A promotion of Mordecai would translate into a demotion for Haman. Although Mordecai's promotion is yet to follow, the king's favor visibly rests on Mordecai. This social fact automatically destabilizes the honor of the Agagite.

The reader notices a transition from Mordecai's identification with his people in sackcloth to Mordecai's

---

[40] E. J. Langdon (1979:297–311) discusses the association between clothing and positive and negative life forces in a Colombian village (see especially pp. 309,310).

[41] See Milgrom's (1983:61–65) insights regarding the symbolic meaning of the priest's tassels.

[42] Other useful sources on the anthropology of clothing include J. C. Flugel (1976), F. Kiener (1956), M. S. Ryan (1966), R. A. Schwarz (1979) and J. Schneider (1987).

identification with the king in royal robes. As one example of clothing's "limitless" communicative power, Weiner and Schneider (1989:1) describe its capacity for "homogenizing difference through uniforms or sackcloth..." Mordecai had renounced his individual identity and his court prerogatives when he joined the Jewish population in the democratic solidarity of sackcloth. He is later granted the privilege to wear the "uniform" of the king by "putting on royalty" as Esther had done.

We should be aware that Mordecai is not only presented as one wearing the king's robes; he is *given* them. This is important, as Weiner and Schneider point out (ibid., 3), because:

> [After cloth manufacture itself] the second domain in which cloth acquires social and political significance is that of bestowal and exchange. ... The cloth-givers ... generate political power[43] as well, committing recipients to loyalty and obligation in the future.[44]

The system of patronage and benefaction described above often uses the currency of cloth to honor publicly its obligations and expectations. The king's "gift" represents a reciprocation for the courtier's loyalty.

Weiner and Schneider (ibid.) describe a third domain of meaning for clothing in "ceremonies of investiture and rulership":

> ... powerholders or aspirants to power declare that particular cloths transmit the authority of earlier possessors or he sanctity of past traditions, thus constituting a source of legitimacy in the present.

---

[43] On power and clothing, see also Schneider (1987:409).

[44] Matthews (ibid., 34) points out some ANE parallels to the ceremonies of Genesis from the annals of Sargon II and a campaign account by Ashurbanipal. In the latter, the Assyrian king presents Neco a multicolored garment and gold chain as part of a treaty following a military confrontation. All the other kings in the area were condemned for treason and their corpses were hung from stakes. See the translation in ANET (295). These associations of loyalty-royal clothing and treason-exposure/hanging are evident in Esther.

This "domain" is true for succession occasions as well as for the
investiture ceremonies recorded in Gen. 41:42–43[45] and in Esther
6 and 8 (cf. I Kgs. 19:19). Authority is transferred through the
bestowal of particular clothing. The wearing of royal apparel is a
public statement of royal representation. Haman had received
this authority when the king gave him his ring earlier in Esther.
But he would be accused of conspiring against the throne were
he to presume too much on this relationship and seek more
prerogatives. The degree and timing of such a transfer is solely
at the discretion of the sovereign. Mordecai's faithful service and
patience make him a more suitable candidate to represent the
king than the self-serving, impatient Haman.

Haman quickly covers (חפוי) himself as soon as he
completes the odious task of honoring Mordecai (v. 12). This is
an attempt to dissolve from public view. His accompanying
mourning (v. 12) is a sign of grief (cmp. 2 Sam. 19:4). From a
literary point of view, Haman is symbolically taking on the same
shroud of death with which they will cover (חפו) his head again
in chapter 7.[46] Haman is beginning, like Ishtar, to disintegrate
through the various stages of death. However, his journey
downward will not include a return back to life.

Haman is also mourning over the loss of his honor. David
similarly went into mourning with his head covered (חפוי) as a
result of his humiliating displacement by Absalom (2 Sam.
15:30). The king's supporters then covered (חפו) their heads and
joined the king in his weeping. The connotation of shame
implicit in the gesture of covering is also clear in Jer. 14:3: "They
are ashamed (בשו) and humiliated (הכלמו); they cover (חפו) their

---

[45] See the comments of Matthews (ibid., 33).

[46] We do not know the details of Haman's head covering in chapter 7. The
Greek and Roman sources describe scenes in which the head of an accused
person is covered. In Quintus Curtius (*History of Alexander* VI. viii. 22) the
condemned Philotas is led to the king's quarters with veiled head. Livy (I.
XXVI) similarly records the head veiling of one tried and found guilty of
treason. There are references also in these sources to the covering of one's
head in mourning, as Haman had done in chapter 6. See, for example,
Curtius (IV. x. 34 and X.v. 19, 24).

heads" (cmp. Jer. 14:4).[47] Targum Rishon confirms this understanding when it describes Haman covering his head, "as one mourning for shame and disgrace."

The author is making it painfully clear that Haman no longer participates in the royal life, as it were. Mordecai had preempted the call of death on the Jewish people by ritually enacting its shame before God. Like David, he ritually shared this shame state in solidarity with his people. Haman stood alone in his well-deserved humiliation. Mordecai, again, like David (cf. 2 Sam. 16:10ff.), could wait for vindication. Haman could expect nothing but judgment. Mordecai now symbolically and systematically regains the lost world of honor, power, and life. Just as Haman will fall lower than the position he originally occupied, Mordecai will rise higher than the place in which he began.

Haman's self-covering represents a universal response to shame (Kilborne 1992:231ff.; Deigh 1983:320). Unlike Mordecai's self-initiated humiliation designed for public viewing, Haman's covering is a form of hiding. As Deigh (1983:320) has noted:

> Covering one's face, covering up what one thinks is shameful, and hiding from others are, along with blushing, the most characteristic expressions of shame.[48]

Haman seeks to avoid "painful exposure" (Kilborne 1992: 245) by covering his head, the physiological center of a person's honor.

---

[47] Est. 7:8 ends with a phrase which has troubled some commentators: ‏ופני המן חפו‎. Though the word order is unusual, the image of a (then) well-recognized response to a royal accusation seems likely, especially in light of the parallels mentioned above. Levenson (1997:100) and Fox (1991a:87) both choose to emend the verb to a form of ‏חפר‎. In any case the expression yields an image of humiliation.

[48] Earlier, Deigh (ibid., 243) notes that, "According to many etymologists, a pre-Teutonic word meaning 'to cover' is the root of our word *shame*."

## *Haman's Hubris, Haman's Fall*

> *Do not exalt yourself*
> *Or you may fall and bring dishonor on yourself.*
> *The Lord will reveal your secrets*
> *And overthrow you before the whole congregation.*
>                                           Sirach 1:30

> *No one praises himself but the devil.*
>                           (Arab proverb; Webster 1984:201)

Haman's fall into disgrace follows a pattern. His demise is inevitable not only because of the serendipitous turn of events which readers readily attribute to God, but also because of certain "laws" which inextricably tie choices to their logical consequences.[49] By seeking too much, by overstepping boundaries set by nature, he is calling for his own destruction. This behavior is summed up in the term, "hubris."

The Greek word, ὕβρις, is a term frequently used in the LXX to translate Hebrew words for excessive pride and arrogance. Scholars of ancient Greece traditionally defined this quality in terms of a challenge to the gods, a breaching of divine boundaries. N. R. E. Fisher (1979) challenged this common view with his thesis that ὕβρις was an assault (verbal or physical) of one man *on the honor* of another. While this debate lies outside the scope of the study of Esther, it clarifies two dimensions of honor challenges which are *both* involved in court conflict stories. Honor-seeking is the cause of both *inter*-class and *intra*-class conflict.[50] In fact, these two types often merge.

The uses of יקר in Esther and Daniel illustrate these dimensions. The honor of rivals in competition is central to both stories. Alongside the rivalry among nobles stands a mismatched rivalry between noble and king and, in Daniel's

---

[49] This notion of *Tat-Ergehen-Zusammenhang* was first proposed by K. Koch (1972 [1955]) and should be understood together with a concept of divine retribution rather than in place of it (cf. Fox 1991a: 81).

[50] One wonders if an exclusive distinction in the Greek context is artificial. Challenges between classes, between humans and gods, and between peers may be analogous.

case, between king and God. The perceived threat to the honor of a hierarchical superior is common to both kinds of hubris. In Daniel 1–6 יקר belongs to both divine and royal spheres but in the royal sphere *conditionally*. The glory and honor of kingship is maintained *only as long as* the king recognizes the ultimate glory and honor of God in heaven who is the source of all glory and honor on earth. In Esther יקר is used of both royal and non-royal contexts, but in the non-royal sphere only conditionally. The noble's honor is derived from the king's honor and is enjoyed only as long as his loyalty to the king's honor is primary. When, in either case, an individual's honor-seeking ambitions become primary, the honor of his superior is automatically threatened.

MT Esther features a competition between two "equal" courtiers of foreign birth. There is not, as in Daniel, a separate "unequal" competition between king and God. In both stories, however, the conflict between courtiers exposes the non-Jew's lack of loyalty to the king. A breaching of *royal* boundaries is perceptible. Daniel's conspirators find themselves in the "pit they had dug" (cf. Prov. 26:27) for Daniel once the king realized that their plot against the king's favored advisor showed disrespect for the king himself. In Josephus' account (Bk. XI. 6. 11–12; cmp. LXX Add. E 16:2ff.), the king publicly rebukes Haman for abusing the honor which the king had given him. For this reason, the speech continues, he fell into the pit he had dug.

This subtle dimension to the king's honor reveals an expected linkage between honor-as-status and honorable behavior (honor-as-self). Haman wants the formal benefits of loyalty to the king without demonstrating the loyalty it presumes. To seek the destruction of the Jews meant taking away from the king his queen and one of his benefactors. Such a plan shamelessly placed Haman's own honor above the king's.

The "wisdom" embedded in these stories is found in proverbial form elsewhere in Scripture. "Anyone who tends a fig tree will eat its fruit, and anyone who takes care of a master will be honored." (Prov. 27:18) Honor needs to follow good service; it must not be an end in itself. "It is not good to eat too much honey, or to seek honor on top of honor." (Prov. 25:27). When

Haman answers the king's question in 6:6ff., his addiction to royal יקר becomes embarrassingly evident.

> He does not mention wealth or power; those he has already. He craves honor and recognition; those he has too, but his appetite for them is insatiable. (Fox 1991a:76)

Mordecai, unlike Haman, patiently waits for reward and promotion. In LXX Add. C 13:12-14 Mordecai disclaims all self-seeking:

> You know, O Lord, that it was not in *hubris* or pride or for any love of glory that I did this, and refused to bow down to Haman; for I would have been willing to kiss the soles of his feet to save Israel! But I did this so that I might not set human glory above the glory of God, and I will not bow down to anyone but you, who are my Lord; and I will not do these things in pride.

Mordecai's disclaimer does not perfectly resonate with hints in the MT that an ethnic rivalry was behind the earlier episode in chapter 3. It does, however, illustrate well his respect for the biblical order of honor.

The fall of Haman is, then, something which he brings upon himself by disregarding the "laws" of honor. Stated, again, in proverbial form, "*Hubris* goes before destruction, and a haughty spirit before a fall" (Prov. 16:18 [LXX]; cmp. Prov. 18:12 and 29:23). This "inevitable" outcome to the ways of the proud constitutes the prayer of the afflicted in many laments:

> Repay [those workers of evil,
>> Who speak peace with their neighbors,
>> While mischief is in their hearts].
> Repay them according to their work,
>> And according to the evil of their deeds;
> Repay them according to the work of their hands;
>> Render them their due reward.   (Ps. 28:3,4)
> Let them be confounded (יחפרו) who devise evil against me
>> Let ruin come on them unawares.
> And let the net that they hid ensnare them;
>> Let them fall into it—to their ruin. (Ps. 35:4, 8)

The common petition in the laments to confound one's enemies and bring them to shame is a call for God to bring upon them that very evil which they had planned for the righteous.

The creative use of the root נפל illustrates this pattern throughout the book of Esther (cf. Levenson 1997:104–5). Its first (3:7) and last (9:24) uses in the book refer to the *falling* of the lot. As one of the central images included in the story's chiastic structure, this falling symbolizes chance or, more likely, divine providence. In chapters 6 and 7 the root is used specifically of Haman's *fall* from grace. In 6:13[51] the prediction of his wife and counselors turns on a word play using נפל: "If Mordecai, before whom you have begun to *fall* .... you will surely *fall*." This assessment at the center of the book hints at the divine hand mysteriously behind the fall of Haman. In the next episode the prophecy comes true literally when Haman *falls* on the couch before Esther to plead for his life (7:8). In 8:17[52] and 9:2 the fear of the Jews *falls* on all the people. In 9:3 it is specifically the fear of Mordecai which *falls* on all the officials. The very response Haman had so desperately wanted both inside and outside of the court is now one rightfully enjoyed by those who understand the order of honor. The irony is complete when Haman's fall dramatically climaxes as he is finally elevated — with his own petard.

---

[51] נפל is also used idiomatically in 6:10 where the king tells Haman to makes sure that nothing he has suggested *falls*.

[52] נפל is also found in 8:3 where Esther shows her continued deference to the king by falling at his feet to plead for protection from the edict which is still in effect.

# Chapter 4

# *EXALTATION*
## *The Status and Security of the Jews Ensured*

## (ESTHER 8–10)

### Esther 8: Authority Granted to Mordecai and Esther

*Summary of the Narrative*

With the end of chapter 7 comes a change in the dramatic action of Esther. There are, still, edicts to send, battles to fight and the sons of Haman to hang. But these are details recounted in a journalistic style reminiscent of chapters 1 and 2 (Moore 1971:77). This change in narration granted, there is still a host of terms and motifs in the final chapters which contribute to the development of the characters, themes and structure of the book.[1] A whole set of reversals is underway and not until each one comes full circle does the plot reach its denouement.[2]

---

[1] Moore (1971:77) correctly insists that the change in style at the beginning of chapter 8 gives no basis, by itself, for assuming that an original version of Esther ended with chapter 7. The overall structure of the story requires much of the content of chapters 8–10 in order to complete its various reversals.

[2] See the discussion of Clines (1984:27 ff.; 39 ff.) about the various endings of Esther. Clines (ibid., 12) agrees that the collection of different "endings" to the story is related to the number of sub-plots each of which must be brought to conclusion (8:1–2, 8:15–17, 9:19).

Chapter 8 beings with a new power triangle in the court: King Ahasuerus, Queen Esther and Mordecai, the Jew. Now that Haman is executed, the king grants Mordecai the prime minister's position. Haman's sizable estate (cf. 3:9, 11; 5:11; 9:10) is immediately given[3] to Esther who, in turn, puts it under the care of her cousin. The signet ring worn by Haman since 3:10 is also transferred to Mordecai. These symbolic details highlight an exchange of roles for the court rivals.

This reversal also highlights Haman's "fall" which his hubris had necessitated. In 5:11-12, he had boasted of his monetary wealth, his sons, his unique status among the nobles, and his privileged relationship with the queen. All of these possessions disappear with surprising rapidity. The final banquet with the queen cost him his life. The loss of his wealth and position is underscored in 8:1-2. What is more, his sons will die — and be hanged — in the next chapter.

> Their death completes Haman's downfall: not only is he killed, but his honor, his position, his wealth and now his sons — all his boasts from his days of glory — are stripped away. (Fox 1991a:110)

The author found it necessary to insist on this comprehensive dismantling of Haman's honor, even after his death.[4] All the items which defined his life and gave him honor are either destroyed or transferred to Mordecai and Esther.

Esther is not satisfied simply to be rid of "a foe and enemy, this vile Haman" (7:6). In her most effusive display of emotion she falls weeping at the king's feet, begging for Haman's edict to

---

[3] The state's confiscation of the property of convicted criminals is mentioned by Herodotus (III. 128,129) and Josephus (*Antiquities*, 11. 17). Interestingly, the Greek word in the LXX corresponding to נתן in 8:1 is not from the common root δίδωμι (which is used in 8:2) but rather from the relatively rare δωρέομαι. This latter term is used in the LXX to refer to presentations of tribute or cultic offerings, the kind of official gifts through which honor is implicitly granted.

[4] Given the typical ANE view of a person's "name" as something which bears honor or disgrace after death, it seems that the writer is at pains to strip Haman of every source of potential honor after his death.

be annulled (8:3). Her behavior demonstrates continued deference to the king and dependence on his favor. The use of the root חנן effectively recalls the charge of Mordecai in 4:8 to "... *entreat* the king for her people" (Fox 1991a:92).[5] Her role as their deliverer is not over. Previously she had asked for her own life together with those of her kin. Haman is eliminated as a threat to the king but not completely as a threat to Esther. Ahasuerus needs to be reminded that the queen's kin are still in grave danger as a result of the edict.[6] Her impassioned speech in vv. 5–6 links his favor toward her with her loyalty to her own people (Levenson 1997:108). Her sense of solidarity with the Jews is now transparent: "How..."(איככה)[7] she asks twice, "How could I watch the calamity ... How could I watch the destruction that is coming on my kindred?" To watch such a destruction passively would clearly betray her ties to her family.[8] Would her husband, the king, want this?

Ahasuerus is kindly disposed to Esther, once again holding out his golden scepter.[9] It is simply unheard of, however, to reverse an edict. The root used in her request for "averting" the evil plot, עבר, has already been used in 1:19 to describe Persian

---

[5] Fox (ibid.) points out that this verb is one of the many links between Esther and the Joseph cycle. It is used to describe Joseph's cries for help from the pit in Gen. 42:21. See also I Kgs. 8:47; Job 8:5; 9:15 and Hos. 12:5, where it appears alongside weeping.

[6] Esther needs not only grace but also law. Like Ruth with Boaz, she has her patron's good intention but she needs to push him respectfully to secure her future legally.

[7] Compare the more common form of this rhetorical interrogative in Gen. 44:34 (cf. Gen. 39:9). איך questions are often posed in shame contexts characterized by social and/or theological irony (cf. Gen. 26:9; Ex. 6:12; Judg. 16:15; 2 Sam. 2:22; Jer. 2:21; 48:39; Hos. 11:8).

[8] G. Anderson (1991:94), as noted in our discussion above, reminds us that for the ancient Jew to "watch" calamity fall on one's kin (both biological and fictive) without helping was tantamount to becoming an enemy. It may have been viewed as something even worse.

[9] It is not necessary to assume that Esther had risked her life again to come before the king. She was not, in this instance, an uninvited guest. According to the narrative, she is still present in the court as the host of the banquet initiated in chapter 7.

law which *cannot* pass away.[10] Like the king in Daniel 6:15, Ahasuerus is bound by his own laws. The plot of their executed enemy still has power over the Jews through the impersonal, bureaucratic administrative system of laws. "Although Haman is dead, his evil influence reaches out even from the grave" (Moore 1971:82). The king finds recourse, in v. 8, by giving Esther and Mordecai the authority to write any counter-edicts which they find necessary to save the Jews.

Mordecai summons the royal secretaries to write letters to all the Jews in every province, authorizing them:

> to assemble and defend themselves, to destroy, to kill, and to annihilate any ... who might attack them, with their children and women, and to plunder their goods on a single day ...
>
> (8:11,12a)

Using the same language as the edict of Haman in 3:13,[11] this notice empowers the Jews for self-defense. A set of royal steeds were sent post-haste ("urged by the king's command" [v. 14]), with the message so that the Jews would have sufficient time to plan their "revenge" (נקם; 8:13).

Mordecai emerges from the king's palace once again in royal apparel. Now he also wears a golden crown. The city of Susa receives him with joyous shouts (cf. Prov. 11:10; 29:2). For the Jews in particular, there is "light and gladness and joy and honor" (v. 16). The day of this new edict was celebrated as a holiday by the Jews and many Gentiles "joined" the Jews (מתיהדים; v. 17).[12]

---

[10] Esther, of course, knows that the law is irrevocable. The use of the root כשר ("fitting") in v. 5 demonstrates her awareness of the king's predicament (Clines 1984:101,102). Without the hesitations which characterized her earlier entreaties (4:11), Esther pushes these limits regardless. Fox (1991a:93) observes that "this time Esther is not going against the man only, but also against the administration of the kingdom itself, and she is forcing the question of how far the king himself is bound by his laws."

[11] Both edicts were delivered in a "hurry" (דחף). The first one was followed by Haman's leisurely feast with the king, the second by the public feasting of the Jews.

[12] This unique participial form of the verb, "to be a Jew", may mean to join sides with the Jews (emotionally, politically, militarily) or to convert to

The systematic reversals and chiastic structure of the story are apparent throughout this eighth chapter of Esther.[13] The promotion/ring and irrevocable edict of Haman in chapter 3 are reversed by the promotion/ring and irrevocable edict of Mordecai in chapter 8. In both cases the promotion is followed by public honor. The first edict caused four expressions of ritual shame: mourning, fasting, weeping and lamenting among the Jews. The second one reversed the four with light, gladness, joy and honor (Clines 1984:97). The rejoicing Susa of 8:15, the reader remembers, was the formerly confused Susa of 3:15. The first edict sent Mordecai into mourning clothes. The second one finds him in royal robes. Haman's wealth, which financed the plot against the Jews in 3:9, is given to the Jews in 8:1 as part of their rightful estate. Behind Haman's promotion lies the secret ethnic identity of Esther (2:10). Before Mordecai's official promotion, Esther openly informs the king about their relationship (8:1). Finally, the replacement of Vashti by Esther stands behind the replacement of Haman by Mordecai.

At most points of reversal in the story there is also a form of enhancement. "Duplicate or exceed" seems to be the rule (cf. Moore 1971:83). Mordecai wears not only the ring Haman had worn but now also a purple robe and golden crown. Members of the court had bowed to Haman, the Agagite, but the whole city acclaims Mordecai, the Jew. Mordecai counters Haman's edict with one similar in language but this time it is sent "urgently and hastily"[14] on elite, royal steeds (הרכש האחשתרנים בני הרמכים;

---

Judaism (the sense it will take on in later literature; see Achior's conversion in Judith 14:10. Cf. the following note on 9:27). This verbal form may also describe "acting as a Jew" in the same way that התנבא refers to "acting like a prophet" (cmp. also the *hithpael* of אבל; R. R. Wilson 1980:138).

[13] Craig (1995:86, 87) charts the reuse of phrases and words from 3:9–4:3 in 8:2–17. Levenson (1997:107–109) mentions not only the reversals and inversions contained in chapter 8; his analysis also includes a description of the reversal of LXX Add. B in Add. E.

[14] Fox (1991a:101) sees a level of enhancement in this phrase which adds to the "hastily" of 3:14.

8:10).[15] One-up-manship is taken to a gruesome level when the stake designed for Mordecai is not only used for Haman but, in the next chapter, also for each of his ten sons. If there were one point of the parallel with chapter 3 missing, it might be Haman's private banquet with the king in 3:15. But this point is merely postponed, notes Levenson (1997:115):

> The Jews are wiser than Haman and thus not so confident as he was. Their feasting will come only when they have attained relief from their enemies. Whereas his celebration was short-lived, theirs will continue to endure from generation to generation (9:20-23).

The private "happy hour" of a smug Haman is replaced by the "carnival" of countless Jews. This enhanced reversal is, thus, magnified annually, *ad infinitum*.

When the king tells Esther and Mordecai in 8:8, "you may write as you please ... in the name of the king," he is sharing his royal authority with them. The description of Mordecai's attire using the terms בוץ, חור and ארגמן clearly echoes the list of the king's hangings in 1:6. Purple is a ubiquitous symbol for royalty and one featured in the promotion of Daniel in Dan. 5:7,16, 29.[16] The crown, like the robe, ring and horses, is clearly a royal symbol. As such, it is one which bears honor (cf. Job 19:9; cmp. Prov. 12:4; 16:31; 17:6; Jer. 13:18. Cf. Ps. 8:6[5]).[17]

Honor is associated, by definition, with these royal accouterments. It is also confirmed by the public acclaim which follows. Mordecai's promotion and the edict together bring a

---

[15] Levenson (1997:110) suggests that the use of exotic animals used for this special assignment is a way of "highlighting the better pedigree of the countervailing edict."

[16] Bevan (1902:280) provides comparative evidence that the giving of a purple garment was, in a later context, a way of marking the king's benefactors.

[17] Herodotus VIII 118 provides an account of Xerxes giving a gold crown as a form of honor.

response of joy (שׁשׂון, שׂמחה) and honor.[18] There is celebration for the beginning of deliverance, to be sure. There is also *yᵉqar* (8:16).

## Honor and Fear

> *When the unrighteous see them,*
> *They will be shaken with dreadful fear,*
> *And they will be amazed*
> *At the unexpected salvation of the righteous.* (Wis. 5:2)

The enhanced reputation and confirmed status of the Jews contributes to a "fear" (פחד;[19] v. 17 and 9:2,3) which falls on the Gentiles.[20] Similar sentiments are expressed by the prophet Jeremiah when he says of Jerusalem:

> ... it shall be to me a name of joy (שׂשׂון), a praise and a glory (תפארת) before all the nations ... they shall fear (פחד) and tremble because of all the good and the prosperity I provide for it. (Jer. 33:9).

This type of fear describes a public perception of divine involvement; it reflects awe and, colloquially, a "healthy respect."[21]

The fear of the nations is not only a motif for Gentile response to divinely produced prosperity. Throughout biblical history פחד is a trope for the terror induced by God and/or Israel in holy war against their enemies. It is a particular awe experienced in the presence of God's power. Fear "falls" on the Egyptians when God first led his people out of their oppressive control (Ex. 15:16 and Ps. 105:38). "No one will be able to stand

---

[18] Light, also mentioned in 8:16, is elsewhere a symbol for prosperity (Ps. 36:10[9]) and joy (Ps. 97:11), but it also participates in the semantic field of honor (i.e., "glory"; Isa. 58:8; 60:1, 19). Terms for joy and glory appear together in Ps. 149:5.

[19] On fear as a kind of heightened respect (i.e., following fame) see I Chr. 14:17.

[20] I follow Moore (1971:81) who translates עמי הארץ as non-Jews. The term has more restricted connotations elsewhere.

[21] Dohmen (1995:17) notes that, in reference to YHWH, כבד is often found in parallel with ירא, the standard verb for fear.

against you;" Moses predicts, "the Lord your God will put the *fear* and dread of you on all the land on which you set foot." (Deut. 11:25; cmp. Josh. 2:9, 24; 2 Chr. 14:14; 17:10; 20:29). פחד is often accompanied by a panic and confusion expressed by the root המם (Ex. 14:24; 23:27; Josh. 10:10; et al.), the same word used to describe Haman's intentions against the Jews in 9:24.

The ancient motif of fear in holy war is still present in the literature of the Second Temple Period. The battle descriptions of Judith (2:28) and the Maccabees (2 Mac. 12:22) use the same language to describe the impression Israel makes on her enemies (cmp. Wis. 5:2; 3 Mac. 7:22). To use these rich images at any point in Israel's history was to engage a whole conceptualization of war, one which assumes divine involvement and, consequently, inevitable victory.[22]

---

[22] Biblical accounts of holy (lit., YHWH) war assume that God is fighting for Israel. In some cases there is no mention of the actual physical combat, and divine/human synergy is hardly apparent. The terror is sent by God and the battle is fought and won by God alone. For this reason many commentators assume that Esther's author is making a decidedly secular statement by excluding the name of God especially at this very moment when deliverance is achieved. A faulty circular reasoning is evident, however, when holy war is defined by a particular list of terms and motifs which rarely occur as a complete collection. It seems much more likely that the Bible shares a pan-Near Eastern assumption that virtually all military engagements reflect divine involvement. This perspective is sometimes more explicit or dramatically described than others, but it is regularly assumed. Furthermore, the very prevalence in Israel's Scripture of holy war accounts with explicit reference to God makes it very unlikely that an ancient Jewish reader could think of anything else but God's hand behind the scenes of Esther 8 and 9. The patterning of Esther after Exodus narratives makes it less likely still. While this understanding does not answer the question of Esther's "non-religious" character (i.e., why does the author refrain from referring to the Divine?) it suggests an appreciation for inference and understatement regarding its religious themes.

## Esther 9: Victory, Vindication and Celebration

ישמח צדיק כי־חזה נקם פעמיו ירחץ בדם הרשע

*The righteous will rejoice when they see vengeance done;*
*They will bathe their feet in the blood of the wicked.*

(Ps. 58:11[10])

### Summary of the Narrative

Esther 9 recounts the details of the actual fighting on Adar 13 and 14, beginning with a thematic recapitulation of the events:

> ... the very day when the enemies of the Jews hoped to gain power over them [was] changed (נהפוך) to a day when the Jews would gain power over their foes

The narrator again emphasizes the fear which had fallen on all the peoples—fear of the Jews (v. 2) and fear of Mordecai in particular (v. 3). This fear inspires widespread official support[23] for the Jews. Mordecai, the account continues, grew increasingly "great" (גדול) in the king's house and his fame (שמעו) spread throughout the provinces (v. 4). The Jews were able— presumably as a result of the empire-wide awe—to kill all their enemies and do to their "haters" exactly as they pleased (כרצונם; v. 5).[24] The anticipated clash between two men, two laws and two forces results in a total victory and complete vindication for the Jewish protagonists.

Vs. 1 is the first occasion upon which the author provides an explicit statement about the plot's reversals. In 9:22 the same verb (הפך) will be used to describe the *change* "from sorrow into

---

[23] Levenson (1997:120,121) translates the Hebrew מנשאים as "gave honor" because of its reversal of the elevation of Haman in 3:1 (where the same term is used). Both Greek versions (A and B) explicitly state that the government officials were "honoring" the Jews in 9:3, using a form of τιμάω where the MT uses a form of נשא.

[24] Nehemiah's review of the conquest similarly describes the subjugation of the Canaanites "... and the peoples of the land, to do to them *as they pleased*." (Neh. 9:24). In Dan. 11:16 doing as one pleases is explicitly connected with overpowering one's enemies.

gladness and from mourning into a holiday."[25] This motif of
reversed fortunes is a common biblical one. In Jer. 31:13 the Lord
promises to *turn* mourning into joy and sorrow into gladness
(cmp. Ps. 30:11; Lam. 5:15; Isa. 61:3). The divine hand stands
implicitly behind the terms "turned" or "changed."[26] Haman,
like Balaam (Deut. 23:5; Neh. 13:2), found his attempts to curse
the Israelites *turned* into a blessing because the Lord was
protecting them.

Another important theme in the story of Esther emerges
again with the root שלט, the term for mastery and domination in
9:1. The same verb is featured in the conflict tales of Daniel. In
Dan. 3:27, the fire had no *power* over the three faithful Jews
thrown into the furnace. In Dan. 6:25[24] the lions *overpowered*
the accusers of Daniel, eating them to pieces. Daniel's "accusers"
(קרצוהי אכלו; lit., "those who ate him to pieces") found
themselves literally eaten to pieces! Just as Haman was hoist
with his own petard, all those who tried to implement his
genocidal scheme received precisely the same treatment they
had intended to dole out. By explaining the slaughter in these
terms of measure-for-measure reversal, the narrator effectively
removes any culpability from the Jewish fighters and justifies a
social order with newly recognized—and increased—Jewish
authority.

After the first day of killing, Esther makes two requests of
the king (v. 13): She asks for a one-day extension of the fighting[27]
and for permission to hang Haman's (now dead) sons. Both
requests were granted. During the following day they gained
"relief from their enemies, and killed 75,000 of those who hated
them" (v. 16). The narrator again emphasizes that the Jews were
acting in self-defense, that there was a tremendous slaughter,

---

[25] In v. 25 the narrator also makes explicit the turn of events for Haman: "...
the wicked scheme that he had devised against the Jews [came] upon his
own head..."

[26] In its active form, the root describes God *overthrowing* his enemies (Gen.
3:24; 19:21, 25, 29).

[27] The careful attention to the law which Esther exhibits in this scene subtly
responds to the accusation of Haman in 3:8 that the Jews do *not* keep the
king's laws (Craig 1995:130).

and that the Jews took none of the plunder (vv. 10, 15, 16).[28] Haman's sons are singled out for public disgrace not only by hanging after death (cf. Josh. 8:29; I Sam. 31:10; Herod. III 125; VI 30)[29] but also, one might argue, by their graphic representation in the MT.[30]

The festivities described in vv. 18,19 set a precedent for the celebration of Purim[31] described in the verses which follow.[32] There is joy and feasting and the giving of gifts (*manot*; vv. 19, 22). These gifts recall the *manot* given to Esther by Hegai in 2:9. Now, however, the Jews were in the position to show favor to those in need. Happily, the object has become the subject. There is also a suitable parallel here to the *manot* mentioned in Neh. 8:10,12 which accompanied rest from military conflict and the celebration of Sukkot.

Est. 9:24–32 summarizes the events of the story and battles once again with a description of the process by which Mordecai and Esther authorized the continued observance of this new

---

[28] The king's edict (8:11) gave the Jews the right to take plunder. Their refusal to do so may reflect the Amalekite story in I Samuel 15 in which the booty that was supposed to be destroyed was taken. It seems very likely that it is also a way of insisting that, *unlike Haman and the other anti-Semites*, the Jews were not out for money in this war. They were strictly defending their lives and their honor.

[29] Some commentators have assumed that the hanging of Haman's sons was purely vindictive (Bardtke, Anderson, Paton) or for practical reasons (i.e., to scare the enemy) (Hoschander, Moore). The element of public humiliation, so central to the idea of crucifixion in Roman times, seems to have escaped these assessments.

[30] There are numerous midrashic speculations regarding the peculiar writing of the names of Haman's ten sons but no explanation for this format (found elsewhere only in Josh. 12:9–23) enjoys the consensus of interpreters.

[31] The debate about the sources of Esther and their various endings is tangential to our analysis of the received text. For the position that the Purim material is extraneous, see Paton (1908:57–60). For an overview of the problems, see S. E. Loewenstamm (1971:117–24).

[32] The Jews celebrate their *rest*, we are told, and not the fighting itself (vv. 18, 22). This emphasis may recall the holy war motif of "rest" found throughout historical narrative (Josh. 1:13, 15, et al. See Clines [1984:162]). The specific root נוח used here is also a play on its first use in Haman's accusation (3:8): "... it is not worth it for the king *to let them remain* (להניחם)."

holiday. An etiology of the name *Purim* is given. A charge to future generations follows.[33] Letters are once again sent to all the 127 provinces of the king. This time they are directed to the Jews wishing them peace (v. 30)[34] and explaining "the regulations concerning their fasts and their lamentations" (v. 31).

## Revenge Revisited

> *Let my persecutors be shamed,*
>     *But do not let me be ashamed.*
> *Let them be dismayed,*
>     *But do not let me be dismayed.*
> *Bring on them the day of disaster;*
>     *Destroy them with double destruction.*
>                 (Jer. 17:18)

> *The ultimate vindication of honour lies in physical violence.*
>                 (Pitt-Rivers 1966:29)

In our earlier discussion of Esther 3 the topic of revenge surfaced in relation to tribal feuding. That scene described a confrontation between Mordecai and Haman as representative heads of two groups in cyclic animosity. The spiral of vengeance which led Haman to plot the genocide of the Jews automatically raised the stakes for the Jews when the account is to be settled in chapters 8 and 9. Was the behavior of the Jews in these final chapters simply malicious vengeance or, rather, exemplary, self-

---

[33] In Est. 9:27 the regulations of Purim are for all generations of Jews and for those who "joined" them (הנלוים). The image of outsiders joining Israel is a frequent one in the Bible and one which assumes religious observance. In Isa. 56:3 the *niphal* of לוה is used to describe foreigners "joined to the Lord" who should not doubt their status among the worshipping Jewish community.

[34] For formally similar greetings, see Isa. 39:8; Jer. 33:6; Zech. 8:19. The context of fasting and feasting in Zechariah 8 (v. 19), its images of nations joining the Jews (vv. 22, 23), and its use of this greeting suggest that an eschatological rubric was in mind in the concluding chapters of Esther. See J. Levenson (1997:130,131), M. Fishbane (1985:503–5) and the following discussion.

sacrificing heroic loyalty to kin? The perspective of the story obviously supports the latter view, but on what basis?

The narrator, first of all, consciously builds a case for the Jewish military action as self-defense. Twice, they "took a stand for their lives" (עמד על־נפשם; 8:11; 9:16) against those who would do them harm. The immediate context for self-defense is the actual attack of the group three times referred to as "their haters" (שנאיהם in 9:1,5,16). The author insists that the Jews were *responding* to the aggression of their enemies rather than initiating it. This aggression may be associated primarily with Haman's plot or may have reference back further into the tribal history described above. The lament categories of "the wicked" and "the enemy" resemble this schematic portrayal of unnamed masses who seek the lamenter's life without cause (Ps. 35:7, 19; 69:4; 109:3; 119:161).

In 8:13 the narrator uses the verbal construction להנקם ("to avenge oneself") which conceptually summarizes the Jewish response. They are seeking not only protection/deliverance but *just recompense*. The root implies a righting of wrongs, measure for measure: "Take vengeance on her (הנקמו)," says the prophet; "*do to her as she has done*" (Jer. 50:15). Pitard (1992) (*contra* Mendenhall 1973)[35] supports the long-held *legal* connotation of the root נקם. This is an important point to emphasize in the narrative of Esther where all of the Jewish military action takes place *according to the king's decree*.[36] The actions of the Jews were *lawful* means of vindication.[37]

---

[35] Mendenhall moved the discussion of נקם beyond the notion of blood-vengeance, providing comparative evidence for understanding the root in terms of extra-legal rescue in covenant contexts. He distinguished between punitive and defensive forms of "vindication." Pitard (1992), finding the linguistic evidence (from Amarna) for Mendenhall's case faulty, prefers the judicial term "recompense." Mendenhall's (1973:72) observation that terms for vengeance in a variety of ancient cultures are "used characteristically only of actions carried out by the highest of social and political authority" is, from either perspective, quite important for our discussion.

[36] The king's law is similarly emphasized in the accounts of Daniel and Nehemiah. Whatever judgment comes on the accusers is *legal*.

[37] The modern concern with an impartial, anonymous executioner is missing in the story of Esther. The offended party itself might be directed,

One wonders what specific wrongs the Jews were seeking to right. The text certainly gives the reader reason to believe that there were many in the Persian empire who wanted the chance to harm the Jews. To call them שׂנִיאהם ("their haters") presumes that there was already a history of anti-Semitism.[38] Haman's plan surely depended on some measure of latent ill will in the general populace.

Perhaps the reader is being led to focus more on the plan to harm rather than on a history of actual physical mistreatment. Chapter 9 describes a reversal of what Haman *intended* to do to the Jews. Just recompense includes not only past misdeeds but publicly planned ones as well.[39] Poetic and moral justice is achieved when Haman is hanged not because he had hanged Mordecai but because he had *planned* to hang him. The slaughter of the enemies of the Jews is not only a response to past grievances but, more likely, a response to present intentions. The narrator has no need to justify Esther's supposed maliciousness because, one can assume, the intended threat itself justified it.

One helpful way to explain such a viewpoint is in terms of the public shame entailed in Haman's accusation and edict. If honor has a near-tangible quality to it, if it is a "commodity" which can be diminished by word or gesture, then certainly there are "damages" to pay for libel. Accusation, as the laments so clearly show, is itself a form of shaming which requires vindication. If thousands of people read the edict and made military preparations for the slaughter of Jews and seizure of their property, then shame was already a social fact for the

---

according to the principle of talion, to take the life of a family member's murderer (cf. Deut. 19:12).

[38] To "hate" (שׂנא) in biblical parlance is to reject, disregard actively or maintain no legal obligations. It is not simply a verb of emotion (cf. Mal. 1:2,3). See the comments of Zenger (1994:32-3).

[39] The laws of Deuteronomy give equal weight to intention and deed. In regard to public witnesses and accusers, Deut.19:19 legislates: "... do to the false witness just as the false witness had meant to do to the other" (cmp. Hammurabi #3-4). Haman had been a public accuser, giving false information to the king about the Jews to get them killed. Their sentence became his by the law of talion. See T. Frymer-Kensky's (1980) discussion of these laws.

Jews.[40] When the Jews went into this day of battle, there was a *debt* in mind. Their lives had been threatened, to be sure, but *their honor had already been diminished.*

This dimension to the activities of Adar 13 and 14 also explains why Haman's property rightfully went to Esther and why his sons were necessarily executed. The very things Haman had sought *from* the Jews had to be given *to* the Jews. His insatiable urge to wipe out every one of Esther's kin created a formal challenge for her, when she was finally able, to wipe out every individual who was (by intention) related to him.[41] Reversals in the story of Esther represent sobering social "laws." Just recompense is one of them.

With these dynamics in mind, it is clear why the prospect of נקם is consistently used in the Bible as a basis for encouragement.[42] "Proclaim the year of the LORD's favor, and the day of *vengeance* of our God; to comfort[43] all who mourn..." (Isa. 61:2). It is a word of freedom from oppressors and a word which promises the public righting of all wrongs. It lies at the

---

[40] In Frymer-Kensky's (ibid., 231) discussion, she assumes that the law of talion is applied to accusation because it would promote identification and prosecution and deter false accusation for monetary gain. In a brief response, L. G. Herr (1981:135) raises the important issue of "personal honor" which is at stake in cases of false witness and accusation. Shame exists when there is public doubt about integrity. True vindication requires the punishment of the accuser for this truly substantial crime. One should recall here that Vashti had "wronged" (עוה) the king by a symbolic act of dishonor in 1:16.

[41] The homologous association between Haman and the haters of the Jews is linguistically reinforced by the epithet "enemy" (אויב) used first of Haman (7:6) and then repeatedly of the thousands who attack the Jews (8:13; 9:1, 5, 16, 22).

[42] Vengeance, like anger, is ascribed most often to God in the Bible. Judges and other public figures who stood in the place of God in Israelite society were expected to render justice and just recompense for those who were oppressed.

[43] The term for comfort (נחם) is often used in parallel to the audibly similar term for vengeance (נקם). The oracle of *Nahum* (נחם) begins three times repeating the root נקם: "A jealous and *avenging* God is the Lord, the Lord is *avenging* and full of wrath; the Lord takes *vengeance* on his adversaries and rages against his enemies." (1:2) So begins this word of comfort.

heart of the prophet's vision of redemption: "For the day of *vengeance* was in my heart, and the year for my redeeming work had come" (Isa. 63:4). The Jews, once "sold," were redeemed ("repurchased") by way of the punitive judgment of their enemies. The salvation of their lives and the restoration of their honor required the disgrace and decimation of their declared enemies, and, as we shall see, the respectful deference of the remaining citizenry.

The equation of recompense with reversal does not, however, fully articulate the dynamics of vindication and vengeance. Vindication, in its fullest sense, apparently required a full public reversal of intended events ... *and more.*" Retribution, therefore, is not only a response to action but surpasses it" (Klinger 1987:368). In the words of the lamenter, "Return *sevenfold* into the bosom of our neighbors the taunts with which they taunted you, O Lord" (Ps. 79:12; cmp. Gen. 4:23-24). A return to the status quo is *not* the goal of the story of Esther. Haman will necessarily lose even more than he had attempted to take and Esther and Mordecai will necessarily gain even more than they might have lost.

### Shame and Honor in Warfare

כי הושעתנו מצרינו ומשנאינו הבישות

> But you have saved us from those who afflict us,
> And have put to shame those who hate us.
>
> (Ps. 44:8[7])

There are a variety of traditions in the Bible which involve military conflict. Virtually every historical and prophetic book features — and interprets — warfare. Warfare is essential not only to the historical descriptions of "holy war," but also to the more forward-looking traditions of Zion and David, the oracles against the nations, and images of the "Day of the Lord."

While even a survey of these eschatological traditions is outside the scope of this study, many common elements can be quickly catalogued: synergy between God and his people in battle, the equivalence of God's enemies and his people's enemies, the efficacious deliverance of God, the peace/rest that follows conflict. One motif which has been relatively unrecognized in the secondary literature is the final, well-deserved shame of the enemy who has first brought shame on the nation of Israel and her God. Images of a coming day of judgment are laced with terms for shame and dishonor, first of Israel and then of her enemies who must suffer for their hubris and mistreatment of Israel.

While the book of Esther shares nothing in common with prophetic oracles or eschatological predictions *formally*, its characterization of the enemies of the Jews and its description of the days of battle and victory are more than subtly reminiscent of such passages. One representative example[44] suffices to illustrate the ubiquitous theme of the shamed enemy.

Jeremiah 50 and 51 is an extended oracle against Babylon, the climax of Jeremiah's collection of oracles against the nations. This archrival enemy of Israel becomes the object of divine vengeance (נקם; Jer. 50:15, 28 and 51:6, 36) — like Tyre (Ezk. 28:2); Moab (Jer. 48:29; LXX Jer. 31:29; Isa. 16:6); Egypt (Ezk. 30:18; 32:12); Pharaoh himself (Ezk. 29:3); and all other tyrants (Isa. 13:11) — because of *hubris* (Jer. 50:32; LXX Jer. 27:32). This indifference to God, most explicit in the form of idolatry, is commonly expressed by a reckless disregard for Israel, God's chosen. A warning is issued to those "*plunderers of my heritage*" who rejoice in their exaltation (50:11). The military abuse of Israel had left Jerusalem "put to shame" (בוש), with dishonor (כלמה) covering their faces (51:51). The prophet now ridicules the pagan gods falsely credited for victory over YHWH's inheritance: Bel is "put to shame" (בוש), Merodach is "dismayed" (חתת), her images are "put to shame" (בוש), her idols are "dismayed" (חתת; v. 2).

V. 2 begins this oracle by calling for a public declaration of the coming demise of Babylon and her gods. The commands to "declare" (נגד), "proclaim" (השמיע; 2x), set up a banner, and not to "conceal" (כחד) insist that the coming destruction must be

---

*public*. And that public destruction is necessarily described in the discourse of dishonor. The consequence (punishment) of their behavior will be *internationally acknowledged disgrace*:

> Your mother shall be utterly shamed (בוש), and she who bore you shall be disgraced (חפרה) ... everyone who passes by Babylon shall be appalled (שמם) and hiss (שרק) because of all her wounds ... How Babylon has become a horror (שמה) among the nations! (Jer. 50:11–13; 23)

An honor/shame reversal is integral to the punishment: "You set a snare for yourself and you were caught ... because you challenged the Lord." The day of God's vengeance is the day when the arrogant will stumble and fall (נפל; 50:3; 51:8).[45] Babylon *must* fall because of the fallen of Israel (51:49). The disgracer *must* become the disgraced. Rest (רגע) for the earth will only come, according to a pun in v. 34, when there is unrest (רגז) for the inhabitants of Babylon. Her whole land will be put to shame (בוש; 51:47) and then everything that is in heaven and earth will shout for joy over Babylon (51:48).

It is not difficult to trace the themes of this passage in the story of Esther. Haman's exulting hubris is a form of personal honor-seeking[46] which threatens the lives and honor of God's chosen people.[47] For order and peace to be restored, Haman and his followers must be publicly rooted out of society. The restoration of the honor of the Jews is built on the shame of their attackers. His shameless joy in secret is replaced by the public

---

[45] Her walls and young men also fall (נפל) in 50:15, 30; 51:4, 8, 44, 47.

[46] Compare the characterization of Haman with that of the king of Babylon in Isa. 14:4ff. Prinsloo's (1981) pattern of hubris and humiliation well suits the antagonist of Esther.

[47] The fact that God's name is not mentioned in Esther has raised a host of concerns about the view on war and revenge the author is promoting. The fasting in chapter 4 and the specific comments of Mordecai in 4:14 have convinced this author that the Jews under threat seek *divine* help. All of the elements which the story shares with both historical and eschatological texts of warfare support the assumption that YHWH is involved in the outcome of these battles.

rejoicing of the Jews and fellow citizens. The words of the psalmist might well be recited here:

> O daughter Babylon, you devastator!
> Honored[48] shall they be who pay you back
>     what you have done to us!
> Honored shall they be who take your little ones
>     and dash them against the rock! (Ps. 137:8-9)

## The Banquet of Honor

*"You prepare a feast for me in the presence of my enemies"* (Ps. 23:5)

The great reversals achieved by Esther and the Jewish people are celebrated in the festival of Purim. This victory banquet brings to a culmination the see-saw series of public and private *mishta'ot* in the story. The first Purim will become, like the original Passover, the precedent for a perpetual re-celebration of deliverance. But deliverance is only a part of the story and only a part of the ritual. More than just the spontaneous merrymaking of victorious survivors, Purim is an orchestrated public celebration of vindication and the resulting increase in Jewish honor. We have already witnessed honor dynamics in the preceding banquets and this final festival will prove no less evocative of such sentiments.

For perspective on the victory banquet in Esther, it is helpful to consider the dynamics of similar celebrations in the ancient world. There are numerous ANE reliefs which illustrate the celebration of military victories. Many depict the procession of booty and prisoners of war before the triumphant king who is either seated on his throne or reclining at his banqueting table.[49] The registers which depict this procession publicize newly acquired wealth and subjects. The captives are presented in a humiliated fashion: in chains, without clothes, and/or bowing

---

[48] I follow the translation of אשרי as "honored" defended by K. C. Hanson (1994).

[49] Two well-preserved examples are the Standard (or "Peace Panel") of Ur (25th c. BCE) and the Black Obelisk of Shalmaneser III (Nimrud; 9th c. BCE).

before the king. In one illuminating relief of Ashurbanipal[50] the neo-Assyrian king is seen feasting with his wife after a battle with the Elamites. Ashurbanipal reclines facing not only the queen but also the hanging head of the defeated Elamite king.

Victory celebrations which relive the humiliation of the enemy as well as the vindication of the victor find parallels in mythic literature.[51] There is evidence of a common ANE combat myth in which a rising deity successfully confronts a cosmic threat and assumes absolute kingship.[52] This myth dramatically traces a suspenseful conflict which threatens to take the lives of the protagonist and his followers. The *Enuma Elish* provides a good example from ancient Mesopotamia.[53] It is the story of the rise of Marduk, the patron deity of Babylon. The threat takes the form of Tia'mat, the goddess of the watery deep who personifies the forces of chaos. When victory is secured, there is great relief and celebration. This celebration is the occasion of public acclaim for the vindicated king in the assembly of the gods. The defeated enemies are permanently dethroned and become the slaves of the assembly. Their task is the building of a temple devoted to Marduk. As the newly acquired status of the Sovereign is celebrated, he is given fifty names of honor which represent his character, roles and achievements.

There is evidence of many of these motifs in biblical poetry. In the ancient hymn of victory over the Egyptians (Exodus 15) the people of Israel celebrate the incomparable splendor (note) of YHWH who defeats his enemies and prepares to reign from his

---

[50] See Plate 451 in *The Ancient Near East in Pictures Relating to the Old Testament* (2nd ed.) by J. B. Pritchard (Princeton University Press, 1969).

[51] For an insightful description of the analogous relationship between ANE myths and various natural, social and political realities, see T. Jacobsen (1976).

[52] To speak of a common ANE myth is simply to refer to a common plot. There are numerous versions of this plot in different literary and historical settings.

[53] Jacobsen (1976:167-168) describes the extent to which this story influenced the myths of other cultures in the Near East and across the Mediterranean. The Ba'al cycle from the Ugaritic texts represents a Canaanite version of the same plot. Jacobsen (1968) argues elsewhere that this West Semitic version may represent the original source of the myth.

sanctuary forever (vv. 17, 18). The song reflects on the Egyptians whose boasting (v. 9) led to their sinking (v. 10; cf v. 5), and whose plans to pursue, overtake, gorge and destroy (vv. 9, 10) became a prescription for divine retribution against themselves.[54]

Mythical language is used to describe YHWH as creator in certain biblical passages (e.g., Psalms 89, 104; Job 40–44). Images of an ancient combat-banquet myth are clearly present:

> You divided the sea by your might;
> You broke the heads of the dragons
> in the waters.
> You crushed the heads of Leviathan;
> You gave him as food for the creatures
> of the wilderness. (Ps 74:13,14)

The final line describes a gruesome feast made up of the carcass of the defeated.

The prophetic literature makes use of these same images. Isaiah 24–27, often referred to as the "Isaianic Apocalypse," presents a vision of a great eschatological feast following a military victory of cosmic proportions:

> On this mountain the Lord of hosts will make for all peoples a feast of rich food, a feast of well-aged wines, of rich food filled with marrow, of well-aged wines strained clear. (Isa. 25:6)

The feast will not only celebrate military victory, but also the Lord's eternal reign on Mount Zion (24:23) and the removal of "the disgrace of his people ... from all the earth" (25:8).

A similar vision is found in Zechariah 14 which also describes a coming *Day* for Zion. The Divine warrior will fight a cosmic battle with his hosts (vv. 3–5). The result will be his eternal reign (v. 9) celebrated by tribute from the nations (v. 14) and the annual, universal celebration of Sukkot in Jerusalem (v. 18). For those nations who do not recognize YHWH as King there will be an ominous curse on human and beast (vv. 12ff).

---

[54] Cross (1973:112–144) was one of the first to provide a detailed discussion of Exodus 15 in the light of the ANE combat myth.

These poetic and prophetic visions reflected the political and military realities of the day. Public celebration with gifts (or tribute) and the honoring of royalty was an expected sequel to military victory. War typically offers the opportunity to redistribute power and such reversals were intentionally celebrated once victory was achieved. After a protracted series of conflicts between Saul and David, the one-time shepherd from Bethlehem was vindicated by God through the death of Saul and his heir on Mt. Gilboa. Divine approval was followed by a public ceremony:

> All these, warriors arrayed in battle order, came to Hebron
> with full intent to make David king over all Israel; likewise all
> the rest of Israel were of a single mind to make David king.
> They were there with David for three days, eating and
> drinking, for their kindred had provided for them. And also
> their neighbors, from as far away as Issachar and Zebulon
> and Naphtali, came bringing food on donkeys, camels, mules,
> and oxen — abundant provisions of meal, cakes of figs, clusters
> of raisins, wine, oil, oxen, and sheep, for there was joy in
> Israel ...                                    (I Chr. 12:38-40 NRSV)

A closer parallel to Esther comes from 3 Maccabees in the Apocrypha. In this story king Ptolemy is the arrogant antagonist to the Jews even though his own life was saved by a Jew (1:3; cmp. Est. 2:21-23). He is repeatedly characterized as impious, profane, puffed up and audacious (2:2 ff.). Because of his own conceit, Ptolemy decides to destroy the Jews (and shame them; 4:5, 11) but, like Haman, he enjoys his victory feast too soon (4:1ff, 16; cmp Est. 3:15). His intention to have drunk (!) elephants feast on the Jews (5:31) during a banquet for the Friends of the king becomes a prescription for the story's great reversal: the animals turned back on the armed forces and trampled them (6:21); the king's anger was turned to pity (v. 22) and praise to God (v. 33); the laments of the Jews were exchanged for praise (v. 32); and while the Jews celebrated a feast of deliverance, their enemies became food for the birds (vv.

30–31, 34).[55] The story is recapitulated in 6:31: "Those disgracefully treated and near to death" were able to enjoy a "banquet of deliverance," but their enemies were "overcome by disgrace."[56] What makes this account particularly useful for our discussion is the subsequent institution of this feast as an annual festival (6:36; cmp. I Macc. 4:56; 7:49; 13:51; 2 Macc. 10:6; 15:36).

## The Unlikely Heroine and the Humiliated Foe

As uniquely captivating as the character of Esther is, she by no means stands alone as an example of female craft and courage in the Bible. There are a number of similar stories about females who outwit and dishonor threatening males. In so doing, they protect themselves and preserve their progeny. An intriguing pattern in both social and literary spheres is apparent.

### Trickster

Analysis of the clever and courageous woman in Israel's literature benefits from a number of different approaches. One recent form of comparative analysis has surveyed "tricksters" in a variety of cultural contexts and compared them with certain biblical characters. A recent *Semeia* volume (Exum and Bos 1988) is devoted to this topic.[57] Although it became clear for a number of the authors that tricksters exhibit quite a variety of characteristics in literature[58] and that they are as often male as female,[59] the venture made some useful observations about a group of female protagonists in Hebrew Scripture. With a focus placed largely on the stories of Rebecca, Tamar, Deborah/Jael,[60]

---

[55] The reader is likely to recall here the words spoken between Goliath and David in I Sam. 17:44, 46.

[56] Interestingly, the "joyful festival" included the "public and shameful death" of apostate Jews as well (7:14, 15).

[57] The analysis of G. Yee (1993) is pertinent to this discussion as well.

[58] See especially the criticism of E. Good (1988:120,121). Compare the comments of C. Grottanelli (1983:117–139).

[59] This point is made by both Fontaine (1988:84 n.1) in terms of the comparative literature and Bal (1988:147) in terms of the biblical.

[60] For a discussion of the parallels between Esther and Judges 4 and 5, see Fewell and Gunn (1991) and Yee (ibid.).

Ruth and Judith,[61] a pattern emerged which includes the following motifs:[62] a threatening crisis/enemy (usually in the form of an aggressive, "foolish" male[63]), some form of deception[64] by an "unlikely" female,[65] stroke(s) of luck/the hand of Providence, the shaming of the man,[66] and the prosperity and progeny of the woman secured. The tricksters in each of these stories typically resort to their sexuality and to their dress as a part of the ruse. The deception also involves some kind of ambiguous statement or other clever use of words. The reader is endeared to these characters because of their courage and cunning in that crisis moment we have called *kairos*. Their well-executed schemes have secured them an entertaining place in

---

[61] Esther figures into some of the discussion along with Rahab, Abigail and Dame Folly.

[62] To the following list one might also add the ironic way in which these liminal figures underscore the vulnerability of those in power (Steinberg 1988:9,10): "The underdog plays the part of power-broker and the one expected to wield authority is under the thumb of the weak." Trickster stories point up the ambiguities of power itself (cf. M. Douglas 1966:3–4; L. W. Radin 1972; Levine 1974; Babcock 1975).

[63] Ruth is different from the other stories in that natural causes (famine, death) constitute the threat she faces. She must, however, secure the protection of an unsuspecting distant-male-relative-by-marriage and her loyalty (to Naomi) and cleverness in so doing provides her a place in the line of king David. Like the king in Esther, Boaz is shown honor as the one who stands in the place of God to provide what "his servant" needs.

[64] The deception may simply be leading a man on in his own self-deception or using the normal expectations of female behavior against him. "...[P]aradoxically, it is precisely in their acting with and against men *as women*, as sexual beings in their own right, that Tamar, Yael, and Ruth accomplish their decisive autonomies." (Good 1988:120) Jael offers desert hospitality and then kills her guest with implements associated with domesticity (cmp. Judg. 9:53).

[65] Compare Esther (the orphan-exile Jewess) with Ruth (the Moabitess), Jael (the Kenite) and Abigail (the wife of *Fool* [נבל]).

[66] Jacob, in Gen. 38:23 , is afraid of being a "laughingstock" (בוז); he is already fooled more than he knows. Sisera ironically disclaims his manhood when he tells Jael, "If anyone asks you if there is a man here, say 'no'." (Judg. 4:20) Haman finds himself begging for his life from a Jewess and then hangs on his own gallows.

the story of Israel's history. They also very clearly serve the higher purposes of God's promises to Israel.

> Each woman steps in at a critical juncture in the life of a family or larger group and brings about a positive turn of events, which were moving in a negative direction. By staying ahead of the males who have power over them, the women thus advance not only their own well-being but also that of the community. (Bos 1988:38)[67]

Esther deserves more attention in such a discussion of female tricksters. She shares with all of them an unexpected threat to which she is an unlikely candidate to respond. Acting upon her deepest loyalties (i.e., to family), she uses a blend of wit[68] and courage to bring down her enemy and secure benefits for her people. A combination[69] of sexuality, food,[70] words, dress—and providence—all together effect the desired reversal. Like Jael, she not only feeds her guest's stomach but also his assumptions about his security with her. Lulled by his own self-deception, he is shocked when she turns against him. In the end, Haman gets what he deserves and Esther gets what she desires.

This characterization of Esther as a type of unlikely-loyal-courageous-crafty female savior of her family is not only a biblical type but also one common in ancient historiography. According to Dewald (1981:107), Herodotus describes a similar kind of figure who departs from the traditional, passive profile

---

[67] While "cunning" (πονηρός) is typically an adjective in Greek tradition for the devil, it is applied as well to women, for they are considered a constant threat to male honor (Campbell 1964:277). However, "cleverness and cunning are legitimate and praiseworthy where their object is the protection or advancement of family interests, but not beyond these limits, or for their own sake." (ibid., 283).

[68] Whether or not Esther technically *deceived* Haman is open to discussion. She certainly set up a "sting," leading Haman along in his own self-deception as Jael did with Sisera.

[69] See Craghan (1982) for a discussion of many of these motifs in Esther, Ruth and Judith.

[70] See Glassner (1987) for an examination of the dynamics of gender and hospitality in the ANE.

in extreme situations and moves into an aggressive, public role. In such cases:

> ... feminine activity is depicted as a creative manipulation of the constraints of the situation in which the woman finds herself, while males frequently ignore such limitations and are brought low in consequence by some factor they have not anticipated. (ibid.,108)

Dewald mentions here Polycrate's daughter and the wives of Sesostris and Intaphrenes as examples of women who make courageous, sacrificial choices to save the lives of those to whom they are fiercely loyal. Their unconventional success is often in the context of excessive male ambition (ibid., 109–110). While these remarkable figures are anomalous, there is a distinct continuity between the characterization of these "heroic" women and the traditional ones which make up the masses.

> They are almost without exception passionately loyal to the family ... not only teaching the conventions of their cultures to their children but reminding their male peers as well of the rules within which the whole society is supposed to act.
>
> (ibid., 97)

All of the women about which Herodotus writes ultimately preserve social order, even while temporarily challenging it. They show respect for social constraints and conventions but as vehicles for cultivating the enduring values of society. Such could easily have been written about the character of Esther.

### Goddess of Love and War

In Carole Fontaine's (1988) contribution to the trickster discussion, she describes a number of deceptive goddesses in ANE myth which resemble the female characters under discussion. The resemblance between goddess myths and biblical stories has previously been explored in the cases of Deborah/Jael (J. G. Taylor 1982) and Ruth (J. M. Sasson 1979:67). Fontaine (ibid., 86) suggests a mythical background for the Zipporah story (Ex. 4:24-26) and other accounts in the life of Moses. She then posits a "banquet-contest type scene" found most clearly in stories of Inanna and Inaras but also in corresponding biblical stories. In the myths the goddess accrues power through the deceptive use of sexuality and hospitality.[71] But there is always a greater purpose. Echoing Bos' comments quoted above, Fontaine (ibid., 98) insists that:

> The goddesses' deception is never mere whim, or worse, moral defect ... she deceives, not on her own behalf, but on behalf of city, high-god, or in Isis' case, on behalf of humankind in general...

A comprehensive redistribution of power is effected.

The mythical figure of Ishtar,[72] the "Queen of the Divine Decrees" and goddess of love and war, may stand behind the characterization of Esther.[73] Her name invites the association[74] and her qualities and strategies provide further intriguing connections. In "The Descent of Ishtar" (discussed above in terms of the symbolism of clothing), the goddess demonstrates her resolve and resilience. In "Inanna and Enki," she outwits the god of wisdom while he is drunk and successfully takes possession of the *me*, a collection of divine attributes. A commentary on the development of the character of Ishtar could easily read as a description of the figure of Esther:

> At the beginning of the story, Inanna flaunted her raw feminine vitality — her wondrous vulva. En route and in battle her powers were tested, and, joining forces with more spiritual resources, Inanna emerged a fuller woman. She

---

[71] Drunkenness is very often the context for the redistribution of power in ANE myth and also in Scripture. Fontaine (1988:98) notes a variety of references.

[72] Ishtar, the principal goddess of Mesopotamia, became associated with Inanna when the Akkadians assimilated Sumerian culture. The West Semitic counterpart, Astarte, is a commonly condemned pagan figure in the OT, one scholars often equate with the Queen of Heaven mentioned in Jer. 7:18; 44:17-19, 25. See W. J. Fulco (1992:521).

[73] Fontaine (ibid., 93) does make reference to the story of Esther (and Judith) as a likely example of goddess influence.

[74] Mordecai is clearly a variant of the Babylonian deity, Marduk. Haman may be the name of the chief Elamite deity.

> passed from vulva to provider, from hero to queen ... She
> offers [her rewards] to the people of Uruk.
>
> (Wolkstein and Kramer 1983:150)

No one particular myth about Ishtar closely resembles the plot of Esther, but the shared motifs of royalty, sexuality, deception and conquest are illuminating.

### Warrior-Queen

The character of Esther invites comparison not only from the world of tale and myth, but, more directly, from the annals of history. Queen Esther can be identified as a type of warrior-queen in history, a culturally anomalous Xfigure but one with wide-ranging attestation. From Semiramis to Cleopatra to Queen Elizabeth I, strong women have taken political leadership into the military sphere with great success. Women, so often viewed as the *protected* in war, are, on such occasions, the *protector*. At the end of chapter 7, Esther demonstrated both courage and craft in the downfall of Haman. In chapters 8–10 she stands in command of a sizable resistance force, albeit with Mordecai's assistance. To the dismay of many a commentator, Esther displays a ruthlessness usually associated with military men (cf. Hoffner 1966; Mazrui 1977).

When historians evaluate the conduct of female military figures, they tend to emphasize the exceptional circumstances which gave rise to a woman in command *or* the savage perversity of the woman herself. The comments of S. Macdonald (1988:56–57) on Boadicea are analogous to the characterizations of Esther in biblical scholarship:

> She has been seen as a cruel, bloodthirsty savage, who would happily torture and kill men, women and children; and also as a decent and honourable British lady, whose righteous actions stem from her motherly sense of propriety.

Because female military leaders in patriarchal societies are exceptions to the norm,[75] they are typically interpreted as

---

[75] While this may be accurate as a general historical statement, societies exhibit distinct versions of patriarchy. There are also different classes and

possessing male qualities.[76] Zenobia, among Arab Queens second only to Cleopatra, was described by the classical historians as one who "ruled Palmyra and most of the East *with the vigor of a man*" (Abbott 1941:13). On the eve of the defeat of the Spanish Armada, Elizabeth I describes herself as one who will fight like a man:

> I have but the body of a weak and feeble woman; but I have the heart of a king, and of a king of England, too; and think foul scorn[77] that Parma or Spain, or any prince of Europe, should dare to invade the borders of my realm: to which, rather than any dishonor should grow by me, I myself will take up arms; I myself will be your general, judge, and rewarder... By your obedience to my general, by your concord in the camp, and by your valor in the field, we shall shortly have a famous victory over the enemies of God, of my kingdom, and of my people. (Elshtain 1987:171-2)

---

conditions within any given society that make exceptions the rule. Pitt-Rivers (1966:71) describes the paradox of women in certain Mediterranean aristocracies: "Thus the lady of the upper class can command men without inverting the social order, since her power derives from her rank not her sexuality... women of high birth are accorded on that account a right to the kind of pride which is a male attribute, an element of masculine honour. They do not thereby forfeit their femininity... they acquire in addition some of the moral attributes of the male. Sexual and class status come together to qualify the rules of conduct which apply to their behaviour."

[76] Circumstances of crisis often push society into a state of flux which often gives rise to the leadership of liminal characters. War is not the only such crisis; it may simply be the clearest. In Mediterranean countries women who are occasionally forced by circumstance to perform the duties of men are often admired for "lacking only testicles." (Blok 1981:429; cmp. Gilmore 1987b:9; 1987a:97). Admiration for such females in patriarchal contexts is comprehensible once we understand that the exception proves the rule. Boundaries may be ironically reinforced by their occasional, conscious, temporary transgression (See I. Kirk 1988).

[77] Queen Elizabeth's speech uses the language of honor and shame associated so commonly with warfare. The threat of invasion is described in terms suggestive of sexual assault: She will not have her borders invaded; she will not be so *dishonored*. She chooses rather to *scorn* such acts which would disgrace England. Her call is one to valor and *famous* victory over their enemies which are synonymous, of course, with the enemies of God.

The warrior queen, like the trickster, exhibits courage but, rather than resorting to cunning and deceit, the queen uses the conventional (male) implements of war to defeat her adversary. The trickster wins by using the informal, nonconventional strategies common to the disadvantaged. Theirs are guerrilla tactics. The warrior queen beats her enemy at his own game with his own strategies. Like Jael and Judith, the Esther of chapters 5–7 is a cunning figure who uses male assumptions about female subservience to outwit them. Like Deborah[78] and a host of non-biblical queens, the Esther of chapters 8–9 successfully wages *war* against her enemies.

One important side-effect of female leadership in war is the enhancement of the humiliation of the enemy. In Judges 9 Abimelech was laying siege to the city of Thebez when he was unexpectedly hit by a mill-stone thrown by a woman on the wall. "Draw your sword and kill me," he commands his armor-bearer, "so people will not say about me, 'A woman killed him'" (Judg. 9:54).[79] Dishonor is feared more than death, and insult more than injury.

The theme of dishonor by a woman is just as explicit in the story of Deborah. The parallel accounts of Judges 4 and 5 honor two women by playing on the dishonor of two men. Because Barak, the general, refuses to go to battle without Deborah, the prophetess and judge, she predicts that he will not get the glory (תפארת) but that Sisera will be handed over to the hand of a woman (Judg. 4:9).[80] The obvious implication is that glory normally belongs to a man in battle. The greater dishonor, however, is reserved not for the man who must be second to the victorious woman. It belongs rather to the real enemy, the man

---

[78] The appellation "mother" for Deborah in Judg. 5:7 may reveal the tendency in some cultures to view warrior women not as pseudo-men but as protective mothers. This is the observation of Sayigh and Peteet (1956) regarding Palestinian women in Lebanon.

[79] See M. Sternberg's (1985:219–22) comments about this passage in his discussion of 2 Samuel 11–12.

[80] This verse uses terms and images also found in Esther: the Lord will, literally, "sell" (מכר) Sisera into the "hand" of a woman. Just as the image of being sold is crucial to the plot in Esther, so is the sending out of the hand (יד; 22x in Esther. See Levenson 1997:109).

who loses his life by the hand of Jael. He will suffer the taunt Abimelech dreaded: "A woman killed him."

Haman, like Sisera, presumes on the hospitality and grace of a woman. Like Sisera who "falls" dead between the feet of Jael, Haman "falls," terrified for his life, at the feet of Esther. The enemy is, in each case, defeated *and disgraced*. The redistribution of social power is symbolically enhanced by the reversal of typical gender roles in the conflict.[81]

### Esther 10: The Permanent Recognition of Ahasuerus and Mordecai

*Summary of the Narrative*

The final chapter of Esther forms a terse conclusion to the story. Taxes are levied throughout the empire (v. 1). The great deeds of the king and his newly appointed prime minister, Mordecai, are recorded in the annals of the kings of Media and Persia (v. 2). Mordecai has power and popularity among the Jews (v. 3).

This conclusion categorically emphasizes the honor of Mordecai, the new "Second" (מִשְׁנֶה) to the king.[82]   What he enjoyed momentarily in chapter 6 and was officially granted in chapter 8 is now recorded permanently in history. We rightly infer the concept of honor in these references to power, public approval, royal favor and loyalty to kin. But the honor of the king is also important, as we have noted throughout the story.

---

[81] In writing about the "Bravery of Women" in his *Moralia*, Plutarch describes the Festival of Impudence which commemorates a battle won through female valor. In this celebration men dress like women and women like men. Purim is a celebration of ethnic survival through a woman's courage and is, likewise, an occasion for gender reversals. The close connection between reversed gender roles and overturned powers is at the heart of *carnivalesque* (Craig 1995:158–59).

[82] One is tempted to create a midrash on this verse by reference to Isa. 61:7: "Instead of your shame you will have a double portion (מִשְׁנֶה), and instead of humiliation they will shout for joy over their portion. Therefore they will possess a double portion (מִשְׁנֶה) in their land, everlasting joy will be theirs."

Royalty is given a place in the book of Esther as the institution of
gentile kingship is honored.

But, the reader asks, what about Esther *the person*? How is
it that the book bearing her name can so abruptly close with
statements of honor only for the king and prime minister? These
questions will receive some fresh light from a final pair of
anthropological excursuses. Before turning to these topics,
however, it is necessary to review one already discussed.

## Mordecai, the Jew

Mordecai's title in the story is most often "Mordecai, the
Jew" (5:13; 6:10; 8:7; 9:29, 31; 10:3). Unlike Esther, who never
leaves the royal compound, Mordecai has been presented
throughout the story as a leader in the Jewish community. More
importantly, he has been presented as the *representative* Jew in
the story. Standing in the royal line of Saul, he refused to show
deference to Amalek, their ancient foe, represented by Haman
(Agag *redevivus*). His explanation was his Jewishness (3:4). Once
Haman sets into motion his plot to destroy the Jews (he also
associates Mordecai with all the Jewish people), Mordecai tore
his clothes and initiated a public fast and mourning. He was
joined in these rites by all the Jews in the empire (4:1-3). The
equation of Mordecai with the Jewish population at large is
made explicit following the reversals in chapters 6 and 7. When
Mordecai was publicly honored in 8:15-17, there was also for the
Jews "light ... and honor." In that context "fear" fell on the
Gentile population. As a result, many of them joined the Jews.
This same fear describes the effect of both Mordecai and the Jews
in 9:2 and 9:3. The happy ending of 10:3 describes a man who
was favored by his people for seeking their good and
"interceding for the welfare of all his descendants." While Esther
had also interceded[83] for her people,[84] Mordecai is the one who
stands as royal representative of the Jews as a whole.

---

[83] There are different Hebrew terms used for intercession: in Esther's case it
is the root חנן, in Mordecai's it is דבר.

[84] The episode in chapter 4 makes it clear that Mordecai's immediate
response to the news of Haman's plot was public mourning. Esther
required persuasion (threat?) before she joined him.

## Honor as Authority and Power

> *The paradox is this: Vashti's insubordination renders her powerless;*
> *Esther's subordination renders her powerful.* (Levenson 1997:131)

The theme of dominion has been present throughout the story and it remains at the center of attention as the plot comes to its conclusion. The issue of control, of having one's way, however this power may be exercised, is one of the book's central themes. It appears in the clash of wills between Xerxes and Vashti, in the description of Esther's malleability and obedience, in Mordecai's refusal to bend to Haman's will and the latter's splenetic attempt to control his enemies by eradicating them, and in other interactions as well. Now, at their moment of triumph, the Jews' not only escape their enemies' power but also impose their own will on *them* (9:5; cf. Fox, 108). Power is not simply an independent theme in Esther (*contra* Berg, 96–98). It is one expression among many of the central theme of honor. Levenson's (1997:120) analysis reveals that, in chapter 9:

> The most important aspect of the great battles of Adar 13–14 is thus not the slaughter, by which the Jews turned the tables on the anti-Semites, but rather their assumption of a new status of honor and dominion, symbolized by the accession of one of their own as prime minister in the previous verses.

Mordecai is presented as a man "growing in greatness" (הולך וגדול; 9:4). Like Moses in Ex. 11:3, this increasing power (demonstrated by freeing his people from bondage) was *publicly recognized*. Esther 10 defines Mordecai's final position as one of authority and power and public recognition: second only to the king in Persia and one who accomplished good for his fellow kinsmen. His deeds of תקף (power) and גבורה (might) were *recorded* in the annals of the kings of Media and Persia. Three times the root גדל is used of Mordecai in the final two verses of the book.

Esther is also a person of power and authority by the close of the book. "The command of Queen Esther," chapter 9 concludes, "fixed these practices of Purim, and it was recorded in writing." As *queen*, Esther gives a command and the matter is permanently settled. The reader is fully aware of the importance of commands and unalterable edicts in the story. They come only from persons in authority. Once issued, they expose the loyalty of one's subjects. Emphasis is given to the counter-edicts written by Esther and Mordecai (chapter 8) and to the regulations of Purim which they also write (chapter 9).[85]

For our discussion, the basic distinction between authority as *right* (or position) and power as *ability* should be maintained.[86] In Esther there is a tension between the formal right (*de jure*) to rule and the true ability (*de facto*) to control. Whether it be the king and all husbands in chapter 1 or the newly promoted prime minister of chapter 3, the question of those in positions of authority having the ability to control their subordinates must be answered. The narrator insists throughout chapters 8 and 9 that Esther and Mordecai *are* able to control their enemies and rule their own people.

The tension between power and authority reflects a facet of the honor and shame dynamic in the world of the ancient narrator. Authority and position are associated with status. They represent honor in its *formal* sense. We noticed a clear example of this perspective in the descriptions of the king's banquets in chapter 1. Status is identified by a label, title, seat, ring, material, or with official written words. Status grants rights. But the prerogatives of formal authority must be publicly tested on occasion to confirm their validity. What a person *may* do is not always equivalent to what a person *can* do.

---

[85] Clines (1984:22) writes, "In Esther, reality tends towards inscripturation, and attains its true quality only when it is written down. What is written is valid and permanent..." He supports this observation by noting that nothing between chapters 4–7 is written; everything is in flux, tentative. Inscripturation is not only a sign of permanency but of authority and authorization. The "right to write" is an important signal of status in Esther. When Mordecai and Esther take up the royal pen and seal in chapters 8 and 9, they are clearly demonstrating royal authority.

[86] See Rosaldo (1974:21) and Dubisch (1986:16–20) who describe how this distinction is usually viewed in relation to gender. Esther's role in the domain of the court gives her the kind of unusual authority noted by Pitt-Rivers (1966:71 [cited above]).

When Haman, for example, does not effectively get Mordecai to bow to him, his authoritative title is potentially a social sham. The *public* awareness of this discrepancy is underscored by the narrator (3:4; cf. 1:16–18). Haman understands fully that, without a visible demonstration of his control over his in-subordinate, his position is in jeopardy. His wife and cohorts clearly comprehend this dynamic (6:13).

As the book comes to a close, Esther and Mordecai demonstrate that there is substance behind their status. Esther is queen not only by title but as a true co-ruler in the kingdom. She effected great change. That change was initiated through the more subtle forms of deception and persuasion which "exceptional" circumstances—and her gender—demanded. But her plan was ultimately executed with the full authority of a queen. Mordecai is the king's *Second* (cmp. Gen. 41:43). This position of authority is granted to a man who effectively saved the king's life and helped saved the lives of all the Jews in the kingdom. He is *gadol* both in terms of his authority and in terms of his power.

### Jewish Honor and World Order

One of the terms featured in our discussion of the final chapters in Esther is the verbal root נקם. This concept of just recompense pictures the oppressed (Jews) not only free from oppression but also holding a more secure and prominent position in the political landscape. A similar root which parallels נקם on occasion is שלם ("to reward, make compensation, make whole"). In Deut. 32:35 the Lord says, "Vengeance (נקם) is mine, and recompense (שלם); In due time their foot shall slip; the day of their calamity is at hand, their doom comes swiftly" (cmp. Deut. 32:41). שלם is also, of course, the root from which the multivalent term for peace, שלום, comes. Letters of *peace* (שלום) and truth (אמת) were sent to all the Jews following the days of fighting (9:30). These were the documents which enjoined the continued observance of the festival of Purim. These linguistic links should prepare us for the subtle association between honor and social order that many biblical writers maintain. In fact, this connection is evident in many societies today (cf. J. Davis 1987:24; J. Fajans 1983:174).

When the United States entered World War II, it was, according to official propaganda, a mission to *liberate* the world, to free it for democracy. The Japanese, notes R. Benedict (1946:27), entered the same war against the U.S. to *restore* the world to its proper order. The ordering of the world which they sought to reestablish placed the Japanese Emperor at the top of a hierarchical socio-political pyramid with the Japanese people immediately below him. The rest of humanity were to be placed under the Japanese. This imperialistic conceptualization is offensive to Western notions of equality and democracy, but it is undoubtedly closer to the cognitive orientation of the biblical writers than to our own.

One key concept in the Japanese perspective is captured in a term Benedict translates as "proper station." Restoring the world to its proper order meant putting each social group back into its appropriate social slot[87] in relation to other groups. Each group would then show proper deference to the groups above it. The greatest honor would be reserved for the Japanese people and their divine Emperor.

Surely there is something of this mentality in the eschatological images of Israel's prophets. Zechariah 14 (discussed above) describes the day of the Lord as a day of battle and vindication followed by the exaltation of Israel's God (v. 9). The city of Jerusalem will experience an endless era of peace and security as a result of victory. All of her enemies will suffer plague and panic (vv. 12,13,15). In the end, respectful Gentile survivors will join the Jews in annual worship of the Lord in Jerusalem, celebrating *Sukkot* with his chosen ones (v.16).

---

[87] C. Schneider (1992:35) notes that the Latin word for shame, *exponere*, means "to put out or place out." One might define shame as "out-of-order" and honor, conversely, as "order." There are hints of this connotation in the verbs כשר (Est. 8:5) and שוה (3:8; 5:13; 7:4).

In Isaiah 56–66 there is a similar[88] eschatological perspective which understands Israel as a community open to Gentiles who join them (Isa. 56:3, 6–8) as a result of seeing the glory of God (60:3). This vision is also built on the defeat of Israel's enemies. The sentiments of Esther are congruous with the following words from Isa. 60:14–16:

> And the sons of those who afflicted you will come bowing to you, and all those who despised you will bow themselves at the soles of your feet; ... Whereas you have been forsaken and hated, ... I will make you an everlasting pride, a joy from generation to generation. You shall suck the milk of nations, you shall suck the breasts of kings ...

In this new era, other nations and their kings will be the servants of Israel (60:10,12). Those who prefer to oppose Israel rather than join them will suffer for it. In the final verse of Isaiah the victors will "go out and look at the dead bodies of the people who have rebelled against me. For their worm shall not die, their fire shall not be quenched."

The social reversal in these accounts serves a purpose more profound than literary peripety or the dramatic constraints of "comedy." A fundamental redistribution of power is envisioned which reorders society around the Jews and their representative head. The memory of a defeated and dishonored enemy is integral to the vision. The honor of the Jews replaces the shame of the Jews which they experienced at the hands of their foes.

While these images, now put in broader perspective, may still elicit little sympathy among Gentile readers, the vision was meant to benefit Jew and Gentile alike. Biblical "imperialism" is not disassociated from its "universalism."[89] When the whole world is put in order, and every group is in its "proper station," there is peace and prosperity *for all*.

---

[88] Levenson (1976) highlights the *distinctions* between the viewpoints of Isaiah and Esther. In spite of the differences—and they are substantial—there are comparable interests deserving of emphasis.

[89] For a useful discussion of this topic, see J. Levenson (1996).

This biblical axiom is inherant in the patriarchal promise:

> I will make of you a great nation, and I will bless you, and make your name great, so that you will be a blessing. I will bless those who bless you and curse those who curse you; *and in you all the families of the earth will be blessed.*[90] (Gen. 12:2,3)

The promise describes three groups of people: blessed and honored Jews, blessed Gentiles (those who honor the Jews) and cursed Gentiles (those who curse the Jews). At the end of Esther there are the same three groups. The enemies have all been killed. The rest of the population has either supported the Jews or at least shows no ill-will. Now that the Jews are given their *rightful* place in the new order of things, there is peace and prosperity. It may be that the increased revenue of king Ahasuerus (10:1) is an example of the blessing promised those who properly honor the Jews[91] (cf. Gen. 39:5; 41:47ff.).

The comparisons above do not mitigate the literary and theological differences discernible between Esther and the prophets. In its description of Purim, Esther does not require the world to observe the holiday *"or else!"* It does, however, share the image of a new world order which has shifted the powers of the known political world. The nations joyfully honor the Jews (and, presumably, their God) and enjoy the prosperity which this honor guarantees.

### The Place of Esther

Esther, like virtually all biblical heroines, finds her place in Scripture not as one who has effectively changed—or even challenged—the social order. Rather, she has contributed, through bravery and intelligence, to the divine purposes for Israel. The social structures and authoritative figures are

---

[90] See the helpful comments of K. C. Hanson (1994) on the relationship between blessing and honor.

[91] Of course taxation is not always viewed as a form of prosperity by the general population. From the narrator's point of view, however, this motif of increased income does suggest the patriarchal promise motif. In the prophetic passages just reviewed there are parallel forms of tribute brought to Zion (Zech. 14:14; Isa. 60:6; cmp. Pss. 45:12; 68:29; 72:10).

parodied to be sure: Haman is ridiculed most strongly, but so also are the king and the Persian system of laws and governance. But Esther takes all of this with a measure of seriousness, mastering the system so that she can use it for higher purposes. When the crisis is over, the deferential queen retires into the background while the king and Mordecai do the business of running the Empire.

Esther is an example of courage and loyalty. She informally represents Jews who must resort, in their liminal state, to the strategies of the threatened, whether with persuasive rhetoric or with sex appeal (cf. Judith 10:3ff.). Mordecai, on the other hand, formally represents the Jews as *the Jew*. Now with ring and crown, he becomes their representative in the court of the king. Esther inspires the Jews; Mordecai stands for them.

One should not assume that Esther is automatically devalued by the author's emphasis on Mordecai and the king in chapter 10 (cf. Dubisch 1986:20–21). The story honors her as a woman and as a queen, but in the author's world her honor is necessarily of a different sort than a man's. Hers is a "muted" honor (Ardener 1975) which maintains (rather than challenges) male dominance (Ashley 1988; cf. Rogers 1975; Sanday 1981). Esther is honored by the narrative for her "subversive submission" (Herzfeld 1991) to the social structure: even while unmasking and exploiting its idiosyncrasies she still supports it. After executing her "exceptional" assignment, she returns to her acquired status ... but also to the status quo.[92]

---

[92] Esther's mysterious absence from the concluding lines of the story named after her may be compared to the absence of other heroines at the end of stories which bear their names. Susanna is an account of a threatened female which similarly ends with praise for her male protector, Daniel. The story of Ruth portrays a woman who, through deference to the patriarchal social structure—and manipulation of it—contributes to the saving plan of God for Israel. She also recedes into the background at the close of the story while Naomi (Mordecai's counterpart; cf. Fuchs 1982) is officially blessed (honored).

# Conclusion

"The book of Esther is many things, so many, in fact, that it would be a capital mistake to view it from only one angle." With this comment J. Levenson (1997:1) appropriately begins his critical commentary. Such a commentary must necessarily explore the entire range of issues in the history of the scholarship of a given book. The preceding analysis, in contrast, has sought to enlarge our understanding of the dynamics of the Esther story by viewing it from one particular, as yet unexplored, angle. This exercise makes no claim to offer the only correct interpretation. Rather, it seeks to supplement the ongoing discussion about the book and character of Esther, and the socio-historical setting of the story.

The analysis to this point has been centered on both literary and anthropological issues. The conclusions which follow summarize the observations made from these two perspectives and suggest the directions future analysis might pursue.

## Literary Issues

The topics of shame and honor are clearly rooted in the vocabulary of the book. The opening scene depicts a royal banquet organized for the display of the king's glory (את־עשר כבוד מלכותו ואת־יקר תפארת גדולתו; 1:4). This purpose is thwarted by Vashti's insubordination. The fear that similar shame (בזה) will come upon all men elicits the first edict. In 3:1 Haman is exalted (גדל, *piel*) and placed (שים) above the other nobles, who then must bow (כרע, חוה) in his presence (3:6). He despises (בזה; 3:6) Mordecai who, alone, dares to deny him proper respect. The tables are turned on Haman, in 6:1, when he has to lead his rival through the streets proclaiming, "This is what is done for the man the king desires to honor (יקר)." His wife and friends understand by this turn of events that Haman will ultimately fall (נפל; 6:13). He does fall, literally, begging for his life at the feet of Esther (7:8). In the chapter which follows, Mordecai is permanently honored and there is joy and honor (יקר) for the Jews (8:16). The final verses of the story emphasize the strength and power of the king and the promotion (גדל, *piel*) of Mordecai to *Second* in the Empire (10:2,3).

The themes of honor and shame are also evident in other related terms and motifs. Honor is implicit in the favor which Esther is shown in the court in chapter 2 and, later, in chapters 5–9. Shame is expressed by ritual humiliation in chapter 4, and by head and face covering in chapters 6 and 7. Honor is associated with clothing in chapters 6 and 8. Shame is associated with anger in chapters 1 and 7. At various moments in the story honor is equated with loyalty, authority, power, obedience, generosity, protection, social order and public recognition. In contrast, shame is equated with disobedience, disrespect, confusion, lack of control, and foolish, self-interested hubris.

Scholarship on Esther must be aware of these connected themes, making use of philological and semantic analysis of various terms and their cognates. It has been our contention that an anthropological approach facilitates the most complete understanding of these terms. Anthropology is used here in its broadest sense, as the science of culture, a science which includes the study of language in context.[1] Although social context is often a matter only tentatively or generally determined in biblical texts, literary context provides a suitable place to begin.

Our analysis has maintained an ongoing comparison between Esther and other examples of the challenge and honor plot (pattern #2). The meaning of words and gestures have been determined primarily by reference to the surrounding context in Esther. Connotations have also been established by reference to their occurrences in comparable texts. This procedure provides

---

[1] This approach follows the interdisciplinary orientation of F. Boaz (1955).

both control and insight for the project. It also highlights the elements of honor and shame in each phase of the pattern.

By looking beyond particular genre designations, we were able to uncover numerous sources of comparative data. Esther is a text in which the cross-fertilization of various genres should be appreciated. Each literary category contributes its own emphasis to the two social values under discussion. Of these types of literature, lament has been the least explored in relation to the book of Esther and, yet, one which offers great potential for intertextual reading.[2]

The laments offer a set of stereotypic characters. Enemies in the psalms are variously described as afflictors, haters, wicked, arrogant, etc. The two most common terms are אויב ("enemy") and שנא ("hater").[3] The narrator of Esther uses these same categorizations to identify the story's antagonists. At the pivotal moment in 7:6, Haman is pronounced "A foe and enemy, this wicked Haman!" (צר ואויב המן הרע הזה) a designation which uses three appellations common to the laments. Haman takes on the title, "the afflictor (צֹרֵר) of the Jews," already in 3:10 (cf. 8:1; 9:10, 24; cmp. Widengren 1937:218). The word for enemy, אויב, used in 7:6, is applied to all those who eventually fight against the Jews (8:13; 9:1,5,16, 22). The opposition are also called "haters" (from שנא) three times in the closing chapters (9:1, 5, 16).

The laments portray a *relationship* of conflict between oppressor and oppressed. The dynamics of this relationship involve the malevolent actions of the enemies who oppress,

---

[2] The plot of the story involves the primary elements and motifs featured in the laments with the exception that God is not mentioned. If the lament "triangle" of God-sufferer-enemies (Westermann 1981a:213) requires *explicit* reference to YHWH for the designation "narratized lament" (Westermann 1981b:6) to be applied, then, of course, Esther does not qualify. Many certainly argue (as I have above) for the implicitly acknowledged involvement of God in MT Esther. But defending one literary categorization of the book over others is not the point of this project. Our interest has been in the common elements of a biblical pattern which suggest certain sociological dynamics.

[3] Botha (1992:256ff) catalogues the occurrences of enemy terms in the Psalms and notes (257) that the most common parallelism (10x) involves these same two appellations, אויב and שנא.

accuse, persecute without cause, lie in ambush, dig pits, insult, attack, and scheme against the innocent sufferer.[4] Deviousness, deception and conspiracy put the lamenter in an unexpected, life-threatening, predicament. Haman functions as the scheming accuser in chapter 3. He obscures the truth about the Jews in order to procure the king's assent to his genocidal plan. On the advice of his wife and friends, he later plots the public execution of Mordecai, his immediate, personal enemy.

The plans of the wicked push the afflicted into a state likened to the grave. Since the days of ancient Sumer laments have constituted a formal grieving response to death. The extension or application of laments to other experiences of grief and loss assumes an essential affinity, or homology, between death, disaster, sickness, disgrace and exile. In Esther 4 the entire community of Jews engages in ritual fasting, mourning and lamentation (cf. 9:31). Esther and her assistants do the same. This is the moment in the story when the community seeks relief from the sentence of death and the disgrace it implies. At this point in the LXX account (Add. C), Mordecai and Esther voice their laments in prayers which proclaim innocence and beg for divine intervention. "Hear my prayer, and have mercy upon your inheritance;" Mordecai pleads, "turn our mourning into feasting that we may live and sing praise to your name." (13:17). These sentiments are implicit in MT Esther as well.

In the depths of despair the lamenter petitions for deliverance from the enemy. Deliverance begins with emancipation, for the afflicted has been sold into the "hand" (Botha 1992:257) of the oppressor. But complete vindication is the goal. Vindication requires that the oppressor becomes the oppressed, that the afflictor becomes the afflicted. This reversal is essential to the pattern.

Lament after lament seeks the return of disgrace upon the head of the mocker. Because both life and honor have been threatened, both life and honor must be restored. The psalmist is only assured that, "You will increase my honor" (Ps. 71:21) when

---

[4] On the enemy's "net" as a symbol of treachery, see the discussion and illustrations in Keel (1997:89–95). For a discussion of several of these images in other ANE laments see Widengren (1937).

he can say with confidence that "...those who tried to do me harm have been put to shame and disgraced." (v. 24). The honor of one is necessarily built on the dishonor of the other.

The laments include requests for the complete destruction of their foes. Without a public display of justice, God could be laughed to scorn.[5] The very memory of those who hate them must perish. While these sentiments seem "devilish" (C. S. Lewis 1958:25) to most modern readers, they are not uncommon in the laments. Nor are they restricted to the laments. The oracles against the nations contain the same vitriol. The ultimate demise of "the enemy" is, in fact, a staple in biblical history, poetry, prophecy and apocalyptic.

The images of the laments are patterned on bipolar moral characterizations. The archetypal images in the conflict between Esther (and the Jews) and Haman (and the haters of the Jews) are expressed by the same contrasting images of the psalms:

> good (us) and bad (them); sacred (us) and profane (them); innocent (us) and guilty (them); truthful (us) and deceitful (them); defenders of honor (us) and aggressors (them)."
> (Hobbs and Jackson 1995:27)[6]

The moral dimension of these sentiments is a crux for the interpreter. Esther, like the psalmist, seeks a violent reversal which is, for the modern, a base human instinct. For the author, however, it is a worthy human desire. Where we see vengeance, they see justice. And they rejoiced without reservation when it was accomplished. Esther is lauded for her loyalty to her people, her bravery and self-sacrifice, *and* for her ability to engineer the death and public shaming of the enemy. Judith, likewise, is hailed as a heroine when she returns to her camp with the head

---

[5] The assumption of the psalmists is that God's "absence" (or non-existence) is a conviction to which the unrighteous can cling if they remain unpunished. See Ps. 14:1 and the whole of Psalm 58.

[6] In Esther there is room for another category of generally supportive non-Jews, of which the king is the principle example. Esther and Mordecai apparently both have favor in the court (cf. 2:9; 2:17,18; 3:3; 7:9). The Jews as a whole also enjoy fairly widespread popular support, as evidenced in 3:15; 8:17.

of the Assyrian general. David, also, when he carries the head of Goliath, is not censured for blood-thirstiness. Rather, he is honored for his faith and courage.

An explanation for the narrator's assessment follows from the order of the action. The unqualified positive portrayal of such characters in laments and narrative *always presumes prior oppression and affliction.* Deliverance, just recompense, justice, and exoneration are sought *in response to* insult and injury. A person fully recovers from attack only when the enemy is placed under a judgment he unwittingly prescribed.

It is also clear that the Bible grants no license for personal revenge in these stories. Esther responds to Haman's edict by seeking *legal* means to defend the Jews. Every act of נקם is not only an act of self-defense, but one carried out according to the laws of the land.


## Socio-Historical Issues

### The Diaspora as a Shame-State

The challenge and honor pattern which Esther shares with other stories transcends not only literary categorization but also temporal periodization. Our analysis has confirmed the enduring resilience of this narrative pattern over time.[7] We have compared the story of Esther with Deborah as well as with Judith, with David as well as with Daniel.

While this pattern is evident in each historical period, it was, however, particularly suitable to the experience of exile. The book of Lamentations articulates a poetic series of laments over the loss of Jerusalem. Nehemiah, as we have noted, follows the movements of the pattern in a post-exilic, historical account. Esther and Daniel contain stories of life in the Diaspora. These also emphasize the movement from humiliation to exaltation.

Of the exilic literature, Esther stands out as being the farthest removed from the center of traditional Jewish activity.

---

[7] Birkeland (1955:93) asserts that the characterization of the enemy in the psalms similarly reflects both a pre-prophetic and post-prophetic perception of the "outsider" in Israel's religion.

Without any reference to Jerusalem or Israel,[8] to laws of ritual purity or priesthood, Esther is *the* book of the Diaspora. "Esther is an Exilic book, written in the Exile, for the Exile," writes S. D. Goitein (1957:62).[9] The story serves well as a window into the concerns of Judaism at the margins of another society.

Exile in the ancient world was considered a state of shame. The curses attached to ANE treaties and covenants typically listed exile as one of the divine punishments a people should expect if they were unfaithful to the terms of the agreement. Exile meant loss of land and central temple, and, through these, a loss of honor. In the closing words of one treaty we read, "May [the gods] exterminate from the earth your name and your seed."[10] In the prophetic words of Moses, "You shall become an object of horror (שׁמה), a proverb (משׁל), and a byword (לשׁנינה) among all the peoples where the Lord will lead you" (Deut. 28:37). Shame is emphasized in other prophetic warnings about the exile as well. The parable of Ezekiel 16 was discussed above as an example of pattern #1 (guilt and reconciliation). In such contexts the message is one of guilt which leads to the shame of exile.

Esther is not about the guilty actions of the Jews which caused their exile. It is, rather, about the tenuous status which characterizes their experience of exile. Nehemiah, Ezra, Haggai and Zechariah seek to regain the lost honor of the Jews and their God by rebuilding the city and its temple and reinstituting the formal worship of YHWH. Esther uniquely illustrates honor regained *outside* of Judah. In either approach, shame is a central concern.

To be separated from land, temple and monarchy in the ancient world was to be separated from one's source of identity as a people. The effort to recreate that identity might take the form of emphasized social or ritual boundaries. In Tobit and Ezra, for example, ritual purity enforces group definition. In

---

[8] The reference to the deportation of Jeconiah of Judah in 2:6 is simply a component of Mordecai's identification of Mordecai as an exile.

[9] This translation of the Hebrew is provided by J. Levenson (1976:446).

[10] This citation comes from the conclusion of the treaty between Suppuliumas and Kurtiwaza (ANET 206).

Esther, acculturation is approved but cultural assimilation is not. Genealogy takes prominence over geography (A. Levine 1992:105).

Psychologists readily equate shame with crises of identity. In contrast to guilt, which is initiated by a particular behavior, "shame cannot be detached from the self" (Lynd 1958:50). "Shame involves one's core sense of identity" (Broucek 1991: 20). "Shame," writes Kaufman and Raphel (1987:38), "presents a challenge and crisis for the self of enormous magnitude."

The association of shame with self is a function of the *Seeing Other*[11] in identity formation. M. Lewis (1992) describes shame as "The Exposed Self." Kaufman and Raphel (1987:38) state, "The awareness of being a Jew in a predominantly non-Jewish society calls attention to the self, *exposing it to view*" (italics added). Shame comes as a result of conspicuousness, of public deviation from the norm. Haman publicly discredits the Jews to the king in 3:8. At the heart of his charge: they are *different*.

## Esther as a Symbol of Israel

The character of Esther provides an appropriate personification of life in Exile. Like Judith (lit., "Jewess"), she was not only a heroine in her own right, but also an example of how one survives in a foreign state. The concerns of the book of Esther are the concerns of the whole Jewish community in Persia—status, power, security, and identity. S. A. White (1989) calls Esther a role-model for Jewish adjustment to political and economic marginality. She is an ideal role-model, for:

> Not only is she a woman, a member of a perpetually subordinate population, but she is an orphan, a powerless member of Jewish society. Therefore, her position in society is constantly precarious, as was the position of the Jews in the Diaspora. (ibid., 167)

---

[11] For a biological perspective on the importance of sight and being seen, see H. Jonas (1966).

Esther is one of many female figures in the Bible who take on paradigmatic proportions. As noted above, Deborah and Jael are important figures during the days of the judges when Israel was in an earlier stage of foreign domination. Female heroes, we noted, also make the downfall of the enemy more shameful. They strategically use their sexual vulnerability to take control of their people's destiny and turn their enemies into a laughingstock. By so doing, these female figures make suitable symbols for the liminal community. They dramatically portray the challenge which the community faces as a whole in its dependent state of exile. The story of Judith functions on the same levels. In the words of Jill Dubisch (1986:38), "Women ... bear a heavy symbolic load."

Another common female metaphor is the harlot, *the* symbol for disobedient Israel (Ezekiel 16; Hosea). In this image sexual impurity is emphasized. A case is brought against Israel because of her reckless disrespect for YHWH, her *ba'al*. Gender underscores the audacity of the harlot's behavior.[12]

Women are not the only representative figures in Israel's historiography. There are numerous examples of male representatives for the nation as well. Joseph and Daniel are exemplary figures from the same genre as Esther—as is Mordecai. We could look to Gideon as well as to Deborah, to Tobit as well as to Judith. Gender is not the exclusive criterion for symbolic utility.

In her discussion of gender and power, Dubisch (1986:35) concludes that "for a true understanding of gender we must move—paradoxically—beyond gender..." She explains (ibid., 35-37):

> Ideas of male and female, inside and outside, are related to conceptions of self and to one's experiences as a member of certain social groups in their relations with other social groups ... concepts of gender are simply the framework upon which

---

12 These examples of pattern #1 are also examples of pattern #2. The movement of Israel away from God's presence and back again is the other side of an account of God's honor challenged and restored. What is necessary for the punishment of Israel's guilt is necessary for the restoration of God's honor.

are hung important social values, as well as expressions and interpretations of life and society. It is through such oppositions as female/male, inside/outside, public/private, intimacy/separation, self/other that people construct a language for talking about and reconciling the diverse experience of their lives, experiences that include life and death, sin and salvation, superiority and subordination, competition and commonality.

The heroes of Scripture are typically individuals without inherited (ascribed) status. They include the late-born, the child of the previously barren wife, the member of the smallest clan, the youngest of the family, the exile, the orphan and the widow. For the nation of Israel, the most unlikely has become the expected and the peripheral has become the central.

P. Machinist (1991:210,211) explains this anomalous national self-perception in the context of other ancient societies:

> It is the fact and problematic of Israel's newness ... that lie at the heart of the Biblical distinctiveness passages ... how to forge an identity for a people that began on the margins of history and thereafter was faced constantly with a return to marginality—whether cultural, political, military, or a combination of all these—as against older societies like Egypt and Mesopotamia on its outside, and Canaanites and others within its midst. Paradoxically, it is this very status as newcomer and marginal, which at first sight looks so negative and culturally unstable, that is taken by our Biblical passages as the basis for a positive picture. In other words, if newcomer and marginal had meant, say, for the Egyptians, barbarian, immoral, and chaotic, in the Bible they became proof of the choice of the 'almighty God'—of new freedom, purity, and power.

The exile pushed Israel back into the margins of the great empires. Her identity as a people was forged not by long centuries of universal recognition but by an experience of God's providence during generations of intertribal conflict and political domination. It is in such contexts that stories like Esther take on significance beyond their own historical particularity. Esther can be more fully appreciated as another chapter in the ongoing story of Jewish survival, another example of the *Heilsgeschichte*. In the words of the NT writer:

*God chose what is foolish in the world to shame the wise;*
*God chose what is weak in the world to shame the strong.*

(1 Cor. 1:27)

# Sources Cited

Abbot, N.
   1941   "Pre-Islamic Arab Queens." *American Journal of Semitic Languages and Literatures* 63(1):1–22.

Abu–Lughod, L.
   1986   *Veiled Sentiments: Honor and Poetry in a Bedouin Society.* Berkeley: University of California.

Adkins, A. W. H.
   1960a   "'Honour' and 'Punishment' in the Homeric Poems." *Classical Studies* 7:23–32.
   1960b   *Merit and Responsibility: A Study in Greek Values.* Chicago: University of Chicago.
   1971   "Homeric Values and Homeric Society." *Journal of Hellenic Studies* 91:1–14.
   1972a   "Homeric Gods and the Values of Homeric Society." *Journal of Hellenic Studies* 92:1–19.
   1972b   *Moral Values and Political Behaviour in Ancient Greece from Homer to the End of the Fifth Century.* New York: Norton.

Anderson, B. W.
   1950   "The Place of the Book of Esther in the Christian Bible." *Journal of Religion* 30:32–43.

Anderson, G. A.
   1991   *A Time to Mourn, A Time to Dance: The Expression of Grief and Joy in Israelite Religion.* University Park, PA: Pennsylvania State University.
   1992   "Sacrifice and Sacrificial Offerings — Old Testament." *ABD* V:870–86

André, G. and Ringgren, H.
   1986   "טמא." *TDOT* V:330–342.

Antoun, R. T.
   1968   "On the Modesty of Women in Arab Muslim Villages: A Study in the Accommodation of Traditions." *American Anthropologist* 70:671–97.

Ardener, E.
   1975   "Belief and the Problem of Women." Pp. 1–17 in *Perceiving Women.* Ed. S. Ardener. London: Malaby.

Arthur, M. B.
   1981    "The Divided World of *Iliad* VI." Pp. 19–44 in
           *Reflections of Women in Antiquity*. Ed. H. P. Foley.
           New York: Gordon and Breach Science.

Asano-Tamanoi, M.
   1987    "Shame, Family, and State in Catalonia and Japan." Pp. 104–120
           in *Honor and Shame and the Unity of the Mediterranean*. Ed. D. D.
           Gilmore. Washington: American Anthropological Association.

Ashley, K. M.
   1988    "Interrogating Biblical Deception and Trickster Themes:
           Narratives of Patriarchy or Possibility?" *Semeia* 42:103–16.

Babcock, B.
   1975    "'A Tolerated Margin of Mess': The Trickster and His Tales
           Reconsidered." *Journal of the Folklore Institute* 11:147–86.

Bailey, F. G. (ed)
   1971    *Gifts and Poison: The Politics of Reputation.*
           Oxford: Basil Blackwell.

Bal, M.
   1988    "Tricky Thematics." *Semeia* 42:133–155.

Bardtke H.
   1963    *Das Buch Esther*. KAT 17/5.
           Gütersloh: Gütersloher Verlagshaus Gerd Mohn.

Barth, C.
   1947    *Die Errettung vom Tude in den individuellen Klage – und Dankliedern
           des Alten Testamentes*. Zollikon:Evangelischer Verlag.

Baroja, J. C.
   1966    "Honour and Shame: A Historical Account of Several
           Accounts." Pp. 79–138 in *Honour and Shame: The Values of
           Mediterranean Society*. Ed. J. G. Peristiany.
           Chicago: University of Chicago.

Bechtel, L. M.
   1991    "Shame as a Sanction of Social Control in Biblical Israel."
           *JSOT* 49:47–76.

1993 "The Perception of Shame within the Divine–Human
Relationship in Biblical Israel." Pp. 79–92 in
*Uncovering Ancient Stones: Essays in Memory of H. Neil Richardson.*
Ed. L. M. Hopfe. Winona Lake: Eisenbrauns.

Bella, M. P. di
1991 "Name, Blood, and Miracles: The Claims to Renown in
Traditional Sicily." Pp.151–65 in *Honor and Grace in Anthropology.*
Cambridge: Cambridge University.

Bellis, A. O.
1991 *Helpmates, Harlots, and Heroes.*
Louisville: Westminster/John Knox.

Benedict, R.
1946 *The Chrysanthemum and the Sword: Patterns in Japanese Culture.*
Boston: Houghton–Mifflin.

Berg, S. B.
1979 *The Book of Esther: Motifs, Themes, and Structures.*
Chico, CA: Scholars.

Berger, P. L.
1974 "On the Obsolescence of the Concept of Honour." Pp. 78–89 in
*The Homeless Mind.* Ed.s P. L. Berger et al.
New York: Random House.

Bevan, E. R.
1902 *The House of Seleucus.* Vol. II. London: E. Arnold.

Bickerman, E.
1967 *Four Strange Books of the Bible.* New York: Schocken.

Bird, P.
1987 "'To Play the Harlot': An Inquiry into an Old Testament
Metaphor." Pp. 75–94 in *Gender and Difference in Ancient Israel.*
Ed. P. Day. Philadelphia: Fortress.

Birkeland, H.
1933 *Die feinde des individuums in der israelitischen Psalmliteratur.*
Oslo: Grøndahl and sons.
1955 *The Evildoers in the Book of Psalms.* Oslo: J. Dybwad.

Black–Michaud, J.
  1975    *Cohesive Force: Feud in the Mediterranean and the Middle East.*
          Oxford: Basil Blackwood.

Blok, A.
  1981    "Rams and Billy Goats: A Key to the Mediterranean Code of
          Honour." *Man* 16:427–40.

Boaz, F.
  1955    *Race, Language and Culture.* New York: Macmillan.

Bos, J. W. H.
  1988    "Out of the Shadows: Genesis 38; Judges 4:17–22; Ruth 3."
          *Semeia* 42:37–67.

Botha, P. J.
  1992    "The Function of the Polarity between the Pious and the Enemies
          in Psalm 119." *Old Testament Essays* 5(2):252–63.

Boulay, J. du
  1976    "Lies, Mockery and Family Integrity." Pp. 389–406 in
          *Mediterranean Family Structures.* Ed. J. G. Peristiany.
          Cambridge: Cambridge University.

Bourdieu, P.
  1966    "The Sentiment of Honour in Kabyle Society." Pp. 191–241 in
          *Honour and Shame: The Values of Mediterranean Society.* Ed. J. G.
          Peristiany. Chicago: University of Chicago.

  1984    *Distinction: A Social Critique of the Judgement of Taste.* Tr. R. Nice.
          Cambridge: Harvard University.

Brandes, S.
  1987    "Reflections on Honor and Shame in the Mediterranean."
          Pp. 121–134 in *Honor and Shame and the Unity of the Mediterranean.*
          Washington: American Anthropological Associationiation.

Brenner, A. (ed)
  1994    *A Feminist Companion to Esther, Judith and Susanna.* The Feminist
          Companion to the Bible, 7. Sheffield: Sheffield Academic.

Broucek, F. J.
  1991    *Shame and the Self.* New York: Guilford.

Browne, L. E.
  1962    "Esther." *PCB*. New Series. London: Thomas Nelson.

Burton, L. A.
  1989    "Original Sin or Original Shame." *Quarterly Review* 8(4):31–41.

Cairns, D. L.
  1993    *Aidos: The Psychology and Ethics of Honour and Shame in Ancient Greek Literature*. Oxford: Oxford University.

Camp, C. V.
  1987    "The Three Faces of Esther: Traditional Woman, Royal Diplomat, Authenticator of Tradition." *Academy* 38(1,2):20-25.

Campbell, J. K.
  1963    *Honor, Family and Patronage: A Study of Institutions and Moral Values in a Greek Mountain Community*. Oxford: Clarendon.

Cazelles H.
  1961    "Note sur la composition du rouleau d'Esther." Pp. 17–30 in *Lex Tua Veritas*. Ed. H. Gross and F. Mussner. Trier: Paulinus–Verlag.

Chance, J. K.
  1994    "The Anthropology of Honor and Shame: Culture, Values, and Practice." *Semeia* 68:139-51.

Childs, B. S.
  1971    "Psalm Title and Midrashic Exegesis." *Journal of Semitic Studies* 16(2):137-50.

Clines, D. J. A.
  *1987*   *The Esther Scroll: The Story of the Story*. JSOT Supplement 30. Sheffield: JSOT.

Coleman, M.
  1987    "Shame: A Powerful Underlying Factor in Violence and War." *The Journal of Psychoanalytic Anthropology* 8(1):67-79.

Collins, J. J.
  1976    "The Court Tales in Daniel and the Development of Apocalyptic." *JBL* 1975:218-34.
  1993    *Daniel*. Hermeneia Series. Minneapolis: Fortress.

Coombe, R. J.
    1990      "Barren Ground: Re-Conceiving Honour and Shame in the Field
              of Mediterranean Ethnography." *Anthropologica* 32:221-38.

Craghan, J. F.
    1988      "Esther, Judith and Ruth: Paradigms for Human Liberation."
              *Biblical Theology Bulletin* 12:11-19.

Craig, K. M.
    1995      *Reading Esther: A Case for the Literary Carnivalesque.*
              Louisville, KY: Westminster/John Knox.

Creighton, M. R.
    1990      "Revisiting Shame and Guilt Cultures: A Forty-Year Pilgrimage."
              *Ethos* 18(3):279-307.

Cross, F. M.
    1973      *Canaanite Myth and Hebrew Epic: Essays in the History of the
              Religion of Israel.* Cambridge: Harvard University.

Danker, F. W.
    1988      *Benefactor: Epigraphic Study of a Graeco-Roman and New
              Testament Semantic Field.* St. Louis: Clayton Publishing House.

Daube, D.
    1969a    *Studies in Biblical Law.* New York: KTAV.
    1969b    "The Culture of Deuteronomy." *Orita* 3:27-52.
    1972      "Disgrace." Pp. 301-24 in his *The New Testament and Rabbinic
              Judaism.* New York: Arno.

Davis, J.
    1977      *People of the Mediterranean.*
              London: Routledge and Kegan Paul.
    1989      "The Sexual Division of Labor in the Mediterranean." Pp. 17-50
              in *Religion, Power and Protest in Local Communities of the Northern
              Shore of the Mediterranean.* Ed. E. Wolf. New York: Moulton Pub.
    1987      "Family and State in the Mediterranean." Pp. 22-34 in
              *Honor and Shame and the Unity of the Mediterranean.*
              Washington: American Anthropological Association.

Day, L. M.
    1995      *Three Faces of a Queen: Characterization in the Books of Esther.*
              JSOT Supplement 186. Sheffield: JSOT.

Day, P. L. (ed)
1991    *Gender and Difference in Ancient Israel*. Minneapolis: Fortress.

Deigh, J.
1983    "Shame and Self-Esteem: A Critique." *Ethics* 93:225–45.

Delaney, C.
1987    "Seeds of Honor, Fields of Shame." Pp. 35–48 in *Honor and Shame
        and the Unity of the Mediterranean*. Ed. D. D. Gilmore.
        Washington: American Anthropological Ass.
1991    *The Seed and the Soil: Gender and Cosmology in Turkish Village
        Society*. Berkeley: University of California.

Dewald, C.
1981    "Women and Culture in Herodotus' *Histories*." Pp. 91–125 in
        *Reflections of Women in Antiquity*. Ed. H. P. Foley.
        New York: Gordon and Breach Science.

Dohmen, C.
1993    "כבד - Etymology." *TDOT* VII:13–17.

Dommershausen, W.
1968    *Die Estherrolle*. SBM 6. Stuttgart: Katholisches Bibelwerk.

Dorothy, C. V.
1989    *The Books of Esther: Structure, Genre, and Textual Integrity*.
        Ph.D. Dissertation, Claremont Graduate School.

Douglas, M.
1966    *Purity and Danger: An Analysis of Concepts of Pollution and Taboo*.
        London: Routledge and Kegan Paul.

Dubisch, J. (ed)
1989    *Gender and Power in Rural Greece*.
        Princeton: Princeton University.

Durkheim, E.
1961    *The Elementary Forms of Religious Life*. New York: Collier.

Eaton, J. H.
1986    *Kingship and the Psalms*. 2nd Ed. Sheffield: JSOT.

Edelman, R.
1987    *The Psychology of Embarrassment*. New York: Wiley.

Eddy, S. K.
1961    *The King is Dead*. Lincoln: University of Nebraska.

Eissfeldt O.
1965    *The Old Testament: An Introduction*. Tr. P. R. Ackroyd.
        New York: Harper and Row.

Elshtain, J. B.
1987    *Women and War*. New York: Basic.

*Esther Rabbah I: An Analytical Translation*.
1989    Brown Judaic Studies 182. Atlanta: Scholars.

Evans-Pritchard, E. E.
1965    *Theories of Primitive Religion*. Oxford: Clarendon.

Exum, J. C. and Bos, J. W. H. (ed.s)
1989    *Reasoning with the Foxes: Female Wit in a World of Male Power*.
        *Semeia* 42. Atlanta: Scholars.

Fajans, J.
1989    "Shame, Social Action, and the Person among the Baining."
        *Ethnos* 11(3):166–180.

Feldman, E.
1977    *Biblical and Post–Biblical Defilement and Mourning: Law as Theology*.
        New York: KTAV.

Fewell, D. N. and Gunn, D. M.
1992    "Controlling Perspectives: Women, Men, and the Authority of
        Violence in Judges 4 and 5." *Journal of the American Academy of
        Religion* 58(3):389–411.

Fishbane, M.
1985    *Biblical Interpretation in Ancient Israel*.
        Oxford: Oxford University.

Fisher, N. R. E.
1979    *Hybris: A Study in the Values of Honour and Shame in Ancient
        Greece*. London: Aris and Phillips.

Flugel, J. C.
1976    *The Psychology of Clothes*. New York: AMS.

Foley, H. P. (ed)
1981    *Reflections of Women in Antiquity*. New York: Gordon and Breach.

Fontaine, C.
1988    "The Deceptive Goddess in Ancient Near Eastern Myth:
Innanna and Inaras." *Semeia* 42:84–102.

Foster, G.
1967    "The Image of Limited Good." Pp. 300–323 in *Peasant Society:
A Reader*. Ed.s J. Potter, M. Diaz, and G. Foster.
Boston: Little, Brown and Company.

Fox, M. V.
1991a    *Character and Ideology in the Book of Esther*.
Columbia, SC: University of South Carolina.
1991b    *The Redaction of the Books of Esther: On Reading Composite Texts*.
SBL Monograph Series 40. Atlanta: Scholars.

Freedman, D. N.
1972    "Tsubat Bashti: A Robe of Splendor." *Journal of the Ancient
Near Eastern Society of Columbia University* 4:91–95.

Friedrich, P. F.
1972    "Defilement and Honor in the Iliad."
*Journal of Indo-European Studies* 1:119–126.
1977    "Sanity and the Myth of Honor: The Problem of Achilles."
*Ethos* 5(3): 281–305.

Frymer-Kensky, T.
1980    "Tit for Tat: The Principle of Equal Retribution in Near Eastern
and Biblical Law." *Biblical Archeologist* 43:230–34.

Fuchs, E.
1982    "Status and Role of Female Heroines in the Biblical Narrative."
*Mankind Quarterly* 23:149–60.

Fulco, W. J.
1992    "Ishtar." *ABD* III: 521.

Funaki, S.
1957    "The Significance of the Old Testament Concept of 'Losing
Face'." Master of Arts Thesis, Wheaton College Graduate
School.

Gan, M.
    1961    "The Book of Esther in the Light of the Story of Joseph in
            Egypt." (Hb) *Tarbiz* 61:144-149.

Gaster, T. H.
    1950    "Esther 1:22." *JBL* 69(4):381.

Geertz, C.
    1972    *The Interpretation of Cultures*. New York: Harper Torch Books.
    1978    "'From a Native's Point of View': On the Nature of
            Anthropological Understanding." Pp. 22-34 in *Meaning in
            Anthropology*. Ed.s K. H. Basso and H. A. Selby.
            Alburquerque: University of New Mexico.

Gellner, E. and Waterbury, J. (ed.s)
    1977    *Patrons and Clients in Mediterranean Societies*.
            London: Duckworth.

Gerleman, G.
    1973    *Esther*. Neukirchen-Vluyn: Neukirchener Verlag.

Gerstenberger, E. S.
    1982,3  "Enemies and Evildoers in the Psalms: A Challenge to Christian
            Preaching." *Horizons in Biblical Theology* 4(2)/5(1):61-77.

Gilmore, D. D.
    1987a   "Honour, Honesty, Shame: Male Status in Contemporary
            Andalusia." Pp. 90-103 in *Honour and Shame and the Unity of the
            Mediterranean*. Ed. D. D. Gilmore.
            Washington: American Anthropological Association.

Gilmore, D. D. (ed)
    1987b   *Honour and Shame and the Unity of the Mediterranean*.
            AAA Special Publication 22.
            Washington: American Anthropological Association.

Ginzberg, H. L.
    1945    "Psalms and Inscriptions of Petition and
            Acknowledgment."*Louis Ginzberg Jubilee Volume*.
            New York: American Academy for Jewish Research.

Giovannini, M. J.
    1981    "Woman: A Dominant Symbol within the Cultural System of a
            Sicilian Town." *Man* 16:408-26

1986  "Female Chastity Codes in the Circum-Mediterranean:
      Comparative Perspectives." Pp. 61–74 in *Honor and Shame and the
      Unity of the Mediterranean*. Ed. D. D. Gilmore.
      Washington: American Anthropological Association.

Glassner, J. J.
1988  "Women, Hospitality and the Honor of the Family." Pp. 71–90 in
      *Women's Earliest Records*. Ed. B. S. Lesko. Atlanta: Scholars.

Godley, A. D.
1982  *Herodotus*. Loeb Series Vol. IV.
      Cambridge: Harvard University.

Goitein S. D.
1957  "Esther." *Bible Studies* (Hb). Tel Aviv: Yavneh.

Goldman, S.
1990  "Narrative and Ethical Ironies in Esther." *JSOT* 47:15-31.

Good, E. M.
1981  *Irony in the Old Testament*. Sheffield: The Almond.
1988  "Deception and Women: A Response." *Semeia* 42:117-132

Goode, W.
1978  *The Celebration of Heroes: Prestige as a Social Control System*.
      Berkeley: University of California.

Gordis, R.
1976  "Studies in the Esther Narrative." *JBL* 95(1):43–58.
1981  "Religion, Wisdom and History in the Book of Esther:
      A New Solution to an Ancient Crux." *JBL* 100:359–88.

Görg, M.
1975  "בוה, בוז, בזה." *TDOT* II:60–65.

Gottwald, N. K.
1978  *The Tribes of Yahweh–A Sociology of the Religion of Liberated Israel*.
      Maryknoll, New York: Orbis.

Greenstein, E. L.
1987  "A Jewish Reading of Esther." Pp. 225–43 in *Judaic Perspectives on
      Ancient Israel*. Ed. J. Neusner et al. Philadelphia: Fortress.

Grottanelli, C.
1983    "Tricksters, Scapegoats, Champions, Saviors."
        *History of Religions* 23(2):117–39.

Gruber, M.
1980    *Aspects of Nonverbal Communication in the Ancient Near East.*
        Rome: Biblical Institute.

Gunkel, H.
1916    *Esther.* Tübingen: Mohr.

Hanson, K. C.
1992    "'How Honorable! How Shameful!': A Cultural Analysis of
        Matthew's Makarisms and Reproaches." *Semeia* 68:81–111.

Hanson, P.
1975    *The Dawn of Apocalyptic.* Philadelphia: Fortress.

Harrelson, W.
1990    "Textual and Translation Problems in the Book of Esther."
        *Perspectives in Religious Studies* 17:197–208.

Hatch, E.
1993    "Theories of Social Honor."
        *American Anthropologist* 91(2):341–353.

Haupt, P.
1906    *Purim.* Leipzig: J. C. Hinrichs.

Heidegger, M
1962    *Being and Time.* Oxford: Blackwell.

Heller, A.
1982    "The Power of Shame." *Dialectical Anthropology* 6:215–28.

Henderson, F.
1994    *Honor.* Chicago: University of Chicago.

Herr, L. G.
1981    "Retribution and Personal Honor." A response to T. Frymer-
        Kensky (1980). *Biblical Archeologist* 44:135.

Herzfeld, M.
1980    "Honour and Shame: Problems in the Comparative Analysis of
        Moral Systems." *Man* 15(2):339–351.

1984    "Horns of the Mediterraneanist Dilemna."
        *American Ethnologist* 11(3):439-54.
1985    "Gender Pragmatics: Agency, Speech, and Bride-Theft in a
        Cretan Mountain Village." *Anthropology* 9(1-2):25-44.
1987    "Within and Without: The Category of 'Female' in the
        Ethnography of Modern Greece" in *Gender and Power in Rural
        Greece.* Ed. J. Dubisch. Princeton: Princeton University.
1988    "'As in Your Own House': Hospitality, Ethnography, and the
        Stereotype of Mediterranean Society." Pp. 75-89 in *Honor and
        Shame and the Unity of the Mediterranean.* Ed. D. D. Gilmore.
        Washington: American Anthropological Association.
1991    "Silence, Submission, and Subversion: Toward a Poetics of
        Womanhood." Pp. 79-97 in *Contested Identities: Gender and
        Kinship in Modern Greece.* Ed.s P. Loizos and E. Paptaxiarchis.
        Princeton: Princeton University.

Heschel, A. J.
1955    *The Prophets.* New York: Harper and Row.

Hillers, D. R.
1964    *Treaty-Curses and the Old Testament Prophets.*
        Rome: Pontifical Biblical Institute.

Hobbs, T. R. and Jackson, P. K.
1994    "The Enemy in the Psalms." *Biblical Theology Bulletin* 21(1)22-29.

Hobbs, T. R.
1997    "Reflections on Honor, Shame and Covenant Relations."
        *JBL* 116(3):501-3.

Hoffner, H. A.
1966    "Symbols for Masculinity and Femininity: Their Use in Ancient
        Near Eastern Sympathetic Magic Rituals." *JBL* 85:326-34.

Holy, L.
1989    *Kinship, Honour and Solidarity: Cousin Marriage in the Middle East.*
        Manchester: Manchester University.

Homans, G.
1961    *Social Behavior: Its Elementary Forms.*
        New York: Harcourt, Brace and World.

Huber, L. B.
1983    *The Biblical Experience of Shame/Shaming.*
        Ph.D. Dissertation, Drew University.

Huey, F. B.
    1989    "Irony as the Key to Understanding the Book of Esther."
            *Southwestern Journal of Theology* 32(3):36–39.

Humphreys, W. L.
    1973    "A Life-Style for Diaspora: A Study of the Tales of Esther and
            Daniel." *CBQ* 92:211–23.
    1985    "Novella" and "The Story of Esther and Mordecai: An Early
            Jewish Novella." Pp. 82–96 and 97–113 in *Saga, Legend, Tale,
            Novella, Fable: Narrative Forms in Old Testament Literature.*
            Ed. G. W. Coates. JSOT Sup. 35. Sheffield: JSOT.

Jacobsen, T.
    1967    "The Battle Between Marduk and Ti'amat." JAOS 88:104–08.
    1976    *The Treasures of Darkness.* New Haven: Yale University.

Jensen, P
    1892    "Elamitische Eigennamen. Ein Beitrag zur Erklärung der
            elamitsichen Inschriften." WZKM 6: 47–70, 209–206.

Johnson, A. R.
    1961    *The One and the Many in the Israelite Conception of God.* 2nd ed.
            Cardiff: University of Wales.
    1964    *The Vitality of the Individual in the Thought of Ancient Israel.* 2nd ed.
            Cardiff: University of Wales.
    1968    *Sacral Kingship in Ancient Israel.* 2nd ed.
            Cardiff: University of Wales.

Jonas, H.
    1966    "The Nobility of Sight." Pp. 135–51 in his *The Phenomenon of Life.*
            New York: Harper and Row.

Jones, B. W.
    1977    "Two Misconceptions about the Book of Esther." *CBQ* 39:171–81.

Kaufman, G. and R.
    1987    "Shame: A Perspective on Jewish Identity."
            *Journal of Psychology and Judaism* 11:30–40.

Kiener, F.
    1956    *Kleidung, Mode und Mensch, Versuch einer psychologi schen
            Deutung.* Munich: E. Reinhardt.

Kilborne, B.
    1995    "Fields of Shame: Anthropologists Abroad."
            *Ethnos* 20(2):230–253.

King, L. W.
1912    *Babylonian Boundary Stones.* London: British Museum.

Kirk, I.
1986    "Images of Amazons: Marriage and Matriarchy." Pp. 27–39 in
        *Images of Women in Peace and War.* Ed. S. Macdonald et al.
        Madison: University of Wisconsin.

Klein, L. R.
1996    "Honor and Shame in Esther." Pp. 149–75 in *A Feminist
        Companion to Esther, Judith, Susanna.* Ed. A. Brenner.
        Sheffield: Sheffield Academic.

Klinger, E.
1987    "Revenge and Retribution." Pp. 362–68 in *Encyclopedia of Religion*
        V. 12. Ed. M. Eliade. New York: Macmillan.

Klopfenstein, M.
1972    *Scham und Schande nach dem Alten Testament.*
        ATANT 62. Zurich: Theologischer Verlag.

Koch, K.
1972    "Gibt es ein Vergeltungsdogma im Alten Testament?" Pp. 130–80
        in *Um das Prinzip der Vergeltung in Religion und Recht des Alten
        Testments.* Ed. K. Koch. (orig. 1955, ATK 52)
        Darmstadt: Wissenschaftliche Buchgesellschaft.

Kressel, G. M.
1992    "Shame and Gender." *Anthropological Quarterly* 65(1):34–46.

Kugel, J.
1986    "Topics in the History of the Spirituality of the Psalms." Pp. 113–
        144 in *Jewish Spirituality from the Bible through the Middle Ages.*
        Ed. A. Green. New York: Crossroad.

LaCocque, A.
1990    *The Feminine Unconventional: Four Subversive Figures in Israel's
        Tradition.* Minneapolis: Fortress.

Langdon, E. J.
1978    "Siona Clothing and Adornment, or, You are What You Wear."
        Pp. 297–311 in *The Fabrics of Culture.* Ed. J. M. Cordwell and R. A.
        Schwarz. The Hague: Mouton.

Lebra, T. S.
  1983 "Shame and Guilt: A Psychocultural View of the Japanese Self."
  *Ethnos* 11(3):192- 209.

Lemche, N. P.
  1995 "Kings and Clients: On Loyalty Between the Ruler and the Ruled
  in Ancient Israel." *Semeia* 66: 119–32.

Levenson, J. D.
  1976 "The Scroll of Esther in Ecumenical Perspective."
  *Journal of Ecumenical Studies* 13(3):440–52.
  1996 "The Universal Horizon of Biblical Particularism."
  *Ethnicity and the Bible.* Ed. M. G. Brett. New York: E. J. Brill.
  1997 *Esther: A Commentary.* The Old Testament Library.
  Louisville: Westminster/John Knox.

Lever, A.
  1988 "Honour as a Red Herring." *Critique of Anthropology* 6(3):83–106.

Levinas, E.
  1979 *Totality and Infinity: An Essay on Exteriority.* Tr. A. Lingis.
  Boston: M. Nijhoff.

Levine, A. -J.
  1992 "Diaspora as Metaphor: Bodies and Boundaries in the Book of
  Tobit." Pp. 105–17 in *Diaspora Jews and Judaism.* Ed.s J. A.
  Overman and R. S. MacLennan. Atlanta: Scholars.

Levine, L. W.
  1974 "Some Go Up and Some Go Down: The Meaning of the Slave
  Trickster." Pp. 94–124 in *The Hofstadter Aefis: A Memorial.* Ed.s S.
  Elkins and E. McKitrick. New York: Knopf.

Lévi-Strauss, C.
  1966 *The Savage Mind.* Chicago: University of Chicago.

Lévy-Bruhl, L.
  1923 *Primitive Mentality.* London: G. Allen and Unwin.
  1926 *How Natives Think.* London: G. Allen and Unwin.

Lewis, C. S.
  1958 *Reflections on the Psalms.* London: Geoffrey Bles.

Lewis, M.
  1992 *Shame: The Exposed Self.* New York: Free.

Loader, J. A.
1979    "Esther as a Novel with Different Levels of Meaning."
        ZAW 90(3):417–21.
1991    *Esther.* Nijkerk: Callenbach.

Loizos P. and Paptaxiarchis E. (ed.s)
1991    *Contested Identities: Gender and Kinship in Modern Greece.*
        Princeton: Princeton University.

Luther, M.
1914    *Tischreden* 3. 3391a:302 in *D. Martin Luthers Werke.* Weimar ed.
        Weimar: Hermann Böhlaus.

Lynd, H.
1958    *On Shame and the Search for Identity.* New York: Harcourt.

Macdonald, S.
1989    "Drawing the Lines–Gender, Peace and War: An Introduction."
        Pp. 1–26 in *Images of Women in Peace and War.* Ed.s P. Holden and
        S. Ardener. Madison: University of Wisconsin.

Machinist, P.
1990    "The Question of Distinctiveness in Ancient Israel: An Essay."
        Pp. 196–212 in *Ah, Assyria ...: Studies in Assyrian History and
        Ancient Near Eastern Historiography Presented to Hayim Tadmor.*
        Ed. M. Cogan and I. Eph'al. Jerusalem: Magnes.

Malina, B. J.
1981    *The New Testament World: Insights from Cultural Anthropology.*
        Atlanta: John Knox.
1986    *Christian Origins and Cultural Anthropology: Practical Models for
        Biblical Interpretation.* Atlanta: John Knox.
1993    *The New Testament World: Insights from Cultural Anthropology.*
        Louisville: Westminster/John Knox.

Malina, B. and Neyrey, J.
1990    "Honor and Shame in Luke–Acts: Pivotal Values of the
        Mediterranean World." Pp. 25–65 in *The Social World of Luke–
        Acts: Models for Interpretation.* Ed. J. Neyrey.
        Peabody, MA: Hendrickson.

Malina, B. and Rohrbaugh, R. L.
1992    *Social Science Commentary on the Synoptic Gospels.*
        Minneapolis: Fortress.

Matthews, V. H.
   1991a   *Manners and Customs in the Bible.* Revised Ed.
           Peabody, MA: Hendrickson.
   1991b   "Hospitality and Hostility in Judges 4."
           *Biblical Theology Bulletin* 21:13-21.
   1993    "The Anthropology of Clothing in the Joseph Narrative."
           *JSOT* 65:25-36.

Matthews, V. H. and Benjamin, D. C.
   1993    *Social World of Ancient Israel: 1250-587 BCE.*
           Peabody, MA: Hendrickson.
   1994    *Honor and Shame in the World of the Bible. Semeia* 68.

Mauss, M.
   1990    *The Gift.* Tr. W. D. Halls. (First pub. 1950)
           New York: W. W. Norton.

Mazrui, A. A.
   1977    "The Warrior Tradition and the Masculinity of War."
           *Journal of Asian and African Studies* 12(1-4):69-81.

McKane, W.
   1961    "Note on Esther 9 and I Samuel 15."
           *Journal of Theological Studies* 12:260-1.

Meinhold, A.
   1975/6  "Die Gattung der Josephsgeschichte und des Estherbuches: and
           Diasporanovelle, I, II." *ZAW* 87:306-24; 88:79-93.
   1983    *Das Buch Esther.* Zurcher Bibelkommentare AT 13.
           Zurich: Theologischer Verlag.

Mendenhall, G.
   1973    *The Tenth Generation.* Baltimore: Johns Hopkins University.

Milgrom, J.
   1983    "Of Hems and Tassels." *Biblical Archeological Review* IX(3):61-65.

Miller, P. D.
   1974    *The Divine Warrior in Early Israel.*
           Cambridge: Harvard University.
   1986    *Interpreting the Psalms.* Philadelphia: Fortress.

Moore, C. A.
   1967    "A Greek Witness to a Different Hebrew Text of Esther."
           *ZAW* 79:351-58.

1971   *Esther.* The Anchor Bible. Garden City, New York: Doubleday.

Moran, W. L.
1987   "Gilgamesh." Pp. 557–60 in *Encyclopedia of Religion* Vol. 5.
        Ed. Mircea Eliade. New York: Macmillan.

Mott, S. C.
1975   "The Power of Giving and Receiving: Reciprocity in Hellenistic
        Benevolence." Pp. 60–72 in *Current Issues in Biblical and
        Patristic Interpretation.* Ed. G. F. Hawthorne.
        Grand Rapids: William B. Eerdmans.

Mowinckel, S.
1962   *The Psalms in Israel's Worship.* 2 Vols. Tr. D. R. Ap–Thomas.
        New York: Abingdon.

Nadel, S.
1947   *The Nuba: An Anthropological Study of the Hill Tribes of Kordofan.*
        London: Oxford University.

Naveh, J.
1982   "*mkbrm* or *mkbdm.*" *Eretz Israel* 15:301–2 (Hb).

Neusner, J.
1973   *The Idea of Purity in Ancient Judaism.* Leiden: E. J. Brill.

Neyrey, J. (ed)
1991   *The World of Luke–Acts: A Handbook of Social Science Models
        for Biblical Interpretation.* Peabody, MA: Hendrickson.

Neyrey, J.
1994   "Despising the Shame of the Cross." *Semeia* 68:113–137.

Nickelsburg, G. W. E.
1972   *Resurrection, Immortality, and Eternal Life in Intertestamental
        Judaism.* HTS 26. Cambridge: Harvard University.

Niditch, S. and Doran, R.
1997   "Esther: Folklore, Wisdom, Feminism and Authority." Pp. 26–46
        in *A Feminist Companion to Esther, Judith and Susanna.*
        Ed. A. Brenner. Sheffield: Sheffield Academic.

Odell, M. S.
1991   "The Inversion of Shame and Forgiveness in Ezekiel 16:59–63."
        *JSOT* 56:101–112.

Ogden, G. S.
1982    "Prophetic Oracles against Foreign Nations and Psalms of
        Communal Lament: The Relationship of Psalm 137 to
        Jeremiah 49:7–22 and Obadiah." *JSOT* 24:89–97.

Olyan, S.
1996    "Honor, Shame, and Covenant Relations in Ancient Israel and Its
        Environment." *JBL* 115(2): 201–18.

Patai, R.
1958    *Sex and Family in the Bible and the Middle East.*
        Garden City, NJ: Doubleday.

Paton, L. B.
1908    *A Critical and Exegetical Commentary on the Book of Esther.*
        The ICC Series. Edinburg: T and T Clark.

Pedersen, J.
1963    "Honour and Shame." Pp. 213–44 in *Israel: Its Life and Culture.*
        Vol. 2. London: Oxford University.

Peristiany, J. G.
1966a   "Honour and Shame in a Cypriot Highland Village." Pp. 171–
        190 in *Honour and Shame: The Values of Mediterranean Society.*
        Ed. J. G. Peristiany. Chicago: University of Chicago.
1967    *Contributions to Mediterranean Sociology: Mediterranean Rural
        Communities and Social Change.* Paris: Mouton.

Peristiany, J. G. (ed)
1966b   *Honour and Shame: The Values of Mediterranean Society.*
        Chicago: University of Chicago.
1975    *Mediterranean Family Structures.* Cambridge Studies in Social
        Anthropology 13. Cambridge: Cambridge University.

Peristiany, J. G. and Pitt-Rivers, J.
1992    *Honour and Grace in Anthropology.*
        Cambridge: Cambridge University.

Pfeifer, R. H.
1941    *Introduction to the Old Testament.* New York: Harper.

Phillips, A.
1986    "The Book of Ruth: Deception and Shame."
        *Journal of Judaic Studies* 37(1):1–17.

Piers, G. and Singer, M.
1953    *Shame and Guilt: A Psychoanalytic and Cultural Study.*
        New York: Norton.

Pitard, W.
1992    "Vengeance." *ABD* VI: 786-7.

Pitt-Rivers, J. (ed)
1963    *Mediterranean Countrymen: Essays in the Social Anthropology of the
        Mediterranean.* Paris: Mouton.

Pitt-Rivers, J.
1954    *People of the Sierra.* (Rev. 1955, 1961, 1971)
        New York: Criterion Books.
1965    "Honour and Social Status." Pp. 19-77 in *Honour and Shame:The
        Values of Mediterranean Society.* Ed. J. G. Peristiany.
        Chicago: University of Chicago.
1968a   "The Stranger, The Guest, and the Hostile Host: Introduction to
        the Study of the Laws of Hospitality." Pp. 13-30 in *Contributions
        to Mediterranean Sociology.* Ed. J. G. Peristiany. Paris: Mouton.
1968b   "Honor." Pp. 503-11 in *The International Encyclopedia of the Social
        Sciences.* Ed. D. L. Sills. New York: Macmillan/Free Press.
1977    *The Fate of Shechem or the Politics of Sex: Essays in the Anthropology
        of the Mediterranean.* Cambridge: Cambridge University.

Porter, J. R.
1965    "Legal Aspects of Corporate Personality." *VT* 15:361-80.

Pospisil, L.
1968    "Feud." Pp. 389-93 in *International Encyclopedia of the Social
        Sciences* Vol. 5. Ed. D. L. Sills.
        New York: The Macmillan/Free Press.

Prinsloo, W. S.
1983    "Isaiah 14:12-15: Humiliation, Hubris, Humiliation."
        *ZAW* 93(3):432-38.

Prouser, O. H.
1998    "Suited to the Throne: The Symbolic Use of Clothing in the
        David and Saul Narratives." *JSOT* 71:27-37

Rad, G. von
1959    *Der Heilige Krieg im alten Israel.*
        Götingen: Vandenhoeck and Ruprecht.

Radday, Y. T.
    1973    "Chiasm in Joshua, Judges and Others."
            *Linguistica Biblica* 27/28:6–13.

    1989    "Esther with Humour." Pp. 295–313 in *On Humour and the Comic
            in the Hebrew Bible*. Ed. Y. T. Radday and A. Brenner.
            Sheffield: Almond.

Radin, P.
    1972    *The Trickster: A Study in American Indian Mythology*.
            New York: Schocken.

Renfrow, C. and Shennan, S. (ed.s)
    1982    *Ranking, Resource and Exchange: Aspects of the Archaeology of Early
            European Society*. Cambridge: Cambridge University.

Roach, M. E. and Eicher, J. B.
    1979    "The Language of Personal Adornment." Pp. 7–21 in *The Fabrics
            of Culture*. Ed.s J. M. Cordwell and R. A. Schwarz.
            New York: Mouton.

Robinson, H. W.
    1963    "Corporate Personality in Ancient Israel." *Facet Books, Biblical
            Series*. Ed. J. Reumann. Philadelphia: Fortress.

Rogers, S. C.
    1976    "Female Forms of Power and the Myth of Male Dominance: A
            Model of Female/Male Interaction in Peasant Society."
            *American Ethnologist* 2:727–56.

Rogerson, J. W.
    1970    "The Hebrew Conception of Corporate Personality."
            *Journal of Theological Studies* 21:1–16.

Rosaldo, M. Z. and Lamphere, L. (ed.s)
    1973    *Woman, Culture, and Society*. Stanford: Stanford University.

Rosaldo, M. Z.
    1983    "The Shame of Headhunters and the Autonomy of Self."
            *Ethnos* 11(3):135–151.
    1989    *Culture and Truth: The Remaking of Social Analysis*.
            Boston: Beacon.

Rosenblatt, P. C. , Walsh, R. P. and Jackson, D. A.
    1976    *Grief and Mourning in Cross-Cultural Perspective*. HRAF.

Rosenthal, L. A.
1895    "Die Josephgeschichte mit den Buchern Ester und Daniel
        verglichen." *ZAW* 15:278–85.
1897    "Nochmals der Vergleich Ester, Joseph, Daniel." *ZAW* 17:125–28.

Ryan, M. S.
1966    *Clothing: A Study in Human Behavior.*
        New York: Holt, Rinehart and Winston.

Sanday, P.
1980    *Female Power and Male Dominance: On the Origins of Sexual
        Inequality.* New York: Cambridge University.

Sandmel, S.
1972    *The Enjoyment of Scripture.* New York: Oxford University.

Sakenfeld, K. D.
1978    *The Meaning of Hesed in the Hebrew Bible: A New Inquiry.*
        Atlanta: Scholars.

Sasson, J. M.
1979    *Ruth: A New Translation with a Philological Commentary and a
        Formalist–Folklorist Interpretation.* Baltimore: Johns Hopkins.
1985    "*WE/O'YITBOSASU* (Gn 2:25) and its Implications."
        *Biblica* 66(3):418–21.

Sayigh, R. and Peteet, J.
1955    "Between Two Fires: Palestinian Women In Lebanon." Pp. 106–
        37 in *Caught Up in Conflict.* Ed.s R. Ridd and H. Callaway.
        London: Macmillan Education.

Sawyer, J. F. A.
1972    *Semantics in Biblical Research: New Methods of Defining Hebrew
        Words for Salvation.* Studies in Biblical Theology.
        Second Series 24. Naperville, IL: Alec R. Allenson Inc.

Schlegel, A.
1991    "Status, Property, and the Value of Virginity."
        *American Ethnologist* 18(4):719–34.

Schneider, C.
1992    *Shame, Exposure and Privacy.* New York: West Norton.

Schneider, J.
1971　"Of Vigilance and Virgins: Honor, Shame and Access to Resources in Mediterranean Societies." *Ethnology* 10(1):1–24.
1987　"The Anthropology of Cloth." *Annual Review of Anthropology* 16:409–48.

Schwarz, R. A.
1980　"Uncovering the Secret Vice: Toward an Anthropology of Clothing." Pp. 23–45 in *The Fabrics of Culture*. Ed.s J. M. Cordwell and R. A. Schwarz. The Hague: Mouton.

Siegel, M.
1985　"Book of Esther: A Novelle." *Dor Le Dor* 14(3): 142–51.

deSilva, D. A.
1995　*Despising Shame: Honor Discourse and Community Maintenance in the Epistle to the Hebrews*. SBL Diss. 152. Atlanta: Scholars.

Smith, W. R.
1889　*Lectures on the Religion of the Semites*. Edinburg: A. and C. Black.

Stansell, G.
1989　"Honor and Shame in the David Narratives." Pp. XX–YY in *Was ist der Mensch?* Beitrage zur Anthropologie des Alten Testament. Munich: Chr. Kaiser Verlag. (Revised version in *Semeia* 68 [1994]).

Steinberg, N.
1988　"Israelite Tricksters: Their Analogues and Cross-cultural Study." *Semeia* 42:1–13.

Stone, K.
1995　"Gender and Homosexuality in Judges 19: Subject-Honor, Object-Shame?" *JSOT* 67:87–107.

Talmon, S.
1963　"Wisdom in the Book of Esther." *Vetus Testamentum* 13:419–55.

Tapper, R. and N.
1992-3　"Marriage, Honour and Responsibility: Islamic and Local Models in the Mediterranean and the Middle East." *Cambridge Anthropology* 16(2):3–21.

Taylor, J. G.
1982    "The Song of Deborah and Two Canaanite Goddesses."
        *JSOT* 23:99–108.

Thiselton, A. C.
1992    *New Horizons in Hermeneutics.*
        Grand Rapids: Zondervan.

Tucker, G.
1980    "Introduction." Pp. 7–13 in H. W. Robinson's *Corporate
        Personality in Ancient Israel.* Philadelphia: Fortress.

Turner, V. W.
1969    *The Ritual Process: Structure and Anti-Structure.*
        Chicago: Aldine.

*The Two Targums of Esther.*
1992    The Aramaic Bible, V. 18. Collegeville,
        Minneapolis: Liturgical.

Valeri, V.
1985    *Kingship and Sacrifice: Ritual and Society in Ancient Hawaii.*
        Tr. P. Wissing. Chicago: University of Chicago.

Vaux, R. de
1967    *Ancient Israel.* Vol.s 1 and 2.
        New York: McGraw–Hill.

Vogelzang, M. E. and van Bekkum, W. J.
1986    "Meaning and Symbolism of Clothing in Ancient Near Eastern
        Texts." Pp. 265–84 in *Scripta Signa Vocis: Studies about Scripts,
        Scriptures, Scribes and Languages in the Near East Presented to J. H.
        Hospers.* Ed. H. L. J. Vanstiphout, et al.
        Gröningen: Egbert Forsten.

Wagner, S.
1990    "יקר." *TDOT* VI: 279–87.

Walcot, P.
1970    *Greek Peasants, Ancient and Modern: A Comparison of Social and
        Moral Values.* Manchester: Manchester University.

Wallace-hadrill, A. (ed)
1989    *Patronage in Ancient Society.* London: Routledge.

Webster, S. K.
    1984    *The Shadow of a Noble Man: Honor and Shame in Arabic Proverbs.*
            Ph.D. Dissertation, Indiana University.

Weiner, A. B. and Schneider, J. (ed.s)
    1989    *Cloth and Human Experience.*
            Washington: Smithsonian.

Weinfeld, M.
    1995    "כָּבוֹד." *TDOT* VII: 22–38.

Westermann, C.
    1974    "The Role of the Lament in the Theology of the Old Testament."
            *Interpretation* 28(1): 20–38.
    1981a  *Praise and Lament in the Psalms.* Tr. K. R. Krim and R. N. Soulen.
            Atlanta: John Knox.
    1981b  *The Structure of the Book of Job.* Philadelphia: Fortress.

White, S. A.
    1988    "Esther: A Feminine Model for Jewish Diaspora." Pp. 161–77 in
            *Gender and Difference in Ancient Israel.* Ed. P. L. Day.
            Minneapolis: Fortress.

Wikan, U.
    1984    "Shame and Honour: A Contestable Pair." *Man* 19/4:635–652.

Wills, L.
    1988    *The Jew in the Court of the Foreign King: Ancient Jewish Court
            Legends.* HDR 26. Minneapolis: Fortress.
    1995    *The Jewish Novel in the Ancient World.*
            Ithica: Cornell University.

Wilson, R. R.
    1977    *Genealogy and History in the Biblical World.* YNER 7.
            New Haven: Yale University.
    1981    *Prophecy and Society in Ancient Israel.* Philadelphia: Fortress.
    1992    "Genealogy, Genealogies." *ABD* II:929–32.

Winter, B. W.
    1988    "The Public Honoring of Christian Benefactors."
            *Journal for the Study of the New Testament* 34:88–90.

Wolkstein, D. and Kramer, S. N.
    1983    *Inanna, Queen of Heaven and Earth.* New York: Harper and Row.

Wurmser, L.
1982    *The Mask of Shame.* Baltimore: Johns Hopkins University.

Wyatt-Brown, B.
1982    *Southern Honor: Ethics and Behavior in the Old South.*
        Oxford: Oxford University.

Yamauchi, E. M.
1990    *Persia and the Bible.* Grand Rapids: Baker Book House.

Yee, G.
1993    "By the Hand of a Woman: The Metaphor of the Woman Warrior
        in Judges 4." *Semeia* 61:99–132.

Zelditch, E.
1968    "Social Status." Pp. 250–57 in *The International Encyclopedia of The
        Social Sciences* Vol. 15.  New York: Macmillan.

Zenger, E.
1993    *A God of Vengeance? Understanding the Psalms of Divine Wrath.*
        Tr. L. M. Maloney. Louisville: Westminster John Knox.

Printed in the United States
83075LV00002B/436-453/A